ALEX WADE is a freelance journalist and Fleet Street lawyer. He concentrates on law, sport and travel, and contributes to a number of national newspapers including *The Times*, the *Independent*, the *Independent on Sunday* and the *Guardian*, as well as various magazines. He has advised *The Times*, the *Sunday Times*, the *Independent*, the *Independent on Sunday*, the *News of the World*, the *Sun* and the *Mirror* on media law issues. He has been a licensed bookmaker and a sports rights consultant, and his media appearances include Sky News, BBC Five Live, BBC World Service, BBC Radio London, BBC Radio Gloucester, BBC Radio Swindon and Talksport. He lives with his wife and two children in the West Country, and is currently writing his second book, which is on surfing in the UK.

WRECKING MACHINE

A TALE OF REAL FIGHTS
AND WHITE COLLARS

ALEX WADE

POCKET
BOOKS

LONDON • SYDNEY • NEW YORK • TORONTO

This book is a true account of certain parts of my life.
For reasons of diplomacy the names of certain individuals
have been changed.

First published in Great Britain by Scribner, 2005
This edition published by Pocket Books, 2006
An imprint of Simon & Schuster UK Ltd
A CBS COMPANY

1 3 5 7 9 10 8 6 4 2

Simon & Schuster UK Ltd
Africa House
64–78 Kingsway
London WC2B 6AH

www.simonsays.co.uk

Simon & Schuster Australia
Sydney

A CIP catalogue record for this book
is available from the British Library.

ISBN 1-4165-2253-0
EAN 9781416522539

Typeset by M Rules
Printed and bound in Great Britain
by Cox & Wyman Ltd, Reading, Berks

This book is dedicated to
Walcot Amateur Boxing Club

CONTENTS

CONTENTS

There were things, he said mournfully, that perhaps could never be told, only he had lived so much alone that sometimes he forgot – he forgot. The light had destroyed the assurance which had inspired him in the distant shadows. He sat down and, with both elbows on the desk, rubbed his forehead. 'And yet it is true – it is true. In the destructive element immerse.' ... He spoke in a subdued tone, without looking at me, one hand on each side of his face. 'That was the way. To follow the dream, and again to follow the dream – and so – *ewig – usque ad finem* ...'

Joseph Conrad, *Lord Jim*

PART ONE

PART ONE

1

ON THE CANVAS (1)

I caught Harold with a left jab, hard enough to make his eyes flicker in irritation. Novice that I was, I moved inside, to my right. Big mistake. Harold threw out a powerful straight right, connecting hard on my chin. My legs buckled and I hit the canvas. Or rather, the scruffy, frayed carpet that passed for canvas. Only later did I notice that it wasn't the real thing, the energy-sapping canvas of places like York Hall in Bethnal Green, the spiritual home of British boxing, a place where the Krays fought and which seems to have faced the axe for years, only to stagger on like a punch-drunk fighter, refusing to go quietly.

There was a momentary hush as I went down. I felt like a child, so vulnerable that I wondered if I'd lose bodily control. Taking a hard punch removes you to a world where you float, where time is frozen. How long did it take for me to hit the deck? No more than a second. It felt like forever. Down there on the tatty, off-green carpet, I could feel the eyes of the other boxers on me. Strangely I didn't think of Harold, the man who had just floored me. He had nothing to do with how I felt, in the split second that I fell and as I lay there for only an instant or two. Of course, he had everything to do with it; this big, heavyweight fighter, to whom I was giving away about three stone, had put me down, dropped me; as an orthodox boxer his instinct after taking a left jab and seeing his opponent move *inside, the wrong way*, into the danger zone, had been to throw out that strong, unerring straight right. Maybe he should have had more control; after all, I was light years away from his level. Perhaps he should have pulled his punch, just given me a gentle cuff. But I didn't think any of this; down there on the floor, I didn't mind that Harold had hit me and I didn't even register where he was standing, what he was doing. Was he smiling, laughing? Was he concerned? Did he feel that he'd taught me a lesson, that he had avenged the miraculous left jab that had got through his guard?

Later, Harold told me I had *walked* on to his right, that the force of my own momentum had put me down. Certainly, I had done what no boxer should ever do, move into range with no defence, inviting an orthodox fighter's best punch. But I have a feeling a hint of pride may have helped things along. A boxer like me shouldn't get through to Harold: it just shouldn't happen. And pride, in boxing, is everything. It may be one of the seven deadly sins but try telling that to anyone who takes the noble art seriously. Pride meant that when Harold dropped me, despite a pounding headache and with wobbling legs, I got up almost as quickly as I'd gone down. I didn't know what Harold was doing, and I didn't care. I couldn't be sure how many of the other boxers had seen the incident, but some of them would have done. And I wanted them to know that even if I was next to useless, I had a heart as big as Harold's straight rights.

I was on my feet within seconds. Harold asked me if I was all right. 'I'm fine,' I said, with a hint of nonchalance, as if being punched to the ground was an everyday occurrence. 'You sure?' said Harold. 'Yeah,' I said. We continued sparring. Harold took it easy. I had nothing left but tried to throw some jabs. Pride. You have to keep going, even when you can't, when everything is telling you to stop, to give up, to quit, to admit that you're not man enough for boxing. The relief was immense when the bell sounded. One or two of the other boxers grinned at me as I climbed out of the ring. Someone slapped me on the back, and I heard the words: 'Well done, mate, good one.' Had I passed some obscure kind of test?

If so, I hoped my experience at Walcot Amateur Boxing Club in Swindon would spare me the fate of Paul 'Mad Manx' Beckett, whose debut as a white-collar boxer at the Mermaid Theatre on 20 March 2003 I had witnessed two weeks or so earlier. Mad Manx was billed as a lawyer with Carters, a firm on the Isle of Man. With his heavily tattooed right arm, he looked more like a TT die-hard than a lawyer. Still, there were one or two boos when his profession was announced by the MC. The legal profession never ceases to inspire dislike verging on hatred. Comments such as 'He's a lawyer, give him a good kicking!' and 'Deck him!' were clearly audible as Mad Manx walked down the aisle to the ring set up on the Mermaid's stage. What have lawyers done, historically, to deserve such universal opprobrium? I have been one myself, one way or another, for over ten years, and have a fair idea.

If the anti-lawyer barbs were not of manic import, they were still loud enough to put a lesser man off. *A lesser man like you*, I heard a voice say. How would I feel come my fight if I was greeted like Mad Manx? Would I crumble before the bout had even begun? Perhaps I was being too sensitive. On the night, surely you hear nothing, are absorbed in nothing but the looming confrontation. How else can you climb into the ring?

If he heard the scattered bursts of invective, Mad Manx took them in his stride, and his combination of height, short hair and singlet, not to mention the tattoos, made him look fearsome enough. He was up against Lee Short 'Fuse', the managing director of an electrical firm. This was the second fight on the card, and it proved to be a terrible mismatch.

Mad Manx came out of his corner looking doomed. Something must have happened to him before the bell sounded, some inner fragility must have surfaced. He exuded a palpable lack of confidence as he tiptoed towards Lee Short, a solid man who appeared at ease with everything and who proceded to land a series of straight rights and lefts on Mad Manx. Those who had booed Mad Manx, or at least his profession, had plenty to cheer about as the blows rained in on him with increasing ferocity. He had no idea how to cope with Short. Within fifteen seconds he was in a neutral corner, eyes radiating sheer terror, proffering a flurry of punches that a man behind me described as 'like a woman's'. He held his fists at face height and tried to palm away Lee Short's blows, just as a puppy scoops its paws at a toy out of reach, and was manoeuvred back into the centre of the ring where Short smashed a huge right into his face. Mad Manx dropped like a stone.

The same hush that I felt at Walcot a few days later briefly swept the Mermaid. It's a strange phenomenon, a sharp intake of breath from neutrals and those with feelings for the man going down, which mingles with the cheers of those supporting the victorious fighter. When the punch is a KO, as it was with Mad Manx Beckett, the hush is still there, somehow present despite the noise. How badly hurt was he? He didn't move for at least two minutes. Paramedics and the ringside doctor swarmed on to the canvas. As I looked on from my near ringside seat, I wondered: is this what it will be like? When I step out for my debut white-collar fight, will I look scared and out of place? Will I hit the floor within thirty seconds? And if I do, how bad will it be? Will I get up again?

Paul Beckett lived to fight another day, groggily sitting up after a few minutes. He seemed to have a vague idea of where he was and slunk out of the ring, chaperoned by various people. Where did he go? I didn't see him in the bar later, but by then I was so preoccupied by my own impending foray into the ring that I wasn't noticing much.

Soon the next bout was underway, its own spectacular momentum diminishing whatever shock had been caused by Beckett's KO. In the ring were Johnny 'Bad Boy' Barr, described as a 'singing Lothario', and Mark 'Maverick' Arnold, an IT manager. It's *de rigueur* for boxers to have ring names, all the way from legends such as Jack Dempsey of Manassa, Colorado ('The Manassa Mauler') and Thomas 'Hit-Man' Hearns to modern boxing's *bête noire*, 'Iron' Mike Tyson. The tradition is upheld in the white-collar world. On the card at the Mermaid that night were fighters such as 'Sugar' Jimmy Rogers, Thomas 'The Marauder' Lloyd-Edwards, Jack 'Something For The Weekend' Kielty and Mike 'Bus Pass' Field. As a man in his mid-fifties, Bus Pass had chosen the most self-deprecating nickname of the show. But whatever Mark Arnold was trying to distill in his choice of soubriquet was forgotten as 'Bad Boy' Barr took the fight to him without mercy. Anyone whose view of white-collar boxing is that it is soft, that somehow it can't approximate the real thing, would have revised their view with this fight following Lee Short's annihilation of Paul Beckett. Barr's technique was good, with plenty of solid jabs and wicked hooks and, game though he was, the Maverick wasn't at the same standard. The fight was stopped at the end of the second round by the referee for the night, Charlie Magri, as blood poured from the Maverick's nose. There was supposed to be another bout but the intermission was brought forward so that the 'claret', as it is known in the trade, could be mopped from the canvas.

Among the crowd, no one seemed to care. This was all good fun, and there were another five fights on the card to look forward to. No matter that the slick, well-promoted event had so far proved to be every bit as tough as any boxing show, anywhere. The motley collection of punters, from men with mashed-up faces in flashy suits to City brokers and bankers, not to mention a number of women who would not have disgraced a catwalk, were enjoying their night out. They had no qualms with the odd KO or bleeding nose, they had no issue with boxing, full stop. In this, the world of white-collar boxing, the combatants boxed for fun, not money, and the onlookers came for a good time, not to gamble.

Placing a bet would have been futile since for the most part the participants in white-collar fights do not 'win', as such. Unless they are fighting for a world or British title, which is scored in the same way as an amateur match, their triumph comes from merely taking part, from having the nerve to step inside the squared circle and box. This form of politically correct pugilism is run by The Real Fight Club from an office off Shoreditch High Street in London's East End, just a stone's throw from the space-age City buildings whose white-collar workers have increasingly been taking up boxing. Like a lot of modern fads, white-collar boxing hails originally from the United States. Its spiritual home is Gleason's Gym, New York, the oldest boxing gym in America, a legendary institution that since 1937 has been graced by the likes of Jake La Motta, Roberto Duran, Joe Frazier and Muhammad Ali. Fresh from one of his lesser criminal convictions, following a brawl in a Brooklyn hotel, Mike Tyson worked out a sentence of one hundred hours community service by training awestruck youngsters at Gleason's in 2003. The gym is owned by fiftysomething former Sears Roebuck executive Bruce Silverglade, who, in the mid-1990s, decided to open its doors to allow all-comers the chance to box. Now Gleason's plays host to some two hundred professionals and another seven hundred men and women, some of whom are amateurs, while a great many others enjoy boxing either as a means of keeping fit or with the intention of taking part in white collar fights, which are held in the gym itself. Rumour has it that Gleason's might have gone out of business – like many other old New York boxing gyms – if it hadn't opened its doors to a new, more affluent breed of fighter.

The first white-collar fight at Gleason's has a hint of urban myth about it but, in many ways, is emblematic of the sport in New York and London. Two Wall Street incumbents apparently decided to up the ante of their competitive streak by betting on who would still be standing after a three-round bout. They employed professional fighters as their trainers, and four months later fought in front of colleagues and friends at Gleason's Gym. Word spread, not so much of their remarkable skill but of what a great evening it had been, and now 'White-Collar Fight Night' is a fixture of certain New Yorkers' social lives. Once a month, Silverglade's Gym, in the shadow of Brooklyn Bridge, hosts an evening of pugilism for lawyers, accountants, bankers and brokers – anyone, in fact, who has joined Gleason's, done the training and got in shape. The events are well attended and have become a tangible part of the fabric of the New York social scene; The Real Fight Club is the UK equivalent.

A sign hangs on one of the walls at Gleason's, on which the following lines translated from Virgil appear: 'Now whoever has the courage, and a strong and collected spirit in his breast, let him come forth, lace up his gloves, and put up his hands.'

At the Mermaid on 20 March, sixteen fighters had answered this imprecation. For the most part, they were over thirty-four, the cutoff point beyond which the Amateur Boxing Association decrees that amateur boxers can no longer fight. A professional can go on indefinitely, subject to passing British Board of Boxing Control medicals, but for amateurs there is nowhere to go. Unless, that is, they join The Real Fight Club, whose website declares 'Pugilism is back', and where age is irrelevant. The publicity material on a flyer for the Mermaid show urged support for boxers ranging from twenty-seven to fifty-five-year-old Mike 'Bus Pass' Field, a financial consultant, in unashamedly eve-of-battle rhetoric: 'Join us in supporting these modern-day Corinthians who have taken time out of their busy corporate schedules to take part in our demanding training programmes based on a professional boxer's workout.' The combatants were eulogised: 'Their achievement can only be described as inspirational', before the declaration: 'There are no decisions in white-collar boxing, as you are a winner when you step into the squared circle.' Another two sentences stayed in my mind for a long time after the show: 'The Real Fight Club is not about hurting or humiliating people. We're about commitment, confidence, control, camaraderie and a bit of showmanship.'

Commitment, confidence, control. How many times had I wished that these were attributes of my own? The flyer slipped through my hands, on to the floor by my feet, and for a moment I was lost in memories of times when commitment, confidence and control were as far away from my life as sustained sobriety. Now, things were better, but they weren't perfect; the serenity I craved remained as elusive as the true meaning of The Real Fight's Club's publicity material. And yet, if I joined The Real Fight Club, did I have a chance? Were commitment, confidence and control somehow guaranteed? As I reached to retrieve the flyer, craning my neck and eying the ring, it seemed possible that perhaps control could be acquired, confidence safeguarded, commitment learnt, by embracing The Real Fight Club, whose language promised a home of sorts, a place of expression free of the jibes of the politically correct, a place where the commitment made is to oneself and to the other boxers of the club. From this act of commitment, confidence will flow and control will be learnt. But only provided that a certain code is observed, an optimistic coda to the mantra that 'Pugilism is back.' It is back but only on the grounds that no one is *hurt*. And no one is *humiliated*.

For all that I was taken with a vision of myself tweaked and honed by The Real Fight Club, I couldn't help but ponder the issue of hurt and humiliation in the intermission. What did Paul 'Mad Manx' Beckett think of The Real Fight Club, now that he had stepped into the ring and had his first bout? Or Mark 'Maverick' Arnold, whose nose had bled so profusely that his fight was stopped? Did they feel like winners, simply by virtue of having taken part? Paul Beckett had been badly hurt, and the harsh truth was that he had also been humiliated. He had proved as much a boxer as a parrot on a perch, eyed by a ravenous cat. What would he say to friends and colleagues afterwards? Would he say: 'I feel like a winner because I had the courage to climb into the ring and try and fight. No matter that I put on an incompetent display and was knocked out by a far better fighter, in less time than it takes to say these words. Victory is mine.' Or would he admit to having got it all seriously wrong, would he acknowledge that he had severely misjudged his ability and that he should have contented himself with a ringside seat, where he could look on and cheer, perhaps muttering under his breath: 'I could do better than that.' How many times had he watched other fights, and thought precisely that? Was that what had motivated him to contact The Real Fight Club and convince them to let him box? But now that he knew what it felt like to be knocked out, and for all that being a lawyer had not endeared him to certain sections of the crowd, surely he must have concluded that a sedentary, non-violent occupation such as The Law is not so bad, after all.

Perhaps Beckett and Arnold experienced camaraderie in their fates, discussing in the dressing room just how perilous, at any level, the business of boxing is, once you climb through the ropes. I wondered about this and then, reading more of the flyer, another sentence struck me. In a section headed 'About The Real Fight Club', the following statement appeared: 'Our mission is to resurrect the noble art of pugilism and promote its positive aspects to our members.' The Real Fight Club was suggesting that something had been lost in boxing, that its nobility was at stake. But The Real Fight Club was the real thing. It would safeguard – and resurrect – the purity of the noble art and all those who practised it. Boxing was an art, and a noble one at that, to be restored and cherished; not a science, not even a *sweet science*, as it is sometimes known, but an art, something inexact, intangible, emotional. This was boxing for gentlemen, for 'modern-day Corinthians', for executives and bankers and brokers and lawyers, for 'white-collar warriors', real men with confidence and control who yet restrain their ability to render a lesser man unconscious through their commitment to the code, to the ethics of a boxing mythology that talks only of its positive aspects, never the negative, never the blood and broken jaws and concussion, the ever-deteriorating brain cells of the lifelong fighter, the occasional death of a young man in his prime.

Could a man die fighting in a white-collar bout? As with amateur boxing, it is compulsory for the fighters to wear headguards. The boxers use sixteen-ounce gloves, far larger than those of the professionals and amateurs. Few of the men on the card at the Mermaid looked especially fit, suggesting that huge power punches would be the exception rather than the norm. It was clear that the organisers carefully scrutinised the progress of each fight. The referee was far more involved than at higher levels, often asking the fighters how they were and talking to the organisers, who were ringside. The Real Fight Club will have no hesitation in stopping a fight if it seems someone is about to get hurt. A doctor and paramedics are present and an ambulance was parked less than twenty feet from the ring, at the back of the Mermaid. But still, Mad Manx Beckett had been floored by a punch that no one had seen coming, that was so quick and so strong that no one could have stopped it even if they had wanted to. And he was out for the count for at least two minutes. Could that punch have killed him?

It was impossible not to speculate along these lines, notwithstanding the content of the flyer, which went on to mix the glamorous with the gritty: 'We train our boxers in a number of boxing and normal gyms across the UK, London, NYC and Frankfurt. There is a serious training preparation process rewarded by a professionally matched bout.' Frankfurt was a strange reference point as I watched a man mop up the blood from Mark Arnold's nose. Perhaps there were white-collar boxers exchanging blows in the German city, sparring after a hard day's trading or even boxing in front of five hundred people in an event like the one at the Mermaid. Somehow the idea of Teutonic 'white-collar warriors' was both amusing and terrifying. An awful and regrettable prejudice, with no foundation in fact, justified only by my experience of a German lawyer I had encountered early in my career, a ruthless and unpleasant man with the moral sense of a snake. He cloaked his lust for status and power in a veneer of chic and charm. Nothing he did or said was agenda-free, was not carefully calculated to achieve an end. He would lie with the effortlessness of a Roy Jones jab, and with every bit as much damage. Why did people like him exist? Why are some people simply nasty, to the core, irredeemably? At least what went on in the ring was honest and up front. A boxer knows that his opponent is trying to hit him, hard, and knows that he has to do the same thing himself. There may be skill and subtlety in the hitting, but the fact that the infliction of harm is intentional is known from the start. The German lawyer I found myself thinking of would speak his perfect English and smile as he shafted you, and you'd only realise it had happened three days later.

And yet it is precisely the intentional nature of pugilism that inspires revulsion in many quarters. It struck me that the flyer unconsciously alluded to boxing's outlaw status in its juxtaposition of boxing gyms with 'normal' gyms, as if boxing is by definition already abnormal, beyond the pale and unwanted. In normal gyms, people work out and get fit. They preen and pose and sweat and lift weights, row hundreds of metres on a machine, run for minutes on a treadmill, climb stair after stair never rising more than a foot from the ground. But in boxing gyms, something different happens (something more real?). Boxers smash their gnarled fists into bags or against each other. They train relentlessly for the moment of combat in the ring, the intentional infliction of harm on another human being. This is the illicit, unknown to most 'normal' gyms. Except, that is, those in which The Real Fight Club trains.

With the intermission over, the fourth fight of the night began, and the ringside air was redolent of the unknown and, usually, unknowable. Sezer 'The Geezer' Yurtseven, a broker with Obsideo, threw left hooks of such velocity that if any had connected with his opponent from Deloittes, Michael 'Baby-Faced Assassin' Doris, they would have taken his head off. Surely it cannot be right that people can be allowed to try and hit someone with so fast a punch? Whether at professional or amateur level, is it right that two men hitting each other can be a popular spectacle? That it is tolerated by the law? For that is what it is – *tolerated* by the law, not endorsed, condoned, still less codified, but at least *tolerated*. Could the Baby-Faced Assassin tolerate the left hooks swung wildly at him by Sezer Yurtseven? Ultimately, this was not a question he had to answer. Yurtseven missed repeatedly, and had nothing to show for his wildly aggressive tactics but exhaustion. His body could not *tolerate* the pace with which he began the fight, and soon he was clinching with his opponent at every opportunity. When each clinch ended, he would throw off Doris, as if it were he who was guilty of wearing down his man by holding. Yurtseven rapidly alienated all but a fraction of the audience, and those still cheering for him were clearly friends. Not a neutral in the building could admire his blend of petulance, spite and violent intent. Curiously, of course, the violent intent on its own would be acceptable. But with a mean-spirited campaign of holding and shoving, few were moved to applaud when the fight finished after its customary three two-minute rounds. As usual in white-collar boxing, a winner was not declared, but anyone watching would have had Michael Doris well ahead.

There were three fights left on the card, and as the fighters prepared for the next one I noticed that, according to the *Financial Times*, 'white-collar boxing is the new golf'. This assertion was quoted on the bottom left of the flyer, underneath the boxers' names. As I watched Jack 'Something For The Weekend' Kielty and 'Gorgeous' Paul Burfoot walk down the aisle to the ring, it was conceivable that this quote was more than mere puff. Each man walked out to loud music selected for the bout, to a rapturous greeting from assembled friends and polite applause from neutrals. They looked confident and charged up. Uncannily both were hair-salon owners, though whatever stylish locks were theirs were lost beneath the compulsory headgear. As it turned out, Jack Kielty had had a few fights, while it was Gorgeous Paul's debut. This was not immediately obvious as Paul Burfoot appeared to have the better technique, though his punches lacked power. Honours were about even and I could imagine stressed executives forsaking the golf course for a night of pugilism, from which they would emerge triumphant, battered or otherwise. What would sound more impressive the following day to colleagues and clients? 'Wonderful day's golf yesterday, got my handicap down then had some G&Ts in the clubhouse. Might have got us a new client, too.' Or: 'Tough fight last night. He caught me with a huge right in the second round but I came back, clocked him with a left hook, a right uppercut, and won it in the third.' The abolitionists would moan and the politically correct despair, but in the testosterone-filled world of corporate Britain I had a feeling that three two-minute rounds of combat would carry more kudos than a round of golf.

Upstairs in the bar, after the fights, I sipped a bottle of water with a few friends. They knew that I would be having a fight too, sometime soon. They had enjoyed the evening but none of them was rushing to sign up to The Real Fight Club. 'You must be mad,' said Rob Pickles, a sports rights agent who co-owns KOTV Ltd, whose base then was a building that looks like a World War II bunker in Chipping Norton, Oxfordshire. Chipping Norton's main claim to fame is that, at seven hundred feet, it is the highest town in its county, and it is not known for its links to professional boxing. But Rob had recently signed a deal for a weekly boxing magazine show, *KOTV*, to appear on Channel 4 and had managed to sell it into another seventy-odd countries worldwide. It was, as he proudly told us, the first show of its kind, a news-format, year-round series featuring the best of boxing everywhere. Rob was at the Mermaid with business partner David McConaghie, who had worked on and off with Frank Warren throughout his life. McConaghie knows boxing inside out but this was Rob's first experience of any fight, let alone white-collar boxing. Both of them thought the show at the Mermaid was slick and professional, a damn good night out, but a little too 'colloquial' for *KOTV.* I think Rob meant *parochial*, but he had had a few beers. I kept quiet, and let him continue.

'I thought it was bloody good, that second fight was awesome. Serves that bloody lawyer right! Lawyers shouldn't box, or maybe they should, it would do them some good. Present company excepted ... So come on, Alex, when's your fight? When do we get to see you in the red trunks giving it what for?'

I wasn't sure when the fight would take place, but if all went to plan I would be fighting Alex Mehta, the current holder of the world white-collar light-middleweight title, before the end of the year. 'Isn't he supposed to be a bit good?' asked Rob. Yes, I replied, he's an ex-amateur who had some forty fights, losing only five of them, who was asked to turn pro a couple of times. 'And you're going to fight him! You're mad!' said Rob.

No one disagreed. They all smiled and looked on at me benignly, as if I were an errant child who has done something wrong, again, and yet whom they like too much to reprimand. Rob expounded further on the lunacy of this proposed bout. 'How are you going to cope with someone that good? Have you done any boxing before?' The answer was no, not much. 'You're barking mad! How do you feel about it, after seeing that lot?'

The truth was that I was having major second thoughts. I had my reasons for taking up boxing, but I didn't want to take the kind of punch that had knocked out Paul Beckett, I didn't want to have a bloody nose, and I didn't want to fight a fast and capable tear-up merchant like Sezer the Geezer. And I didn't want to live like a monk for months on end, which was the only way I was going to achieve the fitness to fight. This was also the first boxing match I had ever seen, and, regardless of its white-collar status, it was the real thing. It had left me feeling that I had made the kind of mistake that Mad Manx Beckett made in deciding to chance his tattooed arm against Lee Short 'Fuse'.

I shifted my weight from foot to foot, seeking refuge in hesitancy. Rob was characteristically blunt. 'You look terrified,' he said, turning to have another drink.

He was right.

2

GOOD ENOUGH

Umar's two gold teeth, embossed with diamonds, flashed at me. 'So you're the journalist geezer?' he said, casually offering a hand. That was me. Ten years in the law had been enough and now I was writing for a living. Well, writing and doing a few other things, even some law, anything to pay the bills. Umar was a personal boxing trainer and I was interviewing him for a piece on white-collar boxing for *The Times*. 'Shall we go inside?' I said. 'Good enough,' said Umar.

We met on 26 November 2002 outside a friend's flat in Clapham, curiously enough opposite the house of my first boss, Nigel, a libel lawyer with Peter Carter-Ruck and Partners. Then, at least, the firm was called Peter Carter-Ruck and Partners, after its eponymous founder, CR to those of us who worked for him, a legendary libel specialist who died in late 2003 having made not quite as many enemies as everyone suspected. Now, after CR's death, the firm is simply 'Carter-Ruck'; then and now Nigel had a boyish twinkle so fixed it was almost an affliction. My friend Marc, also a former lawyer, and also, like me, once employed by newspaper proprietor Richard Desmond, had taken up boxing fifteen months before. He raved about the fitness and confidence it gave him, and got on with Umar, too, who would turn up at his flat and take him through his paces for an hour or so as often as he could find the time. Marc had warned me that Umar was a man with a past, but was adamant that he had changed, got his life together, moved on. I'd stay with Marc sometimes when I was in London, and on this occasion he'd given me the keys and the run of the flat so that I could interview Umar.

Outside Marc's flat, on that wet, flat November day, Umar and I shook hands and left Umar's ramshackle Volvo, stuffed with boxing gear, parked among the pristine Audis and Jaguars of a leafy Clapham street. Inside, I told Umar that the piece for *The Times* would focus mainly on Marc and the phenomenon of white-collar boxing, but that I needed some lines from Umar. 'Sure, man, whatever. Ask what you like,' he said, leaning back on Marc's sofa. Upstairs, Marc's cleaner, whom I'd let in a little earlier, went about her work. What she made of Umar and me chatting idly in Marc's absence I had no idea.

Umar told me that Marc was a decent boxer, nearly ready for his first fight. Umar himself wasn't a member of The Real Fight Club, nor one of its accredited trainers, but he was sure Marc was looking into 'all that jazz', and that he'd step up to make his debut soon. Meanwhile, Umar was lining him up for 'some full-on sparring', against someone his own build and weight, though for now he had to take his hat off to Marc; when he and Umar sparred Marc went for it – 'He's come on so much since he began, and I'll tell you, man, he's not bad, not bad at all.' I had an image of Umar and Marc sparring, and for some reason felt that, if it came to it, I'd rather have a fight with Umar than Marc. Umar was huge, about six foot two but two or three stone overweight, and he had a soft, likeable face that didn't readily convey menace. At least, that's what I thought when I first met him. Marc, on the other hand, was in very good shape, a few years younger than me, and looked like he had one hell of a punch. I wouldn't want to have a scrap with him – not least, of course, because he was a mate. But Umar? He was too big to get anywhere near me, and all that flab surely wasn't commensurate with being a hard man? This turned out to be the first of many misconceptions.

I asked Umar if it was true, that he'd been in trouble.

'Yeah, man, heaps of trouble. Mostly strong-arm stuff, some pimping, crack, you know, nothing too heavy.'

I tried to take this in my stride, but it sounded fairly heavy. 'Were you caught?'

'I was banged up a couple of times. The first was for smashing up a DSS office. The second for breaking a copper's jaw with a baseball bat. I still get hassle for it. They stop me all the time.'

'What about crack?'

'I used to score a grand's worth a day. That's a lot of money to find.'

'And girls?'

'Yeah, man, I looked after a couple. Nothing major though.'

Again I acted as if looking after a couple of prostitutes and scoring serious amounts of crack were, indeed, minor misdemeanours, merely nodding before asking: 'What changed you?'

'I got out of prison and realised that everyone I knew was

mad, dead or inside. I'd been boxing since I was eleven but ran into a mate who also boxed. He was clean, man, totally clean. So I started boxing again. And found religion. I'm a Sunni Muslim, not one of those messed-up al-Qaeda types, we're chilled. Boxing and religion sorted my life out.'

Umar went on to tell me about his childhood. His mother had been convicted of the manslaughter of his uncle when he was eighteen months old, and Umar found himself fostered for another eighteen months. He had been in care from the age of three until he was fifteen, moving from one 'School for the Maladjusted' to another. Umar chuckled over the term 'School for the Maladjusted'. 'Just think, man – there's no way a name like that would be allowed today.' When he was fifteen he had been set up in a bedsit and left to get on with it. The obvious career was crime, at which he excelled, swiftly becoming one of the most feared heavies in a number of red-light districts throughout the country, from Derby Road in Southampton to St Paul's in Bristol and Chapeltown in Leeds, eventually ending up in south London. When he straightened himself out in his mid-twenties, he sparred regularly with former British heavyweight champion Julius Francis, and got to the prestigious south-east divisional finals, where Frank Bruno and Gary Mason also first caught the eye. Umar represented the best boxers from the London area, fighting any number of amateur contests, and was good enough to turn pro. He talked of the rigour and discipline of boxing with the evangelical fervour of a Baptist minister. He'd had some amateur fights and had run a few boxing gyms, but the money was no good. Now, though, he was on to a good thing with his own personal boxing training business. He called it 'PBT4U'. He said this so fast that I had no idea what he'd said as we talked in Marc's flat, but he gave me a flyer later and it turned out that 'PBT4U' translated to 'Personal Boxing Trainer For You'. A bit too text-speak for me but fair enough. 'PBT4U' was going well, with a .co.uk website as well, and most of Umar's clients were businessmen like Marc, though he also had writers and actors, male and female. Almost all were middle class and white, successful in their various spheres, and here they were, turning to an ex-con for illumination. Umar would arrive at their houses with an elaborate contraption that could be assembled within minutes, from one side of which hung a bag, the other a speedball. He'd work out with clients for an hour or so, either on the portable bag or holding pads and letting them fire off punches at him. 'Life's sweet,' said Umar. 'I can make some good dough and I'll tell you, all of my clients, bar none, will tell you how fantastic boxing has been for them.' But what about Umar and his demons; had they really gone forever? 'Even after over a decade of being straight, I still cluck. You know what clucking is? It's when you get big-time cravings, when you just want to disappear for a couple of days and score. It's a real battle but I have to fight it. I'm proud of what I've achieved and don't want to go back to that place again.'

As we sat and talked, a curious thing happened. Something long hidden in my past crawled into my consciousness. I realised that if I hadn't previously met Umar, I'd heard a lot about him. Before we continued I asked: 'Did you train someone called Stefan?'

Umar looked startled. 'Yeah, how d'you know him?'

'It doesn't matter,' I said. But I remembered: a few years ago I'd talked to Stefan about Umar, about boxing, about karate, about women. *Umar is so chilled, you'd love him*, said Stefan. *Why don't you try some boxing? Umar says it knocks spots off karate.* How many times had I heard Stefan say *Umar says*?

Was Umar the source of all wisdom? For Stefan, back then, it sounded like it. *He used to be into some heavy shit, but he's clean. He's a Sunni Muslim now. He's really got it together. You should talk to him.*

So here we were, talking, four years later. 'What's up?' said Umar. 'Is Stefan after you?'

I said no, that wasn't the problem. I hadn't heard from Stefan for years, and nor was I likely to. In fact, contacting Stefan – a man I'd liked a lot – was a no-go. 'Listen,' said Umar, 'I'm old-school. Stum is stum. Whatever you tell me goes no further. I won't even say I've met you. But if it makes any difference, Stefan's not here any more. His family went off somewhere, France or Portugal, maybe Spain. He was a good boxer, though. Nice moves. Sweet. I wanted him to help me run a gym.'

There was a pause as Umar had said all he was going to say about Stefan, and as I fumbled for bland phrases to keep our conversation going. But I couldn't concentrate on the reason I was talking to Umar, on boxing, white-collar or otherwise; all I could think about was the bizarre coincidence that Marc's personal boxing trainer was the same man so admired by Stefan, four years earlier, when my life was in a mess. As I looked at Umar, a huge black man taking up all the space on Marc's sofa, wearing a track suit and trainers and with a bag crammed with boxing paraphernalia at his feet, I couldn't help but be reminded of the chaos of earlier years. I looked at Umar and wondered, how had he done it, how had he managed to beat so insidious a drug as crack? I couldn't help it, and hoped he didn't notice, but my lower lip started to tremble ever so slightly. How had Umar managed to beat his problems, while I hadn't? Here I was, interviewing Umar, out of the legal profession but at least this time of my own volition, still cursed by the same old demons. When would things ever change?

'You know,' I said, hesitantly, 'I've had one or two battles of my own.'

'Really?' said Umar, sitting back and folding his arms. 'Like what?'

'Well, a few problems here and there,' I said. 'Mostly to do with booze and women.'

Umar did his best but couldn't hide the surprise on his face. There he was, the ex-con, crack addict, hustler, strong-arm merchant and who knows what else, sitting talking to a nice white middle-class journalist, who was writing something about white-collar boxing for one of the most eminent newspapers in the world, and that journalist was all of sudden visibly a little shaken, as he tried to find the words to explain himself to Umar, a man he'd heard about so often four years earlier, and whom he could never have imagined meeting in these or any other circumstances. 'Go on,' said Umar, 'what's the story?'

It wasn't easy telling Umar what had happened, about how I'd pretty much lost everything a few years earlier, when an affair with Stefan's sister had destroyed my career and my marriage. I say 'an affair' destroyed things but that's a lie – it wasn't the affair (after all, thousands of people have affairs the world over, and no one ever knows, especially, so it is said, in France; which is not to condone affairs but to acknowledge their sometimes uncontroversial existence) – it was me, I alone destroyed everything, and the havoc I'd wrought had been on the cards all my life. I didn't go into much detail with Umar – there was no need, he is a compassionate man and, because of his own experiences, understood what I was trying to say in the absence of any semblance of eloquence from me. I didn't say much at all, really, just enough for Umar to nod with concern as he sank deeper and deeper into Marc's sofa, my voice rising every now and then when the cleaner made too much noise above us or next door in the kitchen, where empty cans of lager and red wine from the previous night stood on the table. I'd been alone in Marc's flat and had filled up the emptiness with writing and booze, enough booze to mean that the writing didn't last long. *If he possibly can, a young writer should refrain from writing.* I'd consoled myself with André Gide's words as the wine meant that I could no longer type with any accuracy, my fingers hitting the keys and spewing out haphazard text, vague approximations of language, nothing of any value. The trouble was, I wasn't young, and if I was writing for a living it was a recent development, not prolonged enough for me to describe myself as a writer. But Gide's words made more sense than anything else as I'd given up trying to accomplish anything and downed what booze was in the flat. As I talked to Umar, I didn't feel hungover, just slightly rough, but the problem was I felt *slightly rough* far too often. If I wasn't hungover so often as I had been in the bad old days, I was still *slightly rough* on a regular basis. Say, every three or four days. This saddened me and yet nothing ever seemed to change, it was always the same, save for the regular heavy sessions that I would throw in to enliven the near-quotidian of being *slightly rough.*

All this, to Umar, was obvious. Compulsive drinkers, addicts, the dangerous and the deranged, all can spot each other a mile off. It takes one to know one. If I left out the finite detail, my unhappiness was apparent to Umar, a man who had been through the mill and come out standing. 'That's fucked, man,' he said, 'that's fucked. Why do you do it? Why drink? You've got everything going for you – wife, kids, good job, I mean fuck, man, *two* good jobs, you can always be a legal eagle again if you want, so why fuck it all up with the booze?' I protested a little, after all, Umar was inferring more than he'd been told, I wasn't drunk the night before (was I?), it was just that I'd had a few, because, well, that's what I tended to do, but I wasn't up to no good, it was all under control, so what was the problem? Sure, things hadn't been so great a few years back, but now? Didn't I deserve a break, every now and then?

'It's fucked,' said Umar. 'You know it is.'

There was a slight hush as both of us took stock of where the conversation had begun, and where it had ended up. Maybe Umar felt sorry for me, because after a moment or two he hauled his vast bulk out of the depths of Marc's sofa, leant forward and looked at me with a blend of conspiracy and sympathy. 'You know, man, drink's one thing, but being a Sunni Muslim keeps me straight, and anyway, I never liked drinking,' he said, 'but you shouldn't worry about women. What you did was natural, it's the way the majority of men are. That's the great thing about my religion, it recognises what it's like to be a man. You should just tell your woman the way it is.'

I wasn't sure about this, but maybe it's a cultural thing. Would my life have been any different if I'd just said to my wife (and every other woman I'd slept with) that the only long-term certainty was that I'd sleep with someone else? *This is the way it is, I'm a man, and as such I'm bound to sleep with other women, to go forth and procreate, if you would like to put a biblical gloss on it, but whichever way you look at it, that's the reality, and you'd better accept it.* If I'd said that, would it have helped?

'I not sure about that,' I said to Umar. 'I reckon my wife would give me a swift right hook in the jaw if I told her that.'

'You'd be surprised,' said Umar, unwilling to relinquish his theory. And then he came up with something unexpected. 'You know what,' he said, as if he'd just solved some complex and demanding algebra, 'you should give boxing a go.'

'What? Me?' Feeling slightly rough as I was, and also, these days, being a pacific individual, I couldn't see it. But Umar was insistent. 'You should definitely box,' he said, voice rising with enthusiasm. 'It would give you focus and confidence. And you know what? How can you write about it if you don't do it? Look at Hemingway.' On Umar's flyer, a quote from Hemingway had been reproduced. 'My writing means nothing to me', so literature's most famous suicide apparently wrote. 'My boxing means everything to me.'

I thought about Hemingway and his love of pugilism, his desire to take on all-comers when drunk; I thought about Robert Cohn in *Fiesta*, a boxer and hardly a pleasant character. But whatever the ambivalence of my feelings for Hemingway, it occurred to me that maybe Umar was right. Maybe a bit of boxing would lessen the *slightly rough* days, maybe it would nail a few other things too.

'OK, you're on. How about one session for free and then we'll take it from there?'

'Good enough,' said Umar, 'good enough.'

I watched Umar sling his kitbag into the boot of his Volvo and lumber round to the driver's door. He's big, I thought, huge, but how the hell could anyone move that bulk around a boxing ring? Still, turning up for one session with him would be interesting, and he had a point – if you're going to write about things, shouldn't you experience them?

Inside Marc's split-level flat his cleaner was finishing up. She was from Eastern Europe and spoke poor English. There was something appealing about her, something that took my fancy. She had soft grey eyes, eyes of a hard life, and a shapely behind, upon which my eyes lingered as she went back upstairs again. It crossed my mind that here, today, was perfect for sex, if she was up for it. No one was around, no one would ever know, we could have gratuitous sex for an hour or so and go our separate ways. And when *slightly rough*, I always feel like sex. But no, this was absurd. After everything that had happened, how could I even think of sex with someone other than my wife, albeit that those thoughts were utterly, irreparably idle, as evanescent as an orgasm? But that, too, was the trouble. I still had those thoughts, even if nothing ever happened, and invariably they arrived after a night's drinking. And however much I loathed myself for my ongoing, if idle, fantasies, always the product of too much wine or lager, a few days later I would crack open a bottle, or down a pint, or say 'yes' to an offer of a drink, because after all one won't hurt, will it, and haven't I done well in not drinking since the last time? And then the same old temptations would arrive, all over again.

The cleaner finished her work upstairs and came down to ask me how to set the alarm. I had no idea. Between us we fiddled around with it incompetently, soon enough setting it off, a great relief in some ways because the hideous sound obliterated all remaining thoughts of sex, not that they were anything more than those that any other man alone with an attractive woman might experience. It was impossible to turn the alarm off and we smiled at one another idiotically. There was nothing to do but leave the flat, lock the doors and scuttle off. She turned right, we said *nice to meet you, have a nice day*, I turned left and we waved goodbye.

Back home I started writing the copy. I had quotes from

Marc, who was yet to join The Real Fight Club but perfect for the piece. He was a debonair, good-looking (not dissimilar to Brad Pitt in *Fight Club*) and a successful businessman, who had found boxing in the last fifteen months or so and loved it. He planned to join The Real Fight Club and have a white-collar bout by spring 2003. I had plenty of good stuff from Umar, and there was heaps of info about The Real Fight Club and white-collar boxing online. But I needed some quotes from an existing white-collar boxer. One man's name came up time and again via online searches, Alex Mehta, Ph.D., barrister and luminary of British white-collar boxing.

It wasn't hard to track him down, and I rang him at work the next day. Mehta worked as the legal director of a company selling prepackaged legal plans, whatever they were. He'd helped set it up and was, it occurred to me within seconds of our conversation, far better at the corporate world than I had been. He had a relaxed manner and a lilt to his voice, and, it soon transpired, a slightly quixotic habit of giggling every few sentences. I explained why I was ringing and asked him a few questions, and throughout he giggled. Since we had never met it seemed a little premature to be collapsing into hysterics at almost everything I said, but each to their own. Perhaps, for all his boxer's mien, he was nervous about speaking to a journalist.

'What's your current role?'

'I'm the legal director here. The company specialises in the creation of legal plans. They're tailored to an individual or company on a prepackaged basis. We then subcontract legal work to barristers or solicitors. We pride ourselves on very high quality control and I'm responsible for the quality of the law firms we use.'

I said that sounded a far cry from his early life in the law – Mehta qualified as a barrister with the prestigious chambers of Christopher Lockhart-Mummery QC. He agreed. 'Yeah, what we're involved in is the commodification of legal services. It's not like standing up in court. But we've got some very heavy duty executives as clients. There are few other companies with such serious City heavy hitters on their books.'

There it was, a hint of boxing, an allusion, amidst the giggles and corporate jargon, to *heavy hitters*. It gave me a nice way in to the main point of our conversation.

'Talking of heavy hitters, I know that you're a regular participant in white-collar boxing bouts, but boxing isn't something new to you, is it?'

'No, not at all,' said Mehta, then thirty-two. 'I started when I was at Oxford.' He giggled before going on to tell me that he was five foot eight, now a middleweight ('I could do with losing a bit of weight'), and had won four Oxford boxing Blues. He'd been unbeaten in fifteen years, had won the British students' title three years in succession, starting at featherweight and boxing for Oxford in what was (so I learnt) the most successful sports team in the history of varsity contests, and had boxed successfully on the UK amateur circuit. He had even been asked to turn pro a couple of times.

'Why didn't you?'

'Because it would have been a step too far. The hunger in the kids who turn pro comes from a different world. It was tempting but it was just too much.'

'But now you're a world title holder at white-collar level?'

'That's right, I'm the world white-collar light-middleweight champion.'

Again, Mehta laughed a little as he said this. I couldn't

decide whether his laughter came from nervousness or was the product of his endeavour to *empathise*, to make me understand that he understood that I could have no comprehension of the stellar world he inhabited, a world of rigour, discipline and combat, where success in the hard world of business is matched, perhaps even exceeded, by brilliance in the ring. *He laughed to turn his own excellence into a joke. It was self-deprecatory and a result both of humility and ego.*

It was difficult to figure out where Mehta was coming from. The cuttings I'd dug up online referred, ironically, to his 'becoming modesty', and in talking to him I was starting to fear that he had an ego the size of a heavy bag. Perhaps it would survive the same kind of pounding similarly unscathed. I asked him whether white-collar boxing was a bit of an anticlimax after his amateur and student triumphs. 'Not at all,' he said. 'I don't care what anyone says, a punch in the face is a punch in the face. I'd give a hundred per cent credit to anyone who gets in the ring with me.'

'But what does boxing give you? What does it mean to you? Why do it?'

Mehta answered with a passion that was a refreshing change from his legalese about prepackaged legal plans and the commodification of the legal industry. 'Boxing provides an essential balance to my life,' he said. 'It counters the arrogance of the City – you must know what I mean, you're a lawyer yourself. There's a lot of ego in the City but boxing is a great leveller. It grounds me. I just couldn't do without it. A lot of people have nothing more exciting than a morning coffee and a review of their pension, but boxing provides an escape.' I asked if he could still remember what his first fight felt like. 'Absolutely. You never forget your first fight. I was nervous, but the emotion I felt was so raw and intense I could taste it.' I told Mehta I had an idea of what that must have felt like, and mentioned that I'd always been attracted to pursuits involving risk of one kind or another, but he didn't take the bait, he didn't latch on to my efforts to establish parity: 'The only thing I can think of that's comparable is the feeling of walking into a bar and seeing a girl who just knocks you sideways.' I wasn't sure that this was quite what he was looking for by way of a comparison – who knows, maybe he was trying to create his own parameters of masculinity in conversation – but there it was, the build-up to a fight was like seeing a beautiful woman. Inwardly sighing at the comparison – there is, so far as I can see, no link between female beauty and pugilism – as much as the fact that, if I were honest, there were some things he said that I agreed with but didn't want to admit, I asked him how much training he did, how fit he kept himself. 'I train every other day, at the Kronk, with guys like Spencer Fearon and Andrew Wallace.' Current pros, decent amateurs, though Fearon had been out for a while. If Mehta was training with pros, he must be pretty handy, but my own ego was kicking in and telling me that he couldn't really be much cop, after all he was five foot eight, giggled too much and probably wouldn't be able to handle a lunatic like me, someone who had been in as many scrapes as Mehta had had amateur fights. 'So when's your next fight?' I said, wrapping up our chat. I think he said Tuesday the 10th, at the Marriott Hotel, but by then the children had got home from school; I wanted to wrap things up and see them, so I scrawled a note of Mehta's answer without paying any attention to what he said. The note does say *Tuesday 10th, Marriott*, but whether Mehta had that fight I have no idea.

What he did do was drop me a line a few days later. It was

long and involved and he took several sentences to get to the point, but he asked me if I would replace a friend of his – an actor of some repute – who had agreed to fight him in an exhibition bout to raise money for Refuge, the charity for battered women. The friend hadn't been well and had some film commitments looming, but the original plan was that they would fight under the auspices of The Real Fight Club and contest a formal International White-Collar Boxing Association world title. Sky were going to film it and there'd be no problem getting The Real Fight Club to agree to the venture because, as Mehta had told me, he was their best fighter and 'had a certain sway' with them. During the course of our earlier conversation, in another recidivistic and unanswered effort to impress Mehta, I'd told him that I used to do karate to a reasonable level, and he said that his would-be combatant was 'like you, ex-karate'.

'So how about it?' Mehta concluded. 'Might you fancy fighting me?'

I read Mehta's email with astonishment. In the meantime, since talking to him and writing up *The Times* piece (later run with an especially creative subeditor's headline, 'Pecs And The City Packs A Punch With Businessmen'), I'd pitched the idea of a New Year column on boxing as a means to lose weight and get fit to the *Independent on Sunday*. They were interested but hadn't yet said 'yes'. Now Alex Mehta had come up with a great piece of journalistic spin, the idea that the purpose of the column be that I train relentlessly for, say, six months, and then climb into the ring and fight him for his world light-middleweight title. This worked, as an idea, and I felt sure that Mike Higgins, the editor I dealt with at the *IoS*, would go for it.

But, deep inside, what I really liked was the combination

of absurdity and risk. Not to mention the challenge. I hadn't met Mehta, I'd just talked to him over the phone, and I couldn't be sure whether I liked him or not. But some atavistic competitive male urge blossomed as I read his email, and I thought to myself: 'You're on. And you have no idea who you're dealing with.' Sure, I'd fight him, and in an emulation of Stallone in *Rocky* I'd come up trumps against all the odds. Maybe I'd even find some carcasses of dead cows to punch until my knuckles were raw.

We spoke later; I said yes, but wasn't the weight difference a problem? I was at least a stone and a half heavier than him, somewhere in the light-heavy division between twelve and a half and thirteen stone. 'Dude, it's not a problem,' said Mehta. 'Six weeks ago I fought a light-heavy who was thirteen and a half stone. I'll wear a tracksuit for the weigh-in.' I asked him to be gentle with me. He laughed that laugh again, and told me he was worried about me. I could tell he was lying and hadn't the slightest doubt that he'd beat the living daylights out of me, if he wanted to. But then again, this was for charity, and it was white-collar boxing. Mehta repeated the mantra: 'I don't want to hurt or humiliate anyone, I just want to raise as much money as possible.' As he wrote: 'Violence against women is something I have zero tolerance for – there is no honour in hurting someone smaller and physically weaker than yourself – if you want to prove how tough you are, pick a fight with someone twice your size.' Mehta was keen to publicise Refuge and its work, owing to an abhorrence of violence against women and a sense that he had seen all too much of it through his own work, in the ostensibly civilised world of the City. Mehta again: 'The other point we were going to make is that domestic violence isn't just restricted to council estates. It's sad, but through my work and the people I know socially, I have come across countless episodes of City domestic violence – basically, university-educated professional men, with good jobs and degrees, who do batter their girlfriends or wives. The whole idea that domestic violence is only for the working classes is so false – and if by being a boxer I can help demonstrate that such male behaviour is inexcusable, all the better, I say . . .' And he mentioned how the only time he'd ever used his fists outside a ring was on a crowded Tube when two young women were being assaulted – 'nobody did a thing, except me, but that's another story'.

I wasn't sold on the Refuge angle. The idea of boxing being used as a vehicle to raise money to help women who had suffered male violence seemed a little tactless. I said I might look to raise money for another charity, maybe the National Asthma Campaign, and Mehta said that was fine.

I put the phone down and turned to my wife. 'Guess what,' I said, 'I'm going to train and fight for the world white-collar light-middleweight boxing title.' She was quite taken with the idea. I rang Umar and told him that I'd be along for that first session soon, but that there was a new plan – he'd be training me to fight Alex Mehta, the white-collar world light-middleweight champion.

'Good enough,' said Umar. 'Good enough.'

3

NOT THE KARATE KID

'If you keep standing like the Karate Kid, you'll get your head knocked off.' To demonstrate the truth of this assertion, Umar cuffed me – gently – with a looping left to the side of the head. I tottered backwards and had to stagger to regain my balance. As I got back into what Umar decreed was a 'proper boxing stance', I reflected that a few years ago the stance into which I kept lapsing was, according to a couple of highly proficient *shotokan* karate instructors, immovable. Left leg pushed forward, bent at the knee virtually to 90 degrees, right leg stretched behind, almost perpendicular; left foot planted on the floor, right angled forwards, almost as if to do groin stretches before a football match. Even if I didn't quite re-enact the classic *shotokan* fighting stance, it was as if my body had its own memory of what to do before throwing a punch, or receiving one: each time, my feet slipped further and further apart, until finally Umar began to lose patience.

'What is it with you, are you some sort of martial arts dude?'

I admitted that I'd spent four years practising *shotokan*. It wasn't enough to make me a 'martial arts dude' but had been long enough to cause a few problems.

'That explains it,' said Umar, shaking his head. He stood back and looked at me quizzically, and again the irresistible thought occurred that he had just solved a tricky equation. Maybe he had, maybe I was a strange, curly-haired and possibly uncalled for equation in Umar's life. After a few moments he spoke. 'You know, when I ran the boxing gym, we used to get karate guys turn up every now and then. Full of it, they were. We'd get some black belt dude come in and ask to fight one of the boxers. You know what?' I had no idea. 'I used to tie one hand behind my back and nail 'em. You know how?' Again, I was clueless. 'With the jab. With a good jab you can do anything. There's no way any martial arts man can beat a boxer. They ain't got a chance. You've got to forget the karate, man, and get with boxing.'

The idea of black belt 'karate dudes' leaving terror-stricken and humiliated by the one hand of Umar sounded all the more outlandish given the surroundings. This, the first day of the training that would supposedly see me fight Alex Mehta in a few months, was taking place in the front room of Umar's flat in Chiswick. It was a miserable day outside and what peculiar satisfaction I'd derived from discovering that Umar's place was just a mile or so along the road from my birthplace (Chiswick Maternity Hospital, now an old people's home) was subdued by the thought that serious boxers did not kick off intense training regimes in the recently cleared front rooms of flats inhabited by huge ex-cons and their many children. But having persuaded the *IoS* to go for the column – on the premise that I'd train and fight Mehta – I'd cut a deal with Umar whereby, sure, the first session would be free, but thereafter each one would be a tenner, some thirty quid or so cheaper than his usual price as a personal boxing trainer. Naturally, Umar would get a plug at the end of each column, which the editor, Mike Higgins, christened 'The Slugger'. The trouble was, a tenner didn't buy access to a boxing gym. What it did buy was access to Umar's flat, and its communal gardens, and what I'd ended up agreeing to was meeting Umar at his flat to start with, then moving up to a gym when Umar decided I was ready. There'd been a bit of chat about this, but Umar had disabused me of my quaint notion that we needed to start the training in a boxing gym and told me that, if I was to do this seriously, I had to accept that he was the boss, that he called the shots, and that if he said we'd start in his flat, that's what we'd do. And anyway, wasn't the first one for free?

Within minutes of arriving at his flat on the kind of drab west London day that always makes me wish I was living on the Costa de la Luz, surfing nice beach breaks all year and taking it easy, not worrying about anything, least of all boxing or anything that smacks of conflict, I was treated to an Umar inquisition.

'How've you been, bro? How was Christmas? Wife well? Kids happy?'

To all these questions, the answer was, just about, 'good' and 'yes'.

'What about the drinking? You still caning it?'

No, I said, I hadn't been caning it at all. I'd been mindful of the regime about to start in the New Year and had had a totally chilled, tranquil Christmas, during which barely a drop had passed my lips. I hadn't smoked either. Not that smoking was one of my everyday vices, it was just something that inevitably accompanied drinking, like sex-line ads to centrefolds, like the fairy on the top of the Christmas tree, or the mistletoe recently revived in my family's festivities. No, I was clean as a whistle.

'I don't believe you for a second,' said Umar. 'Come on, let's go outside and warm up.'

Umar lived in a ground-floor flat in a modern three-storey block just off Chiswick High Road. It was a tidy residential development with nicely laid-out communal gardens, overlooked by many of the other flats and surrounding houses. There was an office block nearby which would also command a fine view of whatever Umar got me doing in the gardens. The idea of being on public display at the outset of my training didn't appeal and I hoped Umar wouldn't have me doing any boxing. I assumed he'd have me running up and down for a few minutes. I didn't feel too apprehensive about this, having put in a few runs over Christmas and in the first couple of weeks of January. Umar slung his kitbag on to the ground while I loosened up. He looked at me. 'Right, you stretched out?' he enquired. I said that I was. 'OK, I want you to run round the block for ten minutes. You're going to sprint when I tell you, then jog, then sprint again. You got that?' It sounded OK to me and off I went.

By the beginning of my second lap Umar had disappeared. His bag was still there, but there was no sign of him. Just as I was wondering whether boxing trainers habitually vanished at the beginning of training sessions I was startled by the sound of a window being cranked open. It was Umar, and he was leaning out of his flat. 'Right – sprint!' he yelled. I gave it what I could, continually slipping on the damp grass until Umar told me to slow down and jog. My lungs were heaving. The countless cigarettes smoked throughout December and into January didn't make an impression on my fitness for four- or five-mile jogs at a steady pace, but were crippling for any kind of sprinting. 'I thought you said you played football?' said Umar, as I heaved into view. This was true. I was a sporadic, perennially injured member of CHQ United, my local team, where I redefined the striker's role by combining an elegance of touch with an absence of speed and total lack of goals. Umar was not impressed. 'You don't look fit enough to play kids' five-a-side. Where do you do your training? In the pub?'

As I completed yet another circuit, I remembered thinking that it all looked easy enough from the vantage point of the bar in my local, where over Christmas we'd watched the BBC's celebrity boxing match between Grant Bovey and Ricky Gervais. The pair had signed up for six weeks of intensive training and slugged it out in a contest that perhaps proved once and for all that six weeks – however gruelling – does not a boxer make. Gervais looked fat and seemed to take a shot badly, going down a couple of times in training to what looked like soft punches. Bovey was as lean as they come but didn't have the look of a fighter, and would probably never have it, whatever he did. On the night, they stumbled around the ring, fists flying haphazardly to the yelps from an eager audience of 'B' list celebrities. Remarkably, Gervais got the nod, to the visible consternation only of Bovey's blonde beloved, Anthea Turner, though in the pub Joe, a former prizefighter, said that though they were both useless Bovey was the better boxer. Was it a fix, if not prefight but after the event, with Gervais the popular hero getting the nod ahead of Bovey, whose boxing was better developed than his charisma? It wouldn't have been the first controversial decision in the history of boxing. Rigged or not, my mates and I thought *Bloody hell, they're useless, any of us could do better than that*, as we said *Yes please, another pint of Stella, thanks, get one in for the next round, mine's a whisky chaser, have you got the fags, go on, hit him!* And in the background there was the occasional shot of Alan Lacey, the founder of The Real Fight Club, which had put the show together for the BBC. If this was white-collar boxing – and presumably it was – it would be a breeze.

Now, as the ten-minute running and sprinting session was coming to an end, I had slowed to a virtual walking pace, which was only marginally increased on the command to sprint. I didn't feel exhausted so much as incapable – my legs and lungs just didn't have the capability for fast running. Maybe this was because of my age, I said to myself, bent double at the end of the session. Then Umar asked me how much I smoked. 'Not too many,' I said, 'and I only ever smoke when I drink.'

'So what's that, every night?' said Umar.

No, it wasn't every night, not usually anyway, but December, well, December had been tough. Maybe an average of ten cigarettes a day had been smoked.

Umar looked at me with barely hidden disgust. 'I don't understand it,' he said. 'Why do people smoke? I'll tell you, man, if you're going to do this seriously you've got to quit the sauce and the ciggies. Cut 'em out completely. They're fucked, it's fucked, you can't smoke and drink and box. If you think you can you'll be wasting my time as well as your own. Now towel down and come inside.'

Inside, Umar repeated his mantra. No smoking, no drinking, I had to take this seriously. He would sort out my diet as well. I felt a little chastened, and maybe looked downcast. 'Come on,' said Umar, 'give me your hands.' He proceeded to tie wraps around them. Then he looked me hard in the eyes and said: 'This is where it starts.'

I looked around Umar's front room, the furniture pushed to one side to make space, a bottle of water on the table, some children's toys on the floor. I had put on a pair of sixteen-ounce boxing gloves given to me by Umar. So this is where it starts, I thought. Who knows, maybe Umar was right. *Thank God for small mercies.*

Umar was right to disbelieve my initial claim not to have been caning it. Since we'd first met at Marc's flat I'd been *slightly rough* too many times to remember. It was, of course, the festive season. Why not have a few and indulge? After all, the rest of the world was doing exactly that. The immense pleasure I have always found in drinking mindlessly had, however, reached its nadir, and early in December 2002 I had forced myself to an AA meeting. The catalyst was a feeling of self-loathing that, used to it as I was, surprised even me.

I'd been up to my local a few weeks before the Gervais–Bovey fight. It's an excellent pub, I still drink there now. It's a traditional boozer but my first visit some two years earlier hadn't augured well. I'd walked in and the pub had fallen silent. The Wild West cliché was alive and well in the Cotswolds, to which my wife and I had moved because circumstances, twice, had dictated a move. In the first place, we'd moved to Cheltenham, where I'd taken a job with a law firm that offered City-type work from the country, because life as a lawyer in London was taking its toll. Too many nights out, too much stress, too much lunacy, too much aggression, too much effortless hypocrisy and a virtually unfettered alcohol intake, a young child and another on the way, and

Karen, my wife, was sick to the back teeth of London and everything that my life there had become. Not hers – she was always different, not a part of it. So I'd got myself a job in the country, where all would be well. For a while it was, but then the same old demons surged back into play, and suddenly I was living in a bedsit in London, out of work, and my wife was with our two boys in Cheltenham. A couple of years passed but we'd patched things up, in fact, made a damn good job of getting back together, and after one or two impermanent forays into the job market I'd found full-time and gainful employment. But it was in London again, and so the second move we made was away from Cheltenham, an elegant, boxing-free, bourgeois town which one would not readily associate with ghosts, further south, near where the Cotswolds ends and Swindon begins, so that I could commute to London with relative ease, gainfully, in my smart-casual slacks and blazer, every inch the responsible, dull and respectable commuter, a man without a past or at least not one that anyone talked about.

On the day of the move to our new and idyllic village, we walked in to the local and asked for lunch. The request met with the suggestion that we would be far better off trying any of the pubs in Fairford, the nearest town. The landlord seemed friendly enough as he said this and as the few silent faces in the bar absorbed the sight of my wife, myself and my boys, the newcomers to the village, the man with a bit of a past because someone, somehow already knew and word had slunk ahead of us along the country lanes, and the possibility that it was this that was responsible for the landlord's suggestion that we dine elsewhere immediately plagued me, as if of course, and inevitably, we were fools, it was impossible ever to escape, ever to erase the traces of mistakes made and paid for, ever to shake off the fetid stench of one's own self-engendered humiliation, and so No, had said the landlord, thanks very much, you can't eat here, even if your children are small and hungry, not to mention you and your wife as well, why don't you just nip down to Fairford which is just about big enough to accommodate the tangled skein of your wrongdoing without anyone gossiping, for a few weeks, at least. As we left the pub Karen said that it was a shame, the landlord seemed nice enough, but let's just head over to Fairford, it'll be interesting anyway, and I nodded and mumbled inarticulately, consumed as I was by paranoia and rage at my endless failings, the failings that meant we couldn't get a bite to eat on the first day of this, our new start in a new village where no one or everyone knew about what had happened, I wasn't sure.

Naturally, there was a perfectly good reason for the landlord suggesting that we went to Fairford. I can't remember what it was but have subsequently drunk in his pub enough times to say that he is a fine man who, despite a tendency to world-weariness, is not known for being unfair to anyone, least of all me. During December 2002, he had every reason to be weary, as he and his wife coped with double their usual monthly custom and, the perfect excuse of Christmas festivities being present, everyone wanted just that one more for the road. I have never needed much by way of an excuse, pretty much anything will do, but that December, having spent two years back with Karen, the excuses were wearing thin as virtually every night I either drank at home or went to the pub. The booze did what it always did. It annulled my sense of self, made me hate what was left of me in the morning, allowed a constant *slightly rough* feeling to dominate, until one day, not long before Christmas

Day, when the bright eyes of my children would dart around our bedroom as they leapt uncontrollably with excitement, I found myself reeling from a booze-related incident, hardly able to believe that I was the same person as the idiot who had blundered into some inappropriate behaviour with a woman I didn't even fancy, forever to leave the blemish of my alcoholism or impulse-control syndrome or personality disorder in yet another part of the world.

I'd been in Cirencester and had got talking to a curvaceous redhead called Lucy. Initially I'd been with some friends but they had seen sense and gone home on time, while I had opted to stay out drinking. Lucy was happy to keep me company. She had had a few, too, and by the end of the evening we were both pissed. I liked her, but she wasn't my type. I had no interest in her, sexually, even on a *slightly rough* kind of a day; more to the point, I was married to Karen, who would be at home, starting to wonder what on earth I was doing. And yet somehow, at the end of the evening, I found myself not merely walking her home, through the less-than-dangerous streets of Cirencester, but staggering through the front door of her house for just the one more lager.

The conversation degenerated with unusual rapidity. It was surreal, too, precisely because *there was nothing there*. There was no interest, I was drunk, hopelessly drunk, as I have been so many times, but something made me twist the conversation towards the sexual, something untoward, something that might have been sinister if it hadn't been so absurd, something certainly inappropriate given my status as a married man. Why was I doing this? What did I possibly hope to gain or achieve? Seduction was the last thing on my mind. If Lucy had said 'I'm yours' I'd have run a mile, just as I would have done if the cleaner in Marc's flat had miraculously sensed my *slightly rough* imaginings and made an overture. Lucy went along with the conversation, drunk and as bewildered as me, until she or both of us or me realised that it was all ridiculous, pitiful and pointless, it was time for me to get up, leave and get a cab home, then to walk down through my village, across its green of endless car-boot sales in the summer and emptiness in winter, down the hill, past the pub, the ever-welcoming pub, down into the darkness, past the old houses with their Cotswold stone and black Labradors, until I reached the door of my house, battered and with fraying, rotten wood that we never got round to repairing, knocked at it imploringly because I would have left my keys at home and Karen would have locked me out, until finally, angrily she would let me in and I would try and tell her that I loved her and was sorry and as usual it would be useless, I'd be drunk and stinking of alcohol and fags and the last thing she'd want would be even to see me, let alone hear my tedious words of regret and love, and so she'd tell me to fuck off and leave her alone, and like every stupid drunk I'd react as if mortally wounded and say What do you mean, I've only been to the pub, it's not as if I've been shagging anyone for God's sake, and Karen would shake her head with fury and contempt and tell me to sleep in the spare room and for two days we wouldn't talk as she mouldered in her despair and I promised to do better next time.

This time, though, Karen didn't bother shouting at me and I didn't bother with my usual litany of excuses, reasons and regrets. Perhaps the lack of a row was because I was even more drunk than usual. I sat at the end of the bed, our bed, our marital bed, swaying and stinking in the darkness as Karen pretended to be asleep, and told her that I knew I couldn't go on like this, that something had gone wrong at the end of the evening but I couldn't remember what. I knew that my conversation with Lucy had been wrong, deeply wrong, not merely because I was married, and shouldn't be having such conversations, but because it showed that nothing had really changed, I was still the same old Alex, just as capable of taking things to the edge and then pushing them over, still possessed by some dark spirit that only ever seemed to leave me in peace for brief interludes. I wished it would go, I wished that whatever was wrong with me would be fixed, and yet *it never was*, all I did was the same old things, again and again. Karen knew this too; if she had told herself that I had changed over the past two years now she knew, the truth was stark and hideous, there had been no real change, everything was just buried and waiting to explode, it was only a matter of time. I slept in the spare room and didn't let myself lie in bed and fester the next morning. I got up early and hated myself more than ever and told Karen that I would go to an AA meeting. I don't think she believed me. But, this time, things had to change.

I went to my first AA meeting a couple of days later.

Umar was holding two pads in front of his face. 'Let's see what you've got,' he said. I threw out a left and a right. 'Again,' said Umar. I put more power into the punches. 'Come on, more, harder and quicker,' said Umar. I gave it all I had, and with each punch Umar's face twitched a little more aggressively. So did mine. My lungs had recovered from the sprinting and I was enjoying this. It was different from karate, where apart from the *makiwara* board one's fists rarely ever connect with full impact on anything, let alone anyone. After about twenty or thirty punches Umar told me to rest. 'Not bad,' he said, 'not bad at all. You've got a good right but that jab needs a lot of work.' As I caught my breath Umar began the first of many lectures about the importance of the jab. 'Look, you do it like this', and at once I was confused because Umar, as a southpaw, used his right hand to jab, not, like orthodox boxers, his left. Umar's being a southpaw always bothered me, right from that first day in Chiswick. The mental effort of inverting everything he did, so that each movement with his lead right foot became one made with my left, with every feint, slip and punch reversed, reminded me of my failure ever to grasp mathematics. It was just *too difficult*, three attempts to pass the 'O' level had all ended with an E grade. At least my incompetence was consistent. That day, I felt again like the class idiot, as in imitation of Umar's carefully delivered, slow-motion jab I sought to emulate it with my right. That's what he was doing, wasn't it, putting out the jab with his right? 'No, man, no, you're orthodox, I'm a southpaw, you throw the jab with your left, come on, like this.' (I didn't register it at the time, but later it struck me that the only other person I had ever heard describe himself as a southpaw was my father. He boxed for his school, ineffectually, as he would have it: 'I was as blind as a bat so they used to just put me in the ring and point me in the right direction.' The alliance of Umar and my father as the two southpaws in my life was as incongruous as it was strangely pleasing.) Umar showed me the jab again and this time I jabbed with my left, my gloved fist landing with a murmur on the pad held out by him. 'Technique's getting there but you've got to get a lot more power into those jabs,' said Umar. 'And always remember one thing.' What was that? 'The words of Frank Maloney. If you can't jab, you can't fight.'

That first session we didn't do much other than jab,

though every now and then Umar would tell me to let go with the right. He liked my straight rights. 'I'll tell you, man, good punchers are born, not made. You've got one hell of a right. Just don't miss the pads with it.' To begin with it was enjoyable, but I was far from fit enough to sustain an hour's worth of punching, however much I liked banging out the rights when Umar would let me, and after a while the pleasure of the repetition of the same movement – left jab, straight right – began to pall. Fortunately Umar is a loquacious man. I realised on that first day that if I could get him talking about something, I could have a rest. I think he worked this out pretty quickly; every speech about whatever I'd prompted would be concluded with a guillotine of a phrase and a rushed exhortation to get on with things again. 'Come on, enough gassing! We've got work to do!' And the pads would be held up again, and I'd punch them again, and again, until I could think of something else to divert Umar or he would look at me and feel merciful.

Or he would, as on that first day, pick me up on all manner of problems with my technique. Hence the diatribe about karate, as he pushed at my legs with his own feet to get them into the correct boxing stance. 'Karate ain't no good, man. It's fine for a bit of exercise and maybe a bit of a feeling of achievement when you get your nice coloured belts, but it ain't nothing to boxing.' Stumbling sideways from a gentle cuff when I'd lapsed into my Karate Kid stance, I was starting to think that Umar had a point. You can master the *kata* – sequences of preordained movements in martial arts – until the cows come home, you can do all the drills with their required responses until you can dream them in your sleep, but a real fight requires elasticity and fluidity, not to mention the nerves honed by actual combat. Unless you're unlucky enough to walk into a *dojo* run by a nutter, you won't, learning karate, get hit in the face, and nor will you ever deliver more than a graze to an opponent. Actual contact is likely to be accidental rather than deliberate, and certainly won't be encouraged by any of the *sensei*. And yet whichever way they're dressed up, the pugilistic 'arts' are about one thing, and one thing only: fighting.

'OK, you've done enough punching for this first session,' said Umar, pulling my gloves off and untying my wraps. He rolled them up swiftly and told me they were on the house, and then examined my knuckles to see if they'd been cut from the punching. The scars on my right fist were more livid than normal, though they weren't cut. Umar looked at them with surprise. 'Man, how'd you get those scars?' he asked. I ducked the question and asked him with a smile how he had come by the scars on his own knuckles. 'Probably the same way you got yours,' said Umar.

I thought that would be it for the first day, but it wasn't. 'Outside,' said Umar, turning towards his window. 'More running. I'll tell you what to do from here.'

Outside I stood next to Umar's kitbag, still there, pointlessly, so far as I could tell. Perhaps it was symbolic in some way. Umar took up his station at the window. 'Five minutes warm-down, around the block, come on, let's go,' he said, turning inside to say something to someone, I wasn't sure who since so far as I was aware the flat had been empty the whole time we had been training. So once again, I set off around the communal gardens of Umar's block of flats in Chiswick. The pace was even slower by now. I couldn't wait to get the whole thing over with. Landing a few straight rights was OK but all this running and sprinting, not to mention the tellings-off about technique, had worn me down.

I was due at the *Independent* later that day, to steer the paper safely through any libel or contempt problems that the next day's news might prompt, and I was starting to worry that I'd be so knackered that I'd drift off to sleep in the middle of the shift. Dejection was probably ripe on my face, but Umar didn't care. He knew that he had to get me through this session and many others that would be far worse if I was to have half a chance of fighting Alex Mehta, or anyone else for that matter.

I looked up at the office block a few hundred yards away. The drab greyness of the day was turning and black clouds now hovered over the building. A little beyond was my uncle's flat on Chiswick High Road, where I'd spent the first couple of years of my life, a place so crammed with music and books that you couldn't have cleared a space for a boxing workout even if you'd wanted to. I must go and see my uncle, I said to myself, it's been ages. About a mile to the north-east was QPR Football Club, which I had supported since a boy. I always feel some weird sense of comfort when I'm in west London, near my uncle's flat, where I was brought up as a small child, and near to QPR.

Maybe this is OK, I said to myself, you're here, in west London, the weather might be shit and you're tired but life's a lot better than it has been. As my thoughts drifted my pace slackened right off. 'Come on!' screamed Umar. 'I used to run faster for my dealer than that!'

4

GO ON, SON!

Alan Lacey came late to boxing. He was forty-four and smoking thirty a day when he decided to give it a try. The smoking was, as he confessed, 'getting worse and worse. I kept looking for ways to stop but nothing worked. Until I decided to walk into a boxing gym, a crazy idea, but it worked. The day I started boxing was the day I stopped smoking. I stopped one drug and replaced it with another.'

We were talking in The Light Bar on Shoreditch High Street, little more than a stone's throw from the futuristic building of City lawyers Herbert Smith. It was a bright and cold February day and I was late for our meeting. I'd trained with Umar in the morning, at the Energise Centre in Hammersmith. The traffic from west London across to the City had been lousy, finding a parking space even worse. Then as I'd hurried to The Light Bar I'd been delayed further by a work call on my mobile. I stood outside the bar, next to the public phone boxes, trying to wrap up the conversation, hoping Lacey himself was late. A scruffy man in his mid-twenties was loitering by the phone boxes. He squinted at me nervously and our eyes locked. He pulled up the hood of his faded grey sweatshirt and turned on his heel.

The Light Bar was virtually deserted. No wonder, it was about 3.00 in the afternoon, and in today's world long City lunches are as rare as contrition. I peered around to see if I could recognise Lacey. No one seemed to fit the bill. I asked at the bar, but, if he was there, they couldn't help me. 'Dunno, mate, he's not a regular,' said a Spanish-looking barman through his designer stubble. I went back outside and the man with the grey sweatshirt was back. He dived into the phone boxes and pasted some tart cards on the glass, by the phones, even on the counter where they used to keep the Yellow Pages before vandals made it pointless. Within seconds the phone box had become a shrine to harlotry. The cards were everywhere, inescapable. There were some old ones on the floor, tattered and scuffed from the feet of the hundreds of people who still use public telephones. Who did still use public telephones? They were always empty and everyone these days has a mobile phone. Maybe the only people who use them are men seeking prostitutes, meaning that the tart cards are a vital part of the British telecommunications industry, for without them the public phone box would become as functional as a sledge in summer. As the man with the sweatshirt finished he caught my eye again, with the same desperate, shifty look. *So that's what a carder looks like*, I thought. After he'd gone I looked at the cards, the man's mid-afternoon gift to the streets of Shoreditch. *Amber, 44DD, loves oral relief* and *Sexy Swedish blonde, all services* adorned images cut and pasted from the kind of soft-core top-shelf magazines I'd once been responsible for as a lawyer for Richard Desmond in his pre-*Express* days. *Asian Babes*, *Big Ones*, *Shaven Haven*, they were just a few of the choice titles that had sat unquestioned and, indeed, requisite on my lawyer's desk on the Isle of Dogs. Women would sell their bodies for a release fee of some £200, and thereafter immutably inviting in celluloid (as if they were never anything other than a willing, characterless object of male sexual satisfaction) would be recycled from magazine to magazine, ultimately in some cases to end up in full view of the passers-by of London's phone boxes, men in raincoats, City gents, lawyers, accountants, bankers, professionals, the homeless, old ladies, children, anyone who happened to be walking the streets.

Back inside I ordered a coffee. Lacey turned up within a couple of minutes. He was tall, about fifty, with a firm handshake and glittering eyes. It didn't take him long to discourse with a disciple's conviction about his master and religion, boxing. 'I started late, but discovered that, well, I was good at it.' He said this with a shrug of the shoulders and tone of apology that seemed more than a little manufactured. One thing Alan Lacey has no doubts about is boxing. He is proud of being good at it and has no problems with what it is. 'Boxing's for warriors, isn't it, and that's what men are underneath all this fucking bollocks' – he waved dismissively at the empty Light Bar, arm swooping in an arc to take in the City – 'I must have had a hundred fights since I started. I love it. The trouble is, now we're so fucking busy I can't get in the ring any more.'

It's true, The Real Fight Club is busy, though whether this fully explains Lacey's own absence from the amateur pugilism he has pioneered is open to doubt. There comes a time for every boxer when he no longer wants to get in the ring, when there is a sense that too many blows will be received rather than landed, when the work involved in being boxing-fit is just too severe, too draining, too hard. Maybe Lacey has reached that point. Lithe and dapper, in a smart grey suit and open-necked white shirt, complete with slicked-back hair and a wispy goatee, he looks every inch the boxing promoter, less so the ex-fighter who still has a bit left in the tank. Still, he skipped and shuffled nimbly in The Light Bar, unable to resist showing me some moves.

We talked about The Real Fight Club and Lacey's plans. He told me that the club had more than 650 members, achieved after just eighteen months, and that a national franchise was on its way, despite opposition from the British Board of Boxing Control. 'They fuckin' hate me,' said Lacey, a former manager as well as promoter, who once had Gary Stretch on his books. With fellow promoter Barry Hearn, Lacey co-promoted Stretch's fight against Chris Eubank in April 1991. 'It was a sellout,' he told me. 'There were nine million people watching on ITV. Those were the days.' Now, as well as the franchise, which would see Real Fight Club gyms up and down the country, he was in talks about opening an ultra-modern boxing gym nearby, in the City. 'It's some space, I'll tell you,' said Lacey, in an East End accent whose huskiness betrayed his now abandoned love of nicotine. 'It's gonna be fantastic, *fantastic*, if it comes off.'

In The Light Bar, Lacey couldn't have been more charming. This was a relief since we'd got off on the wrong foot. A couple of weeks earlier he had rung me on the eve of the publication of my piece in *The Times* about white-collar boxing. I was skating with my two boys on the ice of the water meadow, which often floods and freezes in winter, in our village, when the mobile went. Lacey introduced himself and asked me what I was intending to write. I said I'd written the piece already and had tried to contact him but that he'd been constantly engaged. This was true. However, the piece was less about Lacey and more about people such as Umar and Alex Mehta, so I hadn't been too worried about Lacey's unavailability, and had lifted an existing quote or two of his from The Real Fight Club's website. It was a straightforward, and, what's more, positive, piece – 'nothing to worry about', as I told Lacey that day.

But he wasn't convinced. 'Look, I'm not saying you're going to publish anything that's negative,' he said. 'It's just that I thought you might like to fax over what you've written so that you can give yourself an opportunity of correcting any errors.'

It was about 4.00 in the afternoon, I had worked all day and I was enjoying my time with my sons. I wasn't in the mood to humour Lacey. 'Look, it's a friendly piece, don't worry,' I said. 'Besides, the page will have been set ages ago.'

Lacey didn't like this. He told me that The Real Fight Club had been stitched up by another broadsheet and that he just wanted to give me an opportunity to get things right. 'Otherwise, I've got a highly paid lawyer sitting here who can bang out a legal claim,' he said.

This threat aggravated me. I told Lacey I was a libel lawyer and that there was nothing untoward in the article. He could call the editor for all I cared. Just as I was getting heated the signal died.

Karen asked me what was going on. I said I had to go and went home to ring Lacey on the landline. I didn't want to fall out with him, not just because he was key to the whole idea of fighting Mehta but because I felt I'd been a bit too quick to hit back, a problem that has bedevilled me in various situations. I rang him back and gave him a flavour of the piece. 'That sounds fine, very fine!' he said. 'If that's what you're going to write you're a gentleman, sir! We should meet up sometime!'

In The Light Bar, the discreet shadow-boxing of our first conversation was forgotten amid the espressos and boxing talk. Lacey was open and charismatic. He told me how he had got himself 'ten-round fit' before hearing of the white-collar events being held in New York at Gleason's. He got in touch, flew over and fought a Manhattan dentist by the name of Jack 'Knockout Doc' Gruber. 'It was fantastic, *fuckin' fantastic*,' he said, adding for good measure: 'It was like being reborn.' (This vignette is narrated with typical enthusiasm – and wit – on The Real Fight Club's website, in particular Lacey's line that the Knockout Doc's 'gentlemanly conduct ensured that I stayed out of his surgery'.) A year later, Lacey flew back to New York with some people from the nascent white-collar boxing circuit, which itself included a perhaps mythical individual who trained at the famous Thomas à Beckett Gym in south London, having first parked his Ferrari outside. As Lacey has it, 'it was a kind of weird, underground scene. I kept hearing of this bloke with his Ferrari, who was supposed to be a hairdresser. People said he'd turn up at hardcore boxing gyms and do eight rounds with pros. I never met him, and whether he exists or not, I don't know. Maybe he's the Tyler Durden of white-collar boxing. But there were, for every boxing gym that I knew, two or three blokes who'd rock up in their Porsches or Mercedes and train hard with the pros and amateurs.' It was a few like-minded individuals from this world of 'closet boxing', as Lacey calls it, that he took to New York for a rematch with the Knockout Doc. 'I did well and maybe, just maybe, edged it. But the Doc was a serious fighter. He'd had thirty-odd fights so maybe he'd disagree.'

It was then, during his second visit to New York, that the penny dropped. 'After the rematch with the Doc I thought, you know what, there's something here that I can develop.' As he flew back from the States, Lacey, who had worked in sports event hospitality for most of his life, was already plotting the first British white-collar fight. This turned out to be 'Capital Punishment', a London v. New York event held at the Broadgate Arena on 13 July 2000. It was a remarkable success, with Lacey matching British white-collar boxers with Wall Street's finest, who were provided by Bruce Silverglade. 'We got some amazing press coverage,' said Lacey. 'We even made *The Times*' leader column. I knew I was on to something but the question was, how to develop it as a business?' He chuckled as he admitted 'it's a question we're still trying to answer'.

Lacey spent the next eighteen months building up his business, mainly by word of mouth. 'Another two or three events were held before I got in some help and set up the website.' The help came in the form of Adrian King, a New Yorker with a background in venture capital finance and a degree in Management Sciences from the London School of Economics. King joined what Lacey had already named The Real Fight Club as its executive producer and took a stake in the company. Then the website – www.therealfightclub.co.uk – was created. 'A lot of our members come from the website,' said Lacey. Strategically placed posters helped draw people in, too: 'We've got people who've been sitting at traffic lights and have seen Real Fight Club posters, and they've got in touch.'

I asked Lacey about the name – was it a deliberate nod in the direction of Chuck Palahniuk's 1996 cult novel *Fight Club*, later made into the film of the same name starring Brad Pitt and Edward Norton? 'It was and it wasn't,' he replied. 'I hadn't seen *Fight Club* but I was aware of it subliminally. When I did see it, I thought: "this is a fantasy" but what we're doing is that fantasy made real.' Lacey is acutely aware of the multilayered irony of this statement. As he told me: 'What we do is also fantasy. It's not as if anyone at The Real Fight Club is a world champion. But then again, the gloves are on, and real punches are exchanged. It is what we say it is – *The Real Fight Club* – with one proviso: we don't want anyone getting hurt.'

Inspired by his fervour, I told Lacey that Alex Mehta had suggested I challenge him for his world light-middleweight title. 'Go on, son!' said Lacey, not for the only time. We talked about how much boxing I had been doing, about Umar, about karate and mountaineering. 'I did a fair bit of karate,' I said. 'The guys I trained with were fairly hardcore.' Lacey didn't seem overly impressed but still managed another 'Go on, son!' And mountaineering – I was no expert but had experienced hardship at high altitude, accompanying the army on one Alpine exercise and climbing in France, Russia and Romania. As for Umar – well, he was Umar, I'd had a few sessions with him and he said I was good. Still no real enthusiasm from Lacey, despite plenty of exhortations to 'Go on, son!' I felt like a fool, increasingly out of my depth, as Lacey seemed to lap up my every attempt to fawn and convince. I decided I'd said enough. I felt the urge to smoke and whenever I think of that meeting with Lacey, in my mind's eye I am smoking. But I never smoke unless I drink alcohol, and that day I was drinking coffee.

Lacey studied me for a moment or two. 'The thing is,' he said, 'what are you going to do when someone clumps you? When a punch like this comes in?' He made to throw a straight right at my chin. I said I'd keep coming back for more. 'What if you hit the deck?' I'd get up and carry on. 'Are you serious?' said Lacey. 'I mean, how do you know?' I thought about telling Lacey one or two pugilistic anecdotes but instead settled for telling him about how I'd had altitude sickness on Mont Blanc, up over the ridge of Mont Blanc de Tacul, deep in the Col Maudit at 4.30 in the morning. I'd felt so out of it in the freezing cold, dry retching, stumbling and staggering, head alternately spinning and pounding, that I'd thought I was going to die. I'd survived a perilous descent, at one stage only just avoiding a 1500-metre fall to certain death. A year later I'd gone back and nailed the same route, one which was a walk in the park for a real mountaineer but for a relative novice like me was, as Umar would say, good enough. Surely this tale of relative derring-do but undeniable commitment would have some impact?

'Yeah, but boxing – well, boxing's different,' said Lacey. Again he leant across the table, jarring the coffee cups in their saucers, and made as if to hit me with another right, this time setting it up first with a left jab. 'What are you going to do if one of these whacks you on the button? Like this?'

I was leaning forward, the better to hear Lacey and to spare my aching back (I can never sit up straight – my bad back dates from early maturity and being taller than all my peers between eleven and fourteen; a doctor once said I stooped to engage, as it were, and the habit has endured). I didn't flinch as Lacey's fists came within an inch of my face. I told him that appearances were deceptive. I didn't know whether I looked like a lawyer, or a journalist, or something altogether different. But with my best blue blazer and neat slacks the chances were that whatever I looked like wasn't too scary. Still, I knew what it was like to have a scrap or two. 'Trust me,' I said. Lacey smiled and sat back. 'Go on, son!' he said. Whether he believed me I had no idea.

What was certain was that Lacey was not convinced that Mehta should be the first person I fight. 'He's too good,' he said, 'he'll make a fool of you. He'll dance around and you won't get anywhere near him. You don't want that, do you? You don't want to be humiliated? That's not what The Real Fight Club is about.' He was also worried about the fight as a spectacle. 'I mean, I don't mean to be disrespectful, but it might not be very easy on the eye. Mehta's the Naseem Hamed of white-collar boxing and, not meaning to be funny, you're a raw beginner. I'm not sure what the audience would make of it.'

Lacey's lack of enthusiasm was disheartening. It was also a little irritating. There was Mehta, telling me that he had 'ahem, a certain sway' with Lacey and that if he thought the fight was a good idea Lacey wouldn't fail to agree. Before the meeting with Lacey, Mehta had dropped me a line saying that the guys at The Real Fight Club were up for the fight. And now, when I met him in the flesh, Lacey was pouring buckets of icy cold water on the idea. I thought of my conversations with Mehta and didn't let Lacey see that I was deflated. I told him that I could do it, the training with Umar was intense, the karate helped, I was coming on way quicker than any other novice he might have at the club. Lacey grinned. 'Go on, son!' he said. 'Go on!' It was as if just talking about a fight was enough to excite him.

We shook hands and Lacey told me to get along to the Kronk Gym in Camden for an assessment by one of his trainers. 'We'll take it from there,' he said. He wrapped a scarf around his neck and strode off down Shoreditch High Street. I turned to walk the other way to the car park. A wind had got up and a couple of the cards inviting punters to avail themselves of Amber's talent for oral relief were limping along in the gutter. At the garage by the car park a homeless lad of about twenty sat begging. He was getting grief from a customer. *I'm going to fight Mehta for his world title, I'll prove that I can do it.* That's what I wanted to think. Instead my thoughts were dominated by the image of Amber, or whoever she was, tattered and worthless on the floor. I settled the parking charge with a cheerful black attendant who let me off a theoretical extra hour for going over by a few minutes. As I drove out of the car park, I noticed that one of the phone boxes was being used. Inside was a white man in his thirties, scouring the cards. The homeless lad was being moved on. I flicked on the CD player and heard the awesome bass line to 'Right Off', Miles Davis' tribute to the first black heavyweight champion of the world, Jack Johnson, who unaccountably fought in a staged contest at the tail end of his career against Arthur Craven, Oscar Wilde's nephew. The riff kicked in and before I knew it I'd forgotten all about the melancholia of prostitution and the plight of the homeless, and instead couldn't wait to hear the bit in 'Right Off' when Davis solos even more plaintively than on *Kind Of Blue* until the bass picks up again with that solid, hard-as-nails riff and Steve Grossman's tenor sax kicks the hell out of everything and people like me imagine they too can train like Davis four times a week as a boxer and maybe beat the hell out of the likes of Alex Mehta but even if we can't nevertheless still get up there and give it a damn good go.

*

I'd had no more than a handful of sessions with Umar before my meeting with Lacey, who asked me about Umar, thinking he'd know him from boxing circles. 'Umar Taitt, that's his name,' I said, 'he sparred a lot with Julius Francis and did well as an amateur in the south-east divisionals. I had a session with him earlier, over in Hammersmith. It was great.' Lacey shrugged. 'Don't know him, never heard of him,' he said. I learnt later that Umar had changed his name after his last stretch. But anytime I went to a boxing show with Umar, there were always people who knew him. 'Umar! How ya doin'?' said Spencer Fearon, a pro in the middle of training for a comeback, at the Mermaid on 20 March. Umar said he was fine, and Spencer asked why he was there. Umar gestured at me. 'I'm with this geezer, he's a journalist. He's going to fight Alex Mehta.'

'Nice one,' said Spencer.

'What's Mehta like?' said Umar.

'He's useless, man. A switch-hitter, moves a lot.'

'OK, sweet. But can he bang?'

'Nah, man, but he moves. He's not bad, man, not bad.'

Umar said he'd catch Spencer soon and we moved off from the stairs, where this conversation had been conducted, to the bar. I found my mate, The Irrepressible, and another friend, Ron 'Rocket' Regan. Both worked for the same betting outfit, which was, in a roundabout way, my last permanent home in the law. From the top of Centre Point Tower, they plotted the domination of the world betting and gaming market with their company's unique new software. The Irrepressible was a project manager. Rocket was in charge of European distribution and spent a lot of time flying around from one glam location to another. He said he'd recently joined The Real Fight Club and was going to train seriously for a fight. He'd already chosen a 'proper' nickname, one for white-collar usage only. He would be Ron 'I'm No Nancy' Regan. The Irrepressible, though, doubted he had the wherewithal to see it through. 'He spends all his time thinking about what music he'll walk out to,' he said. 'That's all he's worried about, his bloody nickname and music. Sod the boxing.' I laughed uneasily, terrified as I was of the whole thing, and bemused by how Alex Mehta could go from being 'useless' in Fearon's view to 'not bad, not bad' in a couple of seconds.

I'd taken Umar so that he could see what white-collar boxing was all about. 'Lots of mashed-up faces,' he said, looking around in the bar, where we drank water and my friends drank their lagers. The KOTV boys, Rob and Dave, were way ahead, having been across the road in a pub for a couple of hours. Ron and The Irrepressible did their best to catch up quickly. I wanted to have a drink but knew that Umar would be disappointed and might have a go at me. I felt tense, self-conscious in front of my friends because yes, sooner or later I would be doing exactly that which we were about to experience, vicariously at least. For them, even Ron 'I'm No Nancy' Regan, it was a laugh. They wouldn't dream of doing anything so stupid as climbing through the ropes into a ring, whatever music they walked out to and however relatively low the standard of boxing. It was a relief when the fights started, to get away from the pressure of prefight small talk, but once underway it was worse still, as I saw fists wildly swinging and hitting the right spot, bodies rocked to the canvas, blood pouring from pounded lips and noses, all beautifully illuminated for an ITV documentary subsequently broadcast under the title *Heroes For Six Minutes*. Throughout every fight, Umar kept up an incessant stream of advice, all of it about jabbing. 'Jab! Come on, use your jab! Stick out that left!' He turned to me at one point and shouted above the din: 'What did Frank Maloney say?' I was flummoxed; what the hell had he said? *'If you can't jab, you can't fight!* Remember?' Sure, of course I remembered. 'Don't ever tell me you can't remember what Maloney said again!' Then he turned his gaze back to the ring and screamed at Tom 'The Marauder' Lloyd-Edwards. 'Keep working that jab! Come on, jab! Double jab! Jab!' Umar was loud and didn't give a damn what anyone thought of him. And whatever anyone thought, they kept their thoughts to themselves. 'Not bad, that geezer in the red,' Umar would say, 'but the other geezer, useless, man, useless. You could go in there now and have a tear-up with him.' Every time Umar mentioned me, or whenever Ron or The Irrepressible would turn and say 'Mate, that'll be you!', I'd feel desperate with self-awareness and wonder what I was doing and why the hell I'd brought them along. I was sure I could hear tutting from the row behind. The interludes between rounds were even worse, as the card girls miraculously slunk through the ropes and every male in the audience, and especially those close to me, stared with collective, demonic possession to get a glimpse of what was between their legs in their absurdly skimpy dresses (were they wearing knickers? It was like being at junior school and watching the girls doing handstands) and yet every time, somehow, nothing was ever seen and everyone had to make do with their strutting back and forth, breasts arching forwards, in the squared circle, as much a part of its mythology as the men doing battle.

By the beginning of February 2003, Umar had got me landing some decent jabs and my fitness was good. At the session in the morning before I met Lacey, I'd felt together and strong, working hard for an hour and a half on pads and bags. Amit Lennon, a photographer, had turned up on behalf of the *IoS*. He was impressed. 'You're really good at boxing,' he said. 'Tell me when you have that fight with Mehta, I'd love to see it. By the way, I know him.' Umar and I were all ears. 'Yeah, I saw him fight.' What was he like? 'Small. I think you'd give him a good fight.' This was good news from an unexpected source, but back then I had no doubt that I'd be able to give Mehta far more than he was bargaining for. The booze had been cut right down and I was barely smoking. Just running and the few training sessions with Umar had shed a couple of pounds. Umar was keen on the body beautiful as one of boxing's selling points. 'Listen, bro,' he'd say, 'there's been a survey saying what male physique women find most attractive. You know what it is?' A surfer's? 'No, man, that's fucked.' No, it's not, surfers always look fit and athletic, tanned too from all that time in the sun and the sea. 'Well, that might be right, but they weren't number one in the survey. You know who was?' Go on, tell me. 'A boxer.' Which one? 'Nah, I don't mean one in particular, I mean the lot of 'em. The survey says that women find boxers the most attractive of all men, physique-wise. I tell you, your wife's gonna love me. The babes are gonna love you. You're gonna be in the best shape of your life.' I was a bit put out by this. 'Hang on,' I said, 'I could lose a few pounds, but who couldn't? I'm not completely past it. I might be thirty-six but I'm not some fat old bastard.' Umar put an arm around my shoulder. 'Nah, course you're not. But, man, you are gonna be super-fit. You are going to surprise everyone around you. And I'll tell you something, you're gonna feel better as a man. Your confidence levels are gonna be sky high. You're gonna walk down the street and feel like you've got a spring in your step. More than a spring – *two* springs. You're gonna feel like a king.'

If nothing else, Umar is one of the best confidence tricksters in the business. Whenever I thought about his pep talks in the isolation of my home, or driving to London (anywhere, away from boxing), I found myself shaking my head with disbelief. What was he on about? Surely it was all bluster. Did he really think I'd fall for any of it? But in his presence, or talking on the phone, he'd have me feeling as if I'd been boxing for years. These were the days when talking on a mobile and driving wasn't categorically illegal. On the day of my assessment, I rang Umar en route to the Kronk, one hand turning the wheel through the stacked-up traffic of Camden, the other clutching the phone to my ear. 'Man, you're gonna be beautiful, *beautiful*!' said Umar. 'Just one thing. Don't let go with that right. I want them to think you're a patsy. If you let go with that right you ain't gonna fight Mehta. So be cool, man, be cool.'

The last thing I felt was cool as I got my shorts and singlet on in the changing room at the Kronk. This was a world-famous brand in boxing, and even if Lacey used it for 'squad sessions' for The Real Fight Club (back then, anyway; The Real Fight Club has since moved), there was no evidence of nice middle-class professionals turning their uncalloused hands to the noble art on 6 February 2003. Working out that afternoon were an awful lot of very serious, very fit, very hard looking boxers, professionals and amateurs, men who had the kinds of faces that if you ever chanced upon in an alley, on a dark night, you looked away, unless you were completely deranged or, in my case, drunk. I found it difficult to believe that these men held the 'white-collar warriors' – who would show up on Tuesday and Thursday evenings and Saturday mornings – in high esteem. As I hung up my jacket and hoped it wouldn't get nicked, I felt the confidence Umar had given me ebb away.

I left the changing room and walked past rows of boxers hammering away on bags, skipping, doing press-ups and sit-ups, shadow-boxing. In one of the rings a hefty male in his early thirties was sparring with a woman who was delivering a blitzkrieg of shots, her face so convulsed with concentration it looked like a curse. I found Lacey, dressed all in black. Somehow he seemed a little self-conscious. He introduced me to the man who'd be assessing me, Piero Severini, a dark and wiry Italian-American who spoke so fast I couldn't understand a word he said, other than 'Ciao'. Severini was a professional welterweight for ten years in the States; he had smallish shoulders and large biceps, was about five foot nine, and was in very good shape. He wore a black T-shirt emblazoned with The Real Fight Club's logo.

Severini said something like 'Let's see what you've got' and spent the next thirty minutes putting me through an assessment that felt like two hours' worth of circuit training. But though it was hard, just a month or so of running and not drinking or smoking *too much* had given me the fitness to get through it. I felt fine, drenched in sweat but then I always sweat like a pig when I exercise. 'You OK?' said Lacey, halfway through yet another evil task devised by Severini. These were the only words he said to me that day, once the assessment had begun. 'Yeah, sure,' I replied, grimacing to make it look as if I was more tired than I really was. Throughout it all, Severini kept noting things down and asking me how I felt. When all the press-ups, sit-ups, pull-ups, running on the spot, skipping and the rest of it was finished, he told me to rest for a minute and went off to get some gloves. 'We'll do a light spar,' he said, 'just to see what you're like in a ring.'

While he was gone I watched the woman who continued to blast away at the heavyset man in the other ring. I couldn't see Lacey. I thought: *This is it, you're going to climb into a ring for the first time, through those ropes, and have a fight.* I couldn't wait. I felt strong and more than up for it.

Severini gave me a pair of black gloves, which I pulled on over a pair of white Kronk wraps that Lacey had tied earlier. The first thing I noticed in the ring was how heavy my feet felt. There was something about the surface that made lightness of movement impossible. Or maybe I was more tired than I thought. Severini hunched up into the classic boxer's stance and jabbed at me. He got through effortlessly, tapping me on the forehead. He told me to jab and I hit him back, or rather, tried to. I didn't get anywhere near him. Every now and then we'd stop and he'd take me through the motion of a good jab, or show me how to swivel the hips when you throw a straight right. And slowly but surely, he upped the ante. The pace got quicker and he popped me in the face with a couple of jabs. They weren't hard at all. It was almost as if they were calculated to rile me, like a slap in the face: not a real punch, but an insult.

I clocked Lacey standing by the ropes, watching intently. Whether it was this or another jab that got through just too easily, I don't know, but something clicked and I found myself slinging a couple of punches at Severini for all I was worth. Nothing seemed to connect with any real menace. Severini slipped one punch and left me flailing at thin air, and, just as I was catching my balance, whacked me with a sharp left hook. This time, it hurt. Not enough to make me go down, or even stun me, but enough to make me think. We carried on sparring for another ten minutes or so, and when I looked up, Lacey was gone. I took this as a bad sign.

A few days later, Severini's assessment arrived via email. The text was short and sweet: 'Hello Alex, hope everything is well. I have attached your assessment results. I think you've done well, now it's all about finding time to hone your boxing skills and build "muscle memory" in boxing mode. That will come with a solid blend of boxing tech training and "sport specific" power drills. Ciao, Piero.' Then the results read as follows:

Alex Wade

>posture & coordination Assessment >>

Excellent balance, good coordination.

>tech Assessment >>

Excellent learning skills considering the close to none experience. Fast and effective to put newly acquired data in practice.
Good understanding of the mechanics behind a perfectly executed action, but of course there's a need to mechanize certain actions, good training (technical & 'sport specific' strength/plyometric training) and a methodical approach will take care of that.

>power Assessment >> Good overall strength, good lower body strength and overall stamina.
SportSpecific strength training should be emphasized for the

reasons listed above. Endurance is relative to the activity
done, and you need to build up that 'muscle memory' in
'boxing mode'. That only comes with practice (technical) and
'boxing customized' strength/plyometrics training program in
parallel with – or blended in – your boxing workouts.
Good core strength!

Underneath was a reminder of the times at the Kronk for
white-collar 'boxing squad sessions'. I told Karen proudly of
the content of Severini's email and she was pleased for me.
Later the same day I gave Lacey a ring. We exchanged
pleasantries and I told him that I'd enjoyed the session with
Severini. 'Good man,' he said, 'now what you need to do is
get along to the club. We'll get you in shape in no time.' I
told him that the trouble was I lived a hundred miles outside
London, and that if evenings were difficult, family
commitments meant that Saturday mornings were
impossible. But still, I could train with Umar on the days
when I was in London, and gear up for a fight. 'Go on, son!'
said Lacey.

I sensed it was a tricky subject, but I couldn't resist
mentioning it. 'You know, I'm really up for this fight with
Mehta,' I said. 'I really think I could put on a good show.'

'Go on, son!' said Lacey.

5

AGIM

Umar rang me the day before training. 'I've got a surprise for you tomorrow,' he said, a chuckle trailing after the words. 'No big deal, just make sure you get a good night's kip.'

I've never been a fan of surprises, which always seem only a bodyshot away from humiliation, and did not get a good night's kip. What did Umar have in store? We had progressed from jabs and straight rights, to hooks and even something vaguely resembling an uppercut. All our work had been on pads and bags and I felt that things were going well. But the fact was that I remained a raw novice, and about the only surprise I would welcome was a pat on the back and a declaration that, instead of training, we would do something more relaxing, like go to the pub.

This was not what Umar, who despite his colourful past has never even flirted with the booze, let alone had a love affair with it, had in mind. Welcoming me with a broad smile, he gestured to a tough-looking, shadow-boxing skinhead. 'Say hello to Agim,' he said. 'He's going to be your sparring partner from now until the fight.'

Agim gave me a nice, friendly smile and I tried to manage one back. Sparring? Surely I wasn't ready to try and hit someone, still less be hit? 'Trust me, you're ready,' said Umar. 'Besides, if you're going to have any chance against this Mehta geezer, you've got to be sparring far earlier than a beginner usually would.'

After the session with Severini, I'd had a few more lessons from Umar. We were both talking a good fight. 'It's on,' I said, ringing him after my meeting with Lacey. 'I'll be fighting Mehta, sometime in the summer, maybe in the autumn, but it's happening.' Umar was focused. 'You're gonna do him, man, you're gonna be *beautiful*. When people see you in there with him they're gonna look at you and say "How the hell did this geezer do that?" Meanwhile I want tapes, I want information. I want to know everything about this Alex Mehta geezer. Is he a southpaw? Can he bang? Has he got bottle? What's his record? I ain't never heard of him but someone must have done.' I'd shake my head and think: *this is insane*. But in the early days it all seemed OK. Severini hadn't really hit me, he'd just let go a medium-strength left to let me know he was there, and this boxing lark, consisting of working on technique with Umar, who never hit me back, was a breeze. Agim Tadaj, twenty-three, an Albanian from Kosovo, was about to change all that for good.

Agim wasn't the first Albanian boxer I'd met. A few months earlier, I'd been in Tirana, the capital, and had watched the boxers of Dinamo Tirana, one of Albania's top boxing clubs, as they trained in the Palestra Dinamo. The Palestra Dinamo was a gym annexed to the national football ground, the Stadium Kombetar. Inside the gym, on a warm, sunny morning in November 2002, there had been a ferocity to the blows traded by the club's boxers that was terrifying. If ever there was a country whose boxers are desperate to make the big time, it is Albania.

Professional boxing was outlawed by Albania's Communist dictator, Enver Hoxha, in 1963, and only when his successor, Ramiz Alia, had been ousted in 1992 were Albanians permitted to box again. Quite why Hoxha felt that boxing had to be banned wasn't clear to me. Perhaps it offended some fundamental tenet of Marxist ideology, perhaps its mythology of betterment through individualistic endeavour, thence to a land of riches, outraged Hoxha's egalitarian soul. My trip to Albania did not yield the answer to this question. I was there doubling up as a writer and sports rights agent. I could hardly claim that either was my profession; the mark of the law was still so recently upon me. But I interviewed various Albanian lawyers for the UK legal press, and wrote a piece or two about the Lunxheria Mountains in the south and the extraordinary, garish colours of Tirana. On behalf of Rob from *KOTV*, I hauled a load of boxing tapes around and tried to get Albanian broadcasters interested in boxing. They all said that Albanians loved boxing but that they weren't interested. '*Pac fat*,' they would say, as I left their offices. '*Pac fat*' means 'good luck'. But each Albanian television executive – almost invariably ex-BBC Worldwide – would tell me in fluent English that Albania was moving on, that boxing wasn't 'suitable', or 'appropriate', for where the country was going.

But where was it going? After Alia's downfall Albanians went on the rampage and destroyed almost any physical remnant of the ancien régime. Government buildings, schools, hospitals and even greenhouses had been torn down in an economically disastrous, if cathartic, bloodletting. Those same buildings only had to be rebuilt later by a country with no resources. Then, in 1997, a pyramid selling fraud left thousands of Albanians out of pocket. Riots ensued. The clash of old world and new continues. A place like Gjirokastra in the south – a moody slate and stone town dating from Ottoman times, hatched into the hillside, overlooking magnificent sunsets on the endless ridge of the Lunxheria Mountains – has unemployment running at well over 50 per cent, while Tirana has a vibrant café culture and media scene, with youngsters eager to embrace everything that the West has to offer. It is only a matter of time before Tirana gets its own McDonald's, and, in doing so, becomes a typical Eastern European capital. In Gjirokastra, a place where the men hang about on street corners all day and where not a woman is to be seen, the *KOTV* tapes went down well. 'I think these tapes will be very popular in Albania,' said Drago Kalemi, owner of a guesthouse, as we drank raki from an Evian water bottle. I'd hoped he was right but Tirana's TV execs weren't keen. 'No, Albanians want something different. Can you get us a licence for *Millionaire*?' I'd stall and mutter and think that this trip was a waste of time, that I'd be better off back in a suit, back in the straightjacket of Her Majesty's legal profession. '*Pac fat!*' they'd say, waving me goodbye.

Walking along the streets of Tirana, after yet another fruitless meeting with a broadcaster, it occurred to me that even if I was getting nowhere trying to sell boxing programming, I should at least check out the boxing itself and try to write a piece or two. There couldn't have been too many articles about Albanian boxing in the UK. And who knows, I said to myself, maybe the trainer would know one of the TV execs, perhaps he'd put in a word. God knows I could do with the commission on the sale of some programming. I rang one the broadcasters I'd spoken to earlier, one of the ones who'd been most hearty with his *pac fat*, and asked if he could introduce me to a boxing club. 'Sure, no problem, meet me at ten tomorrow and I'll take you to Dinamo Tirana. They're the best club in Albania.'

I had a hint of the *slightly rough* about me as I made my way to the café in the morning. The previous night had looked set to be lonely but a journalist from *Shekulli*, the country's biggest-selling paper, had met me at my hotel. I had been put in touch with her before I arrived in Albania, through a committee for tourism of which she was a member. I rang the number I'd been given, not wishing to spend the evening alone, and not expecting her to be around. But she was, and said she'd meet me in the lobby of the hotel. I couldn't tell from her voice but had expected someone dour in her fifties. I was surprised by the youthful and attractive brunette who appeared an hour later. With her high cheekbones and classically Italian looks, she reminded me of the woman on the front cover of one edition of Antoni Libera's *Madame*, a relatively obscure, delicately understated novel whose principal theme of continually elusive and ultimately lost love had resonated with me longer than it should have done, perhaps up until the point when I first started boxing in earnest. We'd gone out for dinner, and to my amazement she'd tucked into some succulent roast lamb with as much zest as me. So many English women barely touch their food over dinner, but not the woman from *Shekulli*, and it is true that Albanians male and female love lamb. A few days earlier, in Saranda, a resort town in the south just twenty-five minutes' ferry ride from Corfu, I'd come across a family dressed up in their Sunday best and preparing to slaughter a lamb. I hadn't stayed to watch. En route over the endless potholes on the road that hugs the Ionian and Adriatic seas, from Saranda to Durres and then across to Tirana, I'd stopped and eaten a hunk of lamb, freshly skewered. Lamb seemed to be in every dish, on every menu.

It was enjoyable talking to the *Shekulli* journalist. She told me she was a translator of Jose Saramago's fiction, and I happened to be reading *The Cave*. I walked her home to her 'blue palace', as she called it (a tower block that would have blended beautifully with any 1960s London estate, except that it was painted bright blue), and then ambled with occasional looks over my shoulder back to my hotel. Tirana at night is not especially threatening but it pays to be on your toes. Back in the sanctuary of my faceless four-star hotel I lay in bed watching mindless Western pop videos, smoking and emptying the mini-bar. I was on my own, and I could drink fearlessly. There was no one to tell me to be moderate, or sensible, or not to drink at all and instead allow myself to drift happily off to sleep. And so I drank and smoked until what happiness existed had been eviscerated.

At the café at ten o'clock next morning, there was no sign of the TV exec I'd seen the previous day. Instead a young slim man came up to me and introduced himself as Eric. I vaguely recalled seeing him the day before. He said his boss was busy but that he'd take me to Dinamo Tirana. His English was very good and soon we were making our way around the side of the Stadium Kombetar, dodging the ubiquitous Mercedes and trying to avoid muddying our feet too much. 'First we go to the office,' said Eric, 'then we go to the gym if they say it's OK.' Eric pushed at a couple of doors, only to find them locked, until finally we entered and climbed some steps into a corridor that ran the length of the pitch, just behind the terracing. I could see the parched grass and had the same thrill that I get when I walk through the turnstiles at Loftus Road for a QPR game, a feeling of anticipation and adrenalin and happiness. We walked along this corridor for a while, Eric trying door after door, again with no joy. Eric asked a cleaning woman something in Albanian and she gestured further down the corridor. We got to yet another closed door, and before he knocked on it Eric shrugged his shoulders and gave me a 'who knows what'll happen?' look, the kind that is regularly deployed in places like Albania. A gruff voice bellowed a command and in we went.

We were greeted by three men. One had jet-black hair, a paunch, and was about five foot six. I didn't catch his name but he was courteous and offered me a brandy. *Slightly rough* as I was, I declined, and anyway, I never drink in the mornings. We all have our limits. My refusal was noted with surprise. The man with the jet-black hair poured out two small glasses of brandy, one for himself, the other for a broad-shouldered, solid man with one gold tooth, who sat still and silent throughout, occasionally smiling. Eric also declined and so did sixty-four-year-old Ramiz Reka, the technical director of the Albanian Boxing Federation. Reka beamed proudly as I looked around his office, crammed with mementoes, boxing regalia and the Albanian flag, one of the more sinister and impressive of statements of nationhood with a black double-headed eagle against a red background. *The Land of Eagles*, that's the guidebook tag for Albania, or would be if there were any guidebooks. I took a photo of

Reka – a former national featherweight champion – standing in front of the flag and a red boxing pennant. I had no idea if it would ever be published but Reka was happy to be photographed. He had a quiet dignity and a manner that reminded me of my grandfather, a taciturn yet gentle man who had been a wrestler in his youth. Reka told me that Albanians were a tough, proud people with a great boxing heritage. 'We have come a long way in a short time,' he said. I was welcome to go to the gym and watch his boxers training. The best were Shkumbi Shatrolli, a twenty-four-year-old light middleweight, and lightweight Lutfi Gega. Reka had high hopes for both in the Amateur World Championships in Thailand in 2003, and thereafter at the Athens Olympics. I said I'd be delighted to meet his boxers and thanked him for his time. The man with the jet-black hair raised his glass and downed his brandy. I had a feeling that he might be sinking a few more as the day went on.

By the time we got to the Palestra Dinamo it was eleven o'clock. Inside were about five or six boxers, skipping and hitting the bags. One was lifting weights. There was one ring, empty when I arrived. Their trainer was Hamdi Uka, a tough-looking man with a boxer's sideways nose. Uka was Albania's youngest champion at the age of seventeen, in 1963 – and then boxing was banned. Talking later outside the gym, drinking a coffee brought to me by one of the young boxers (they all jumped at Uka's every word, even outside the gym; he'd clicked his fingers and within a minute I was drinking an espresso), Uka said that no, it didn't bother him that boxing was banned, when he was just seventeen, even before he'd reached his prime. No, it didn't bother him at all, he said, looking utterly bemused at the idea. Instead, he took up wrestling and became a wrestling champion.

Uka organised a sparring session for my benefit. I stood by the ring, taking photos, watching Shatrolli trade blows with a boxer to whom he was giving away about a stone and a good half a foot. It didn't matter. He barely broke sweat and the bigger man, exhausted at the end of three or four hard rounds, clapped him on the shoulder and proffered a complimentary shake of the head. Uka agreed with his boss Reka's assessment. Yes, Shatrolli was the best they had. They hoped he'd do well at the World Championships. But Gega was good, too. They were all good. They had heart and determination. Uka said this and banged his chest.

Shatrolli cut a mean, brooding, Brando-esque figure at the table outside the Palestra Dinamo. Swarthy and simmering, with black eyes and wearing a dark tracksuit with scruffy shoes, he told me, through Eric, that he was paid by the government an allowance of $120 a month and that everything was geared to the Olympics. 'They mean everything to me,' he said, to an approving nod from Uka. That's what he was training for, that's why he was so mean in the gym. He had to take every fight seriously, even the sparring. He had just won a contest in Serbia and, after Athens, hoped to turn professional and compete on the European circuit. It was hard not to conclude that he would destroy anyone he met. He exuded menace in the way that some people exude sex. Throughout our talk, he cradled a cup of coffee with his bandaged hands, ravaged knuckles visible. He looked as if he'd as happily crush his coffee cup as drink from it.

The solid man with the gold tooth had reappeared and joined us. Again he merely smiled once or twice and didn't say anything. Shatrolli told me that he had a friend who had left Tirana to go and train in England. His friend was doing well and Shatrolli gave me his number. I rang the number back in England but no one ever answered it. Shatrolli said the only thing his friend didn't like was the way the media portrayed Albania and its people. 'They say we run drugs and are mafia people,' Shatrolli's friend would tell him. 'It's not true. We are good people.' These words were echoed by Elton Gashi, a twenty-year-old ethnic Albanian driven from Kosovo, in an interview he gave to the *Observer* in February 2003. 'My boxing nickname is Tony Montana, like in *Scarface*,' Gashi told the newspaper. 'He was a refugee from Cuba. Unlike him I haven't got refugee status yet and I don't sell drugs, but I share his determination to get to the top.' Gashi was smuggled to Italy in a speedboat by Albanian gangsters, and had spent £2500 over ten days making his way to England. He was pursuing a judicial review against the Home Secretary, hoping to be granted asylum status, and had been taken under Brendan Ingle's wing in Sheffield. Ingle, who famously trained Errol 'Bomber' Graham and Prince Naseem Hamed, had told Gashi he could be a world champion.

Uka and the other boxers agreed that Albanians got a raw deal in the UK press. I nodded and said that I couldn't understand it, everyone I'd met in my week in the country had been wonderful. One or two bodybuilder types were lurking and I'd run out of questions. I said my farewells and thanked them for their time. As I got up I shook Shatrolli's hand. '*Pac fat*,' I said, and he gave me a wide smile.

Later that day I wandered over to a road called Gjergj Fishta, near the courts. On one side there is an open ditch that goes on forever, on top of which hawkers set up crates and sell anything from plastic knives and forks to scarves, comics and counterfeit toys. On the opposite side is an array of small offices, poking out from crumbling brickwork, doors always open, revealing nothing but a desk and a chair. The words 'Avocat' and 'Notare' adorn one after the other of these buildings, often in bright yellow letters against a black background, giving the feel of a poor man's amusement arcade. These offices are the home of many of Albania's legal profession, 'avocats' and 'notares' who would be very unlikely to pass muster before the denizens of Chancery Lane in London, head office of the Law Society, which regulates the behaviour, criteria for entry and standards of one trunk of England's legal profession, the Solicitors of the Supreme Court, a solicitor's rightful description, as one former partner at Peter Carter-Ruck and Partners never tired of telling me. On the day of my qualification we went for celebratory drinks somewhere in Chancery Lane. 'As of today,' he intoned solemnly, taking hold of the sleeve of my suit, 'you are entitled to call yourself not just *a solicitor*, but *a Solicitor of the Supreme Court*. Think of that, Alex, *think of that*.'

I did, many times, and particularly when I walked through the crowds on Gjergj Fishta. Inside the tiny offices the 'avocats' and 'notares' were busy helping Albanians with tasks such as completing visa applications or writing letters. Elsewhere in Tirana, there is a developed legal marketplace, with Western-educated lawyers handling complex corporate and commercial work, or international arbitration, or issues arising from banking and finance, oil, gas and water, commercial property, telecoms, agribusiness and privatisation, the redrafting of the civil and criminal codes, land reparation, new copyright laws and TV licences, but on Gjergj Fishta the lawyers' work is simple and there are no hourly rates.

As I walked back to my hotel, along the muddy, rubble-strewn streets of Tirana, trying to avoid its endless cars, again astonished by the extraordinary colour scheme introduced by the mayor, Edi Rama (Tirana's five hundred thousand inhabitants look up at predominantly 1960s-style office and residential blocks whose colours range from yellow to brown to puce-green, lime and salmon pink; in their midst are small Italianate villas, whose crumbling plaster bears witness to the yen to paint. They too have become ochre, or mud-brown, or Post-it Note yellow, and the only unpainted buildings are the many under construction. Half finished, adorned with rubble, at least they are a dull, inoffensive white or grey), I thought of Shatrolli and his dedication and the nonsense that goes with the legal profession in Britain and I wished that I didn't feel *slightly rough* and that my life was different.

Agim hit me with a straight right that whipped my neck back and went through me like an electric shock. I didn't even see it coming. All I could do was let out a cry when it connected, and stand rooted to the spot. My spine was tingling and I could feel the pain in the soles of my feet. Agim's pleasant, kind face was twisted into a snarl and I heard him say, 'Come on, box.' After what was probably no more than five seconds (five seconds of pain, throughout which my body was alienated from itself, another thing, nothing to do with me) that's what I did. I came back at him with a flurry and caught him with a couple of rights. Not as hard or effectively as he'd hit me, but I got through and I could see him wince as my right glove smacked against his mouth. At the end of the session we touched gloves and Agim was full of praise. 'You know, man, you could be a good boxer,' he said. 'You just gotta work on your technique and your defence but you know, you punch good.'

Umar had missed this incident, having disappeared inside his flat. It occurred on about the third session with Agim. Up to that point we'd taken it easy, so easy that Agim hadn't been allowed to hit me back. Umar would shout instructions in the communal gardens of his Chiswick flat and Agim and I would run up and down, sprinting, slowing to a jog, doing star jumps, squat thrusts, press-ups, sit-ups, the warm-ups alone taking about half an hour. Then we'd spar, or rather, Agim would block punches while I hit him with all my might. My jabs were nice and stiff, the rights had power, and I had learnt how to hook off the jab. There was just one problem, and that was that hitting someone who doesn't hit you back is not a great test of boxing skill. It wasn't really a surprise when Umar announced that things were going to change.

'If you're gonna fight this Mehta geezer, we need to put you on a fast track,' he said, one bright lunchtime in the gardens. A couple of his neighbours were watching and I couldn't help but think the whole thing was beyond surreal, it was absurd. 'We need to get you sparring a hell of a lot earlier than a beginner usually would. So today, instead of just taking shots from you, Agim is going to hit you back.'

I wasn't sure about this. I'd only been boxing a couple of months and pointed this out to Umar. 'Trust me, you're ready,' he said. To Agim I heard him say, 'Take it easy, nothing too heavy.'

Agim arrived in London in 1997. He had spent a few years in Germany, where he'd had four amateur fights. 'Man, the feeling of having a fight, in front of all the people, is the best,' he once said, showing me some photographs of one of his fights. In England Agim boxed out of Battersea Boxing Club, home of the current class act in UK middleweight boxing, Howard Eastman. Agim was lean and solid, way fitter than his trade as a barman in the West End would have left me, had I been in his shoes, and he had all the time in the world for Umar, who had helped him when he first came to England. He planned to return to Kosovo and build a new house. 'It's my home, why not?' he said, when I asked him whether he really wanted to go back.

Agim was a decent man and a proud one, too. Whenever we'd finish a session at Umar's place, I'd offer him a lift to West Kensington, where he lived, which was no hassle, being on the way to Wapping or the Isle of Dogs, where I'd invariably be heading. Every time, it was with reluctance that Agim got in the car. 'You sure, man, it's not out of your way?' he'd say, with a furrowed brow. No, don't worry, I'd say, each and every time, it's on the way. 'You sure?' Yes, I'm sure. 'OK, if you're sure.' And whenever we got to where I'd drop him off, he said his farewells uneasily, as if embarrassed to have been done a good turn. When I took him to the white-collar show at the Mermaid on 20 March, he insisted on paying for his ticket, even though I explained that it was complimentary, from Lacey. 'No, no, here's the money,' he said, pushing a £20 note into my hand. I had to force him to take it back.

Unlike Umar, Agim kept his thoughts about the white-collar boxers at the Mermaid to himself. By that time, I'd sparred with him a few times. I had no doubt that he'd have half-killed anybody in the ring that night, had he been on the card. He could have been put in with anyone and it would have been as bad a mismatch as Mad Manx Beckett's fight against Lee Short 'Fuse' (Umar took one look at Short Fuse walking down the Mermaid steps to the ring, turned to me and said: 'Watch this geezer. He can bang. I'm telling ya, he can bang.').

After the Mermaid show, I gave Agim a lift back to West Kensington. Umar and The Irrepressible were in the car, too, rattling away. Agim didn't say much and as usual seemed somehow upset – as if his integrity had been compromised – to have been given a lift. He was the first to be dropped off. I drove away and, looking at him shuffle down the street in the rear-view mirror, the thought crossed my mind that if you were an ex-amateur boxer of reasonable ability, you could clean up as a white-collar warrior.

The regime of not drinking, not smoking and boxing was going well. I'd lost about half a stone and the unusually warm and sunny weather, coupled with the fact that training took place in Umar's garden, had given me a tan. I felt together for the first time in a while, fit and strong. Despite one heavy shot from Agim, the sparring was fine. Umar was pleased. Typically, I couldn't sustain it, and one night, staying over in London, went out and got blind drunk. I smoked about thirty cigarettes and felt sick as a dog the day after. Not just from the booze, but from the vile aftertaste of a conversation I'd had with a couple of barflies. Some boxing had been on the pub TV and we'd got talking. They were a couple of Brummies working in London. It was a scruffy pub in Hackney, the kind of place where trouble is only ever a misplaced stare away. A couple of Albanians had come in, to their dismay. 'Bloody immigrants, why don't they fuck off back home to their tinpot country,' said one of the men, to the fervent agreement of his friend. 'Aye, this country's going to pot, letting the likes of them in. You know who could have sorted them out, don't you?' The question was directed at me. I said I didn't find them a problem. 'Why don't you fuck off and live with them, then?' I shrugged and took a sip of my pint. 'I'll tell you who could have sorted them out, Hitler, that's who. He was the one man in the last century who knew what he was doing. Look at the filth we've got running around now, ruining our cities, look at this poxy fuckin' place, full of coons and nignogs and scum from Eastern Europe. They should fuck off and leave our country to us."

It was too much, and despite my love of drink, which has meant that I can drink with anyone, anywhere, I couldn't stand it. I left and got hammered back at a friend's flat. Next day I went for a seven-mile run. I kept thinking about what the men had said. To them, Umar and Agim were scum. They shouldn't be here. They should fuck off back to where they'd come from. They should leave England to its rightful owners, the likes of the two men from Birmingham, a city whose multicultural modernity had failed to influence them for the better.

A few days later, on a Saturday morning, I got a call from the manager of CHQ. 'We're short, can you play?' I'd told him I couldn't play for the rest of the season for fear that an injury would scupper my plan to fight Mehta. Umar had insisted that I give up football. 'Honestly, you've got more chance of getting injured playing football than you have boxing,' he said. 'I want you to lay off and take the boxing training seriously. Saturday is a day of rest, a day for a long walk and time with the family. No football. Besides, I know what you lot do, you go to the pub after every game. You've got to stay off the sauce and forget football until this fight's over.'

I told the manager that I'd meet him at the pitch. It was a rough old game and I had a few tussles with their centre-half. He was a young lad and one clash saw us both fall to the ground. As I went to stand up he kicked at me. I told him to fuck off and gave him a shove back on to the ground. I heard a shout from a player about fifty feet away and looked round. A fat fortysomething was sprinting half the length of the pitch. It turned out the centre-half was his son. He was as protective as I would be, seeing his lad get a shove from a man fifteen years or so his senior, and stormed up to me with fury etched all over his face. He was fat, he was round, and he probably didn't score at every ground, but he grabbed me with both hands around the neck and screamed, 'Come on then, if you want some! *Come on! Fucking come on!*' I stood facing him, staring into his blue eyes, thinking *I bet you think just the same as those two twats from Birmingham.* I didn't move a muscle, save for my hands, which I felt clench into fists. I thought, *Shall I hit him with a left jab? I could whack him with a quick jab then drop him with a right. Before he knew it he'd be on the deck, blood pouring out of his nose.*

I didn't hit him. It felt somehow wrong, despite the provocation, and I didn't want to be prosecuted for assault. Besides, as with all good football confrontations, players from both sides quickly pulled us apart, telling us to 'calm down, calm down'. I spent the rest of the game winding him up, until fifteen minutes from the end I took myself off because I had a feeling he was going to put me in hospital and, beyond that, I could no longer play the role of amateur yob with any conviction. I left the field covered in bruises and we won 6-0.

Umar loved this story, even though he was annoyed that I'd played football. 'So did you hit him?' he said, when I told him that I'd contemplated throwing a stiff jab out of the blue, moreover that I'd felt completely confident about doing so. I told him I hadn't, and why I hadn't, and he said, 'OK, good enough.'

It was time to go. I got my gear together and Umar walked me round to the front of his flat. That day, Agim couldn't make it and I'd sparred lightly with Umar. I put my bag on the back seat of my car and told Umar I'd see him in a couple of days. He put a hand on my shoulder and leant down to look me in the eye. 'I tell you, man,' he said, 'by the time I finish with you, *you're gonna be a wrecking machine.*'

I smiled, embarrassed, and drove away. What Umar didn't know was that I'd been a wrecking machine for a large part of my life. I wasn't at all sure that I wanted to be one again.

6

BIG HARRY SCOTT
AND THE BOYS OF WALCOT ABC

One of the hurdles in the way of my efforts to get in shape to fight Alex Mehta was the fact that I live in the Cotswolds. The area is not renowned for its boxing heritage. Picture-postcard villages and immemorial Middle English landscapes, yes. But boxing? No chance. There would be more chance of finding a mosque in this neck of the woods than a boxing club. Or so I thought.

As the weeks moved along towards spring, I'd clock in as many sessions with Umar as I could, usually at his flat and on the way to either *The Times* or the *Independent*, where I would read the newspapers for libel. Working as a so-called 'night lawyer' was my remaining toehold on the legal profession. I liked the work, being with journalists on a newsroom floor, watching them putting stories together, trying to stop them being sued or, if they were sued, ensuring that they had a half-decent defence. I'd kept my hand in as a night lawyer for most of my career, and when things went badly wrong it had been a lifeline. Much though I would sometimes lament the fact that now, in the relative calm of the present, I had to drive more than a hundred miles to get to work, I couldn't bring myself to give up being a night lawyer, as if being one had somehow become talismanic. But if shuttling up and down the M40 was tiring enough, adding the boxing training left me constantly drained. Surely there was somewhere I could box closer to home? I rang a few leisure centres in Gloucester and Cheltenham but no one could tell me where there might be a boxing club. It was with relief that I greeted the news that there was an amateur boxing club in the centre of Swindon, just twenty-five minutes drive from my house. 'Yeah, it's next to the football club,' said a friend. 'I haven't got a number but it'll be in the book.'

It wasn't but I rang the County Ground Hotel in Swindon. 'Am I right in thinking there's a boxing club near you?' I asked. Sure there is, said a thick West Country voice, it's Walcot Amateur Boxing Club, just round the back. The deep, gruff accent, so familiar to me from my mother's side of the family (she comes from a clan of farmers in east Devon) gave me the number of chief trainer Harry Scott, whose accent was altogether different. Harry had come to England from Jamaica in the 1970s and still spoke with a heavy Jamaican bass drum of a voice, untainted by any hint of a West Country burr. I told him I was a journalist training for a white-collar fight. 'What's that?' he asked. I gave him a brief explanation of white-collar boxing. 'It's boxing for City types,' I said. 'It started in the States a few years ago and now it's really popular in London.' He didn't say anything and I could hear myself rambling on, covering up a silence that I anticipated descending before Harry would pause and then tell me straight that he thought white-collar boxing was nonsense. Instead, though, he heard me out and simply said, 'Right, I see.' I asked if I could come and train at the club and he told me to get there the following Sunday. 'It's a good day to start training, to introduce yourself to the boys,' he said. 'I'll see you at ten forty-five.'

A few days before, I went to the Cheltenham Gold Cup. There I met Marc, whose flat I'd borrowed to interview Umar. He was nursing a boxing injury but looking well, planning to get back in training soon and make his debut as a white-collar boxer. A law firm that I knew all too well was entertaining him, while I was a guest of Betfair, the betting exchange company. The task for me, that day at the Gold Cup, was not to drink, not to make a fool of myself, not to lose it all big time, not to let the ghosts of comfortable Cheltenham unravel everything I'd clawed back in the last three years or so. The one and only time I'd been to the Gold Cup previously was with the same law firm now graciously extending the hand of corporate hospitality to Marc. Inevitably I'd misbehaved and lost a fortune betting on horses whose form I neither knew nor understood. The day was a disaster, a harbinger of things to come, but on 13 March 2003 I managed to attend the Cheltenham Gold Cup, a tent away from my former colleagues, without incident. I arrived home sober, to the astonishment of Karen, who had been fearing the worst. To celebrate having behaved so well, I went up to my local and had a few, talking about boxing with Joe, who had been a prizefighter in his youth, and Mitch, who had fought as an amateur. Both were now in their sixties and still loved boxing. 'It's an art form,' said Mitch, while Joe demonstrated a boxing style alien to me, hands held by his waist rather than tucked up by his face. 'You don't hold your hands up high, do you, like all these modern lads?' said Joe. I couldn't believe that anybody didn't and must have looked bemused when I said that yes, I did, didn't everybody? Joe, still in excellent shape and with tales from his youth of fights against gypsies at fairgrounds, shook his head.

Joe and Mitch were curious about my impending fight, as were many of the other locals. The landlord couldn't understand why I would want to have a fight at all, let alone one against Alex Mehta, whom he recalled seeing on TV once. 'He's bloody good, that lad, are you sure you know what you're doing?' I would grin and nod and say that it'd all be all right on the night, trust me. The landlord would tut disapprovingly before launching into a speech about the stupidity of boxing *per se* and the even greater idiocy of someone supposedly intelligent taking up boxing. 'Why? When there's any number of other things you could do? Things that would help other people? Your bloody mountain climbing was more sensible than boxing.' Joe would listen, unperturbed, and tell me to ignore what anybody else was saying and get on with it. He told me there was even talk of getting a coach together so that he and Mitch and other regulars could come and watch. I said it'd be great if they came and hoped they would forget the idea. I told them I'd discovered a club down in Swindon and that I'd be going there the coming Sunday. 'Good for you,' said Joe, who wasn't sure about Umar's credentials, primarily because he didn't rate Julius Francis and so anyone who sparred with Francis couldn't be much cop.

Outside in the gents, I reflected upon the ubiquitous ease with which fighters are categorised and condemned in boxing; they are, truly, only ever as good as their last fight, until they have retired and all their fights become a blur and only the best, or worst, are remembered. Francis may have become something of a journeyman but had been in with Tyson and achieved a lot more than many British boxers, despite losing every fight since that against Tyson in Manchester, in 1998. Perhaps his achievements, and durability, were because, in his own words, 'I'm still fighting because it's in my heart, it's in my blood. I'm in the fight game, the hurt game. I love being in the gym, I love being in the ring, in the spotlight. I love the thrill and smell of it all, even the fear. It's what I do.' He said this, at the age of thirty-nine, to veteran boxing writer Alan Hubbard a week before his bout for the English heavyweight title against Matt Skelton, a boxer much touted by Frank Maloney.

Back in the pub the boxing talk continued. I was desperate for a smoke but couldn't let Joe and Mitch see me with a cigarette in hand, just days before my foray into amateur boxing in Swindon. 'You'll enjoy it,' said Joe, 'it'll do you a lot of good.' On the fringe of this conversation was Andy, a carpenter, who said he'd be up for coming with me to Swindon. 'You're on,' I said. 'I'll pick you up at ten or so.'

Come Sunday I nipped round to Andy's to pick him up. I didn't expect him to be as good as his word but he was there, just about ready. It was a bright mid-March morning, unusually warm, and we rolled up to Walcot ABC at about 10.45. As I drove into the car park I caught sight of a black man about the same height as me standing outside the club. He had biceps the size of some men's calf muscles, straining at a white T-shirt. It had to be Harry Scott, the chief trainer I'd spoken to on the phone. We parked up and I felt devoured by self-consciousness: there I was, parking my car, not a super-flash car but nevertheless the kind of car that you might expect a *white-collar professional* to have. How many of the boxers I was about to meet would have a car like mine? What did Harry Scott drive? It didn't matter, should never matter, I couldn't give a toss about whether people have flash cars or not (and not too long ago, for a few months, in the midst of the madness, I didn't even have a car; I'd handed the keys back to the featureless, faultless face of corporate indifference and turned on my inadequate heel, bursting with the barely hidden shame of the serial pariah), but what would *they* think? What did Harry think as he watched me driving past him? Later, in the summer, I would sometimes drive into the car park through another entrance, a little further away from the club itself, so that no one would see my car. In the winter it was dark, it didn't matter. But plenty of times I wished I was in a different motor, one altogether *less white collar.*

Harry's words when we met echoed Umar's. 'So you're the writer bloke?' Yep, that was me. 'OK. And who's this?' I introduced Andy, himself in his late-thirties, as a friend keen to try some boxing. Harry is not a man who wastes his breath, as I learnt that first morning: 'OK, in you go' was all he said. There was an Asian man, quite slim, with him, who for some reason I thought was a photographer. He didn't strike me as a boxer.

Inside there was a collection of lads milling around, exchanging banter. Some were as young as ten, though the majority seemed to be in their mid- to late-teens. There were also some men in their twenties and even one or two in their thirties. I couldn't decide whether the presence of some other thirtysomethings was good or bad. On the one hand, it was good because Andy and I weren't the only ones; on the other, maybe they'd been boxing for years, were hard as nails and would give us a good pasting. Before I had time to get too worried, the training started. Everyone lined up in the warehouse loaned out to the club by the owners of the County Ground Hotel, amidst the array of bags, speedballs and floor-to-ceiling balls, some standing in the ring at the end of the rectangular room. There was a hush as Harry Scott walked up and down, between the rows of boxers. Eventually he said 'OK, boys, skip it out', and everyone started shuffling on the spot, some more nimbly than others, almost as if they were dancing, until Harry shouted 'Punch out!' and there was a mass of fists being thrown forward, faster and faster as Harry upped the pace. 'Take it up one!' he would say, everyone running harder on the spot until a minute or two had gone by and Harry would say 'Sprint!' and there'd be a collective stamping of feet as everyone sprinted on the spot as hard as they could, punching the air. Then he'd call time and we'd be back to skipping it out, gently shuffling, throwing our arms from side to side, loosening up the upper body. After between five and ten minutes of this Harry had us standing still, arms outstretched as if to form a crucifix. Then he had us rotating our shoulders in a small circular motion, first one way, then the other, until a leaden, spirit-sapping feeling crept in and some of the younger lads couldn't resist dropping their arms when Harry wasn't looking. Then squat thrusts, snake dives and press-ups, trunk curls and tuck jumps. This warm-up was twice as hard as anything Umar had had me doing, but I counted my blessings in at least having done a fair bit of work with him. An unfit person taking on this kind of exercise wouldn't last two minutes.

The warm-up complete, Harry split the boxers up into various groups. The younger boys went upstairs, where there was another ring but slightly less overall space, to be trained by ex-amateur turned ABA coach, Dave Holyday, now in his sixties. One group, comprising most of the younger fighters and Andy, was taken outside by Harry's son, Harold, for what Andy later described, with more than a little understatement, as 'hard work', a figure-of-eight run through the adjoining park and its Sunday morning drunks and drug addicts followed by sprint work in the car park outside the Arkell's Stand of Swindon Town Football Club. I was put in a group to be trained by Harry and an ever-smiling ex-amateur in his mid-thirties by the name of Kevin Fertnig.

We were divided into two further groups. One would be working the bags while the other sparred in the ring. 'Glove up,' said Harry, and I realised that I'd be sparring within just a few minutes. This time it wouldn't be with a likeable ethnic Albanian in Umar's gardens but with any of several likely looking amateurs. I selected a pair of gloves from the shelves by the floor-to-ceiling bags. They were black and yellow and looked OK. 'Nah, mate, not them,' said Mark, a big heavyset bouncer in his mid-twenties. 'They're bag mitts. Here, try these.' I felt like an idiot but he wasn't taking the piss, he was being helpful. I put my gumshield in and donned a pair of fourteen-ounce black gloves. As it always did in the early days the gumshield made me gag, and soon I'd taken off one glove so that I could hold it until the last moment, when it would be my turn to spar.

Kevin Fertnig took the sparring that day. I watched as he and England Schoolboys boxer Jamie Cox went at it relentlessly. Cox, then sixteen, is a top-rated amateur, the one lad at Walcot who everyone agrees is good enough to turn pro. *Good enough to turn pro* – they were the words that I kept coming across whenever I read anything about Alex Mehta, a man who said he didn't turn pro – 'despite one or two offers' – because *the hunger in the kids who turn pro comes from a different world*. I looked in on that world as I saw Jamie Cox throwing lightning-fast combinations and jaw-breaking left hooks at the perpetually cheerful Fertnig, himself a man who could have been a pro if he had elected to ignore his wife's wishes, and who had recently been offered £70,000 to take part in a bare-knuckle fight in France. So I was told by one of the lads, as I watched Kevin at work, and there was something about his endless smile in the teeth of the storm of blows raining in on him from Cox that made me think that this was a story that was far from apocryphal.

Strangely, despite the huge gulf in ability between Kevin and me – between all the other boxers and me – I wasn't nervous when he waved me into the ring. Perhaps it was that smile again. How could someone who smiled so often beat the hell out of me? Even as I threw the first tentative jabs of the two rounds that first Sunday morning I didn't feel fear, I felt up for it and eager to let fly. So I did, banging out jabs as best I could and trying to land some rights. Still Kevin smiled. He slipped every punch or covered up or feinted to move one way then was nowhere to be seen by the time I'd launched my fists. He landed a few jabs on my head and then, midway through the second round, hit me hard in the sternum. He'd winded me, I gasped and Kevin immediately stopped, asking me if was all right. 'Yeah, sure,' I said. I recovered quickly and resumed trying to hit him, just to get through that guard and maybe make him wince rather than smile. I was aware of the other lads looking on, and heard the voice of Dave Veysey, the club chairman and coach, saying *He needs a haircut and he's sweating like a pig, but he's doing all right*. Finally the bell sounded. It had been just two rounds and I was finished.

The groups swapped. There was a moment or two to rest and I read various press cuttings on the wall. There was a picture of former world champion Charlie Magri, who has refereed some white-collar bouts, with the Walcot boxers, and another piece about how Harry Scott had been honoured with a civic award by Swindon Town Council, headlined 'A Noble Art That Teaches Respect'. I started on the bags and felt good enough. Harry came over and corrected my jab, telling me to look along the arm as the punch is thrown and, with both lefts and rights, make sure the hand is retracted as quickly as it is delivered. 'Get your hands back quickly, like this,' he said. Umar had said the same things, over and over again, and there I was, completely forgetting what he'd told me. Still, so far, so good. Another twenty minutes went by, I wanted to collapse, but I got through it. There was just ground work – sit-ups, mainly – to do, and it was over. I drove home with Andy feeling good about boxing and what it would do for me. I would become fit and healthy and off the booze and virtuous and admired and steady and all the demons would be gone. And if I trained at Walcot, I reckoned I'd be able to handle even the meanest white-collar boxer, Alex Mehta included.

I asked Andy if he'd done any sparring. He hadn't, and he'd found the session tough going, especially the sprinting. But he agreed with me: they were good lads at Walcot, and you had to respect them, whether for their determination or athleticism or the basic courtesy that all of them showed Harry and the other trainers. Yes, said Andy, he'd be coming back for more. The possibility of someone I knew sharing the pain and similarly enjoying a certain subtle kudos energised me yet more and I found myself speeding through a sleepy Cotswold village. 'Slow down,' said Andy, 'people live here.'

*

Andy never turned up at Walcot again and nor did he appear, as he'd promised, for a boxing show hosted by Walcot eight months later. Why should he have done? *A normal, well-adjusted man does not need boxing in his life. The intentional infliction of harm on another human being is odious and anything that legitimises it cannot be regarded as a sport, still less as an 'art' or a 'science'. Give it up. It is pointless and, moreover, abhorrent.*

My mind was mulling over these thoughts as I sat listening to Jonathan Phillips, a pianist who lived nearby, play excerpts from Rachmaninov's Piano Concerto No. 3. I was interviewing Jonathan for the *Guardian*. He had a moustache that reminded me of Proust's and a similarly obsessive nature. A graduate of the Royal Northern College of Music in 1982, where he studied with Sulamita Aronovsky, he had been widely acclaimed as a soloist, competing in the ninth international Tchaikovsky competition in Moscow following the recommendation of Tamás Vásáry. Vásáry, renowned as a pianist and conductor, had praised his 'outstanding technical, musical and sensitive qualities, allied to a strong performing projection'. At the height of Cold War Moscow, where his hotel room had been bugged, Phillips had not vanquished all but his eyes lit up when he recalled the experience. 'It was incredible to walk out on the stage where Rachmaninov himself graduated. Russian audiences have a tremendous appreciation of their musical heritage. One of the most wonderful experiences of my life was playing there and seeing the chairman, Tatiana Nikolayeva, beaming as I finished.'

Phillips played professionally between 1982 and 1995. Then along came children and the need to generate additional income. Despite having a degree in Philosophy from London Birkbeck College, of all things Phillips, whom

I knew through our children, had ended up being a salesman. He too shuffled up and down motorways from the sanctuary of the Cotswolds, selling video conferencing equipment for a succession of corporate monoliths until, a little later, he gave it all up to find a way of playing music again. I was interviewing him during a period when he was a salesman by day and a dedicated pianist for every other hour that he had free. He would rise at 5.00 a.m. to practise for two and a half hours, help his wife, Tani, get the children off to school, then work for the rest of the day, sometimes taking an afternoon off to play again if time allowed. As soon as the children were in bed he would continue, playing on a recently purchased Steinway that dominated his living room. This regime had been followed for the best part of a year, because Phillips knew exactly what was entailed in playing 'the Rach 3', as it is known by its cognoscenti. It is perhaps the most difficult of all piano concertos, dense, savage and relentless, and Phillips would be playing it on 17 May 2003, conducted by Paul Watkins with the Trinity Orchestra. He had decided to perform the Rach 3 in the middle of one particular journey home on the M4, when he had turned on the radio and found himself intoxicated anew by the piece (a work that he had always wanted to play), a moment which, in its combination of high art and ennui, reminded him of the force that music had been in his life and all too emphatically showed him that it was absent and had been absent for a long time. Nearly a year on from this quiet epiphany, it was only a few weeks until he would be performing, and yet the endless practise continued. I asked him if Tani minded the utter absorption in what he was doing, if she objected to the undeniable fact that she and the children had, for a time at least, to take a back seat. A careful, thoughtful man, Phillips took his time, then said that no, she didn't really mind, because she knew that what he was doing defined him, that music made him the man he was, that without it – as he had been for the past few years – he was lost.

As he played some of the Rach 3, it occurred to me that Karen had no real reason to tolerate the obsession that boxing had become. Could she comfort herself by thinking that without it – without its relentless, savage and inexorable violence – I *was not the man I am?* What was I, if boxing was my *métier*, if the language of aggression, not art, was mine, if the medium of violence was how I was perceived and how I perceived the world? Listening to Phillips play, I felt sad and lost, as lost as he must have been in his desert of motorways and meetings, where music is never played and only ever heard amidst traffic or in smooth and shiny corporate lifts, or perhaps on rare afternoons when he had the house to himself. When he'd finished, aware of the way in which boxing had steamrollered itself into my life, he told me that there was one thing that boxing and Rachmaninov had in common.

'What's that?'

'Their physicality. The Rach 3 is exhausting, it takes everything out of you. My shoulders and lat muscles have become massive again, since I started the regime for the Rach 3.'

He is a stocky man and it was easy to agree with him. I asked him whether, like me, he was terrified of getting an injury to his hands, something that meant he couldn't perform.

'No, not at all,' he said. 'That's never crossed my mind.'

As I wrote the piece up, sans boxing comparisons, I realised that Phillips never worried about hurting his hands for the simple reason that he was not engaged in a pursuit that could leave them wrecked, scarred and gnarled by the time he was fifty, or even, on the eve of a fight, a *performance*, broken. His was not a life where the possibility of serious injury was ever-present. Having spoken with him for the article, I doubted as much as ever how anyone could legitimately ascribe to boxing the status of art – surely this was something properly possessed only by the likes of Rachmaninov and his Piano Concerto No. 3, for example? But for all that listening to Phillips interpreting and creating beauty was moving, inspirational, *soothing* even, I knew that I was in a darker realm, one of shadows and ambiguity and pain, one which had little room for anything so evolved as emotion recollected in tranquillity, one where risk and regret and intense physicality still defined the present and the past. I couldn't wait to get back down to Walcot, or to Umar's communal gardens. Anywhere, so long as I could put on some gloves and smack the heavy bag and spar, even if it meant getting hurt – and maybe even humiliated.

Days before I made my first appearance at Walcot I had been trekking in the Fagaras Mountains in Transylvania. This was a trip I had booked in early January but I went with misgivings, Karen's mother having died just two weeks before I was due to go. I had to break the news of her death, just as I had to tell her of her father's death some eight years earlier. Then, I had been working as a newly qualified solicitor for Peter Carter-Ruck and Partners. I was having a miserable time, unable to empathise with the woes of the predominantly Conservative clientele of the firm as they sought to vindicate their maligned reputations and failing to achieve any kind of working *modus operandi* with my boss,

Andrew Stephenson, a man who (with me, at least) seemed to prefer to communicate via memo rather than anything so intimate as speech. At the end of each day I would arrive home and open a bottle of wine (or fail to get anywhere near Karen and just head to the nearest pub), frustrated and depressed yet further, mystified by Stephenson's diffidence. I have come to realise that the character I was must have been an offence to him, that he was the first of various employers in the legal profession to spot that for all my outward badges of honour I just might not be *of the right sort*. As such, having me as an assistant was less than ideal. We were opposites, certain – in a work context – to clash. Back then, I had taken a call from Karen's mother, telling me of the death of her husband. She was distraught and unable to face telling Karen herself. It was early afternoon, and I put down the phone to find Stephenson waiting to talk to me. He handed me a memo, something to do with Neil and Christine Hamilton's libel claim against the *Guardian*. I told him that Karen's father had died, that I needed to go home to her. He said he understood and returned to his office. The memo lay there on my desk, asking for research on one of the many rarefied points of law thrown up by this notorious claim. My heart wasn't in it, but I felt that I had to fiddle around, looking up bits and pieces of The Law; it was as if leaving immediately, in such circumstances, would have offended a certain unspoken protocol. Not one set by Stephenson, but by The Law.

That day, I had finished my work and gone home an hour or so after I had spoken to Karen's mother. Now I was free of The Law, save for my night lawyer work, and at home, able to be with Karen, and yet the trip to Romania had been paid for and set up for over a month. We discussed it and

Karen told me to go ahead, and so two weeks after her mother's death I was on a plane to Bucharest, where I had arranged to interview various Romanian law firms for *The Lawyer* magazine. Then I would head into the mountains and trek for a week, in the hope that I could sell a travel piece subsequently (it was early in my bid to write for a living, and I needed to generate by-lines; few pieces had appeared about the area I would be visiting). In the Fagaras Mountains, in early March, amid the coal-green, deathly quiet forests with their wolves and bears and sodden in the deep and serene snow, I talked a lot about Çeauşescu and politics and the way we live our lives with Andrei, my guide, the first Romanian to climb the north face of the Eiger. And I thought about Karen and my life and how I'd let her down and how she'd loved her parents uncritically, and about how her father had been a schoolboy boxer, so too his brothers, one of them, Alan, being particularly good. Family folklore had it that they'd boxed at the Royal Oak in Canning Town (indeed one of the Royal Oak's owners, some seventy years ago, was Fred Rhodes – Karen's grandfather) and I could imagine her father, John, as a boxer. He was a good-looking, black-haired man with a strong body and velvet-blue eyes who had died, in his early sixties, of a heart attack. Caught by the faded black and white photographs, in a suit or just a pair of shorts, by the sea on family holidays or in the garden of one of the many houses he had lived in (he found it difficult to settle, the family moved often up and down the country, with his jobs, until finally they stayed put in Cornwall), he has the same debonair roguishness as Alan Lacey, and there in the Fagaras Mountains I could imagine him saying 'Go on, son!' in just the same way, with the same slightly quizzical optimism, as if he wanted the exhortation's recipient to succeed but had a feeling that he wouldn't.

I returned from Romania determined to get things right, to *make* everything right. It still wasn't right, I wasn't right. In boxing lay my salvation. If I didn't do it everything would fall apart again. If it hurt, so what? I deserved to be hurt, just as I had hurt others.

'I'm back,' I said, 'and I'll tell you what, being in the mountains for a week is just as hard as boxing.'

Umar laughed. 'Nah, it can't be, nothing's as hard as boxing. When are you next here?'

'How about tomorrow at two?'

'Good enough,' said Umar. The line went dead and I caught sight of my red wraps, hanging down from the wardrobe. I never bothered to roll them up, to Umar's exasperation. I rolled them as neatly as I could and put them, a pair of red sixteen-ounce gloves and my kit in a bag, ready for the next day. I was full of determination to do better, and the means to do so was crystal-clear: to become a boxer.

A routine soon developed, with training alternating between Umar and Walcot ABC. Sometimes Agim couldn't make it, but so long as he was there he tended to do the lion's share of the work, with Umar disappearing inside his flat for long periods and occasionally poking his head out to shout orders. Sometimes I resented this – after all, wasn't he supposed to be the man in my corner? – but there wasn't any real need for him to supervise sparring with Agim. I got on well with Agim, who knew I still played football on weekends but never told Umar, being, like many Eastern European males, football mad. I promised one day to take him to a QPR game and, unlike the way many would have greeted such a treat, he was excited. Until, that is, he realised I was offering to pay for his ticket, and then his pride kicked in. 'No, no, I will pay, it's not right if you do.' I told him not to be so ridiculous, that I'd not accept a penny towards a ticket, but as it was one thing or another kept cropping up and the season was pretty much over before I could be as good as my word.

Occasionally Umar would have a friend come and watch, or he'd have back-to-back sessions with me and another client. His demands for information about Alex Mehta went unanswered – I asked the *KOTV* boys, who asked around in boxing circles, but no one had ever heard of him. Lacey had promised me a video featuring Mehta but this wasn't forthcoming, and he remained sceptical about the fight. Sometime in April, Lacey introduced the notion of fighting someone else – maybe a couple of other fighters – before Mehta. Having seen the event at the Mermaid, I was starting to see the sense in this. Still, I wanted to keep Mehta as my focus: neither my ego nor my body had yet been hit hard enough.

'OK, maybe,' I'd say, 'but Alex says it should all be OK.'

Lacey would sigh. 'Well, what Alex Mehta says is one thing, what The Real Fight Club is going to do is another. I mean, there are political issues as well as all the rest of it.'

'The rest of it' was Lacey's conviction that Mehta would make me look an idiot and thereby devalue his brand. His matchmaking was never idle, always considered. The 'political issues' arose from the fact that other, more experienced white-collar fighters would be put out if I rolled up out of the blue and fought Mehta for his title. Even if it was for charity.

'Well, all right. But how about if I agree to fight another couple of fighters first, then I fight Mehta?'

'Go on, son!' said Lacey.

The boys at Walcot ABC were getting used to me and I was starting to enjoy going to the club. But often, as I drove there, leaving my wife and children at home midway through *The Simpsons* (once I rang Umar to arrange training during *The Simpsons*; he told me to ring back afterwards – no one interrupted his family viewing of Homer, Bart et al.), I would feel terrified. The sense of dread would mount the more I contemplated the sparring to come. Who would be hitting me tonight? Would it be Mark, in his mid-thirties, like me an ex-karate man (though he had his black belt, I did not)? Mark's movement was no better than mine, both of us were heavy on our feet, but he packed a decent punch and rocked me with a few good shots. He was there at the beginning, but, like a few people drawn to boxing, seemed to drop away after a while (we were the same age; perhaps, unlike me, he decided that boxing wasn't the best way for a man past thirty-four to spend his time. After all, this was the age when the Amateur Boxing Association decrees that a boxer can no longer fight. Professionals can go on indefinitely, subject to the rigorous medicals imposed by the British Board of Boxing Control. I came to realise that The Real Fight Club offered a welcome haven not merely to City types who fancied themselves but also, whether knowingly or not, to the lost souls of the amateur world, non-professional men beyond the age of thirty-four who couldn't bear to hang up their gloves.) Or maybe I'd be put in with another Mark, a super-heavyweight, the bouncer who'd pointed out the difference between bag mitts and gloves, a man who'd boxed in his youth and who was taking it up again with the aim of having some amateur fights. In the beginning, I could cope with Mark, but he rediscovered his skills quickly and by the end the disparity in our size wasn't the only reason why sparring with him was hopeless. Other boxers I sparred regularly with were Ben Fitch, fifteen, a Western Counties Schoolboys champion, and Jaggdave, in his early twenties, who'd boxed a lot but hadn't yet had an amateur fight. Sometimes Phil Day, a cruiserweight pro with ties to the club, would turn up. He could have torn me apart but was always fair, always said 'good shot' on the rare occasions I hit him. There were plenty of other fighters, some younger than Ben, and all a complete handful. But the one I dreaded most was Harry Scott's son, Harold. I dreaded getting in the ring with Harold because he was the first boxer to teach me what it felt like to be dropped.

I don't think Harold meant to drop me. *I walked on to his punch, my own momentum put me down.* This is true, save for the nagging thought that Harold's right hand was thrown out unerringly, into my face, the face of someone who had been boxing for just a few months, a face that then collided with the fist of a man three stone heavier who had been boxing all his life, a man who worked as a bouncer in a hard town and was the son of the toughest of them all, his own father, Harry Scott. 'Whatever you might think, you're wrong,' Harry once said, during a pretraining lecture to the assembled boys. He was angry with one young lad, Danny Bharj, whose talent was matched by his cockiness and who had a tendency to clown around just a little too much for his own good. 'I've seen it all before,' said Harry. 'Good young fighters who come here and then throw it all away. Don't make the same mistake as them. Show some discipline and respect. I don't care what anybody says or does outside this club. In here, I'm the man. You do what I say.'

The day that I was dropped was in mid-April 2003. It wasn't the first time in my life, but was the first time since I'd been boxing and had never happened during karate. It was a disconcerting experience, for two main reasons: I didn't even see the punch coming, and I can remember nothing of the four or five seconds from contact with Harold's fist to staggering to my feet from the floor. It is a blank, a void, like a booze-induced blackout but not as bad. I wasn't out like Paul 'Mad Manx' Beckett, but I lost a few seconds of my life to that punch. Both Umar and Alan Lacey were outraged when I told them about it. 'It's a disgrace!' said Lacey. 'It shouldn't happen. A good boxer like that bloke should never drop a raw novice like you. I don't believe a word of this stuff about you walking on to his punch. It's bollocks.' Umar was even more incensed, and for a few minutes talked of coming down to Swindon to have a ruck with Harold. But he calmed down and put a positive spin on what had happened. 'You know what, it's a good thing. Now you know what it's like to be dropped. You can learn from it. But I don't want any macho shit from you when you're down there. You tell that lot that you want to spar with someone your own level, or preferably worse than you. Be strong and say it to them straight.'

This was all very well, but the problem was that there was no one worse than me at the club, save for one or two strays who turned up to give it a go, before deciding boxing wasn't for them. As Harry Scott himself said, at the end of the first session: 'See how you get on. Boxing's not for everyone.' And the very act of walking through the doors of a place like Walcot ABC is an act of commitment to the club's way of doing things. Unless I had an injury that would legitimately prevent sparring, I had to do things their way – whatever Umar said. And so, the closer I got to the club, the more I would start to fear that *this time, you're going to get really hurt*, or that Harold might drop me again. He never did, and we ended up getting on well, Harold often encouraging me, telling me that 'it'll come' when I would bemoan my inadequate defensive skills, or useless left uppercut, or whatever else it was that I just couldn't seem to get right.

Once, in the middle of a lay-off from training, I ran into Harold outside the County Ground Hotel, where he was working as a doorman on the day of a Swindon v. QPR game. He greeted me with a smile and a shake of my hand as if I were a long-lost friend. Like his father, he is a good man. And like his father, he is formidable boxer. Now twenty-nine, Harold started boxing when he was nine. He had a total of fifty-five amateur fights at heavyweight and super-heavyweight, winning thirty-five of them and three times reaching the quarter-final stage of the ABA national championship. 'Funnily enough, I lost my first six fights,' said Harold, who last fought in 2002, stopping his man in the first round. He hasn't ruled out a return to the ring. 'I might have another fight, but Dad needs help with training the lads, so that comes first for now.' Harold admits that he used to get himself into trouble as a young boy. 'I was always getting into fights and used to think I was fairly hard. My first spar changed my views. I was in against a boy called Mark Brown. I looked at him and I thought "this'll be easy". He was smaller than me, but he whipped me. I was crying afterwards.' Brown went on to become an ABA champion, and just as Harold himself progressed through the amateur ranks he also calmed down. He has no time for the abolitionists' arguments about boxing. 'It teaches respect and the value of hard work. And it can keep people out of trouble.' Still, if Harold is calm now – the father of two children of his own – any football thugs who caused trouble at the County Ground Hotel would be making a very big mistake.

Often the lads at Walcot were surprised to see me. I think they expected me to quit at any moment; indeed, Phil Day once said, one Sunday morning, 'Still here? I didn't expect to see you again'. The incongruity of my early efforts was no better illustrated than by an incident one Wednesday evening. Harold Scott took us outside after sparring and bag work, to stand in a circle in the car park next to the football club. He clutched a large red medicine ball, almost protectively, as if it were a baby.

'Right, this is a fun exercise, you'll enjoy this,' said Harold, in the manner of someone who knows full well that what is about to happen will be neither fun nor enjoyable. 'What you're going to do is have one person stand in the middle of the circle, and he's going to throw the ball – hard – to the rest of you, and you just have to throw it back.'

Harold took the centre of a circle of predominantly heavyset boxers and began by hurling the ball at Mark Reynolds, or 'Beano' as he is known, who, even more vigorously, hurled it back. Then to Jamie Cox, the club's ultra-disciplined England Schoolboys international, who again caught it easily and fired it straight back at Harold. All the other lads enjoyed throwing and catching the ball, at maximum speed; unless it was dispatched with the utmost effort, with the possibility of hurting its recipient, it was as if the medicine ball was not being treated with requisite respect. 'Come on, harder!' shouted Harold, and I knew that when he delivered it to me things would take a turn for the worse. Sure enough, Harold, having cradled the ball for a couple of seconds, launched it at me. I caught it as it thumped on to my chest. For a second, I congratulated myself for having held on to it, for having caught it cleanly and avoided the way its packed leather can rip and twist your fingers. But then I realised that it had hit me with such force that I was tottering backwards, step after helpless step, driven remorselessly by the ball until there was nothing I could do but fall in a heap on the concrete. Some of the lads fell about laughing, others looked on with bewildered sympathy. Hitting the deck because of a medicine ball would not happen to any of them, was beyond their comprehension. I picked myself up and said to Harold, the man who had dropped me all those months ago when I first started turning up to Walcot: 'Bloody hell, mate, what have I ever done to you?'

Harold smiled, and said Nothing, Alex, you've done nothing. I threw the ball back at him and on we went.

As the sparring intensified, the urge to quit grew. There is no getting around the fact that getting hit in the face is not fun. Only a lunatic would say that it was. Sometimes I'd turn up and hope against hope that for some unknown reason Harry or Dave or Kevin or whoever was taking training would decide that *tonight, there will be no sparring for Alex*. But, of course, this fantasy was never realised. It just got harder and harder. But by the end of every session, I'd feel good, clean, worthy. I would feel purged.

Alex Mehta had round shoulders, a large head and lots of smiles. If I'd met him cold I'd never have had him as a boxer. I'd made the same mistake at Walcot, figuring the slim Asian man standing next to Harry Scott on that first day was a photographer. God knows why I selected photography as his putative profession. He turned out to be Bobby Gwynne, an ex-amateur in his fifties, who helped with the coaching. He put a lot of work in with me, getting me in shape, and he and everyone at Walcot taught me that, in boxing, looks don't mean a thing.

But this lesson was yet to be absorbed as I sat next to Mehta at another Real Fight Club event at the Mermaid Theatre, on 22 May. Lacey had given me a press pass for the show, the highlight of which was to be a grudge match between East End entrepreneur Danny Mardell and Steve Miller for the British white-collar heavyweight title. I was late, having been night lawyering at *The Times*, and missed Mardell's fight. I didn't know if Mehta would be there but gave him a call when I arrived. Sure enough, he was there, with a non-boxing friend. We met in the foyer and the first thing that struck me was the similarity of his physique to that of someone I had studied law with, a man who much later came to inherit an office that, complete with rather non-lawyerly surfing posters, I was entitled to call mine. No doubt the posters have long since been removed, and this individual's name eludes me, but I will never forget standing in a bar with him and some friends, nascent lawyers all, talking about football and the usual nonsense. The white Mehta lookalike had approached and ventured a few thoughts on Leicester's Asian population, specifically one Asian girl on the course. 'The thing is,' he'd said, lowering his voice to whisper conspiratorially, '*they're not PLU.*' None of us had the faintest idea what he was talking about. 'What's a PLU?' we asked. He grimaced as it dawned upon him that he had chanced his convictions with the wrong crowd, and yet he knew that what he had begun, he had to finish. He looked over his tiny shoulders and then said: 'People Like Us, you know, *she's not a PLU.*' No one said anything and, shortly afterwards, he left to talk to some people like him. I had forgotten all about him until he came to reside in an office that was once mine, and then, aside from a reflection or two on the strange patterns that life throws up, for people like me and him and all of us, had happily obliterated him from my thoughts once again until there, before me in the foyer at the Mermaid, stood his *doppelgänger*, a man who decidedly was not a Person Like Him, at least by the criteria he had tried to advance all those years ago back in Leicester.

But I do Mehta a disservice. It was no more than the juxtaposition of his large head and, by comparison, smallish shoulders that set me thinking he was just like that fool in Leicester. And, no doubt, when I met him – the man I would apparently be fighting for a UK boxing title, albeit a white-collar one – my own ego was playing a role as grand as any that Mehta had ever created for himself. We exchanged pleasantries and went into the theatre to watch the remaining fights, and all the while I was thinking: *I could beat you, you've got small shoulders*. Mehta was pleasant, I was self-deprecating, but inwardly what were we thinking, as two heavyweight boxers lumbered around the ring, barely stirring a ripple in the somnolent crowd? 'You look in great shape,' said Mehta at one point, as we discussed how my training was going. I felt much larger than him, physically, and I couldn't see how, if something kicked off there and then, I could lose. Not least, as he had told me, because he had done all his fighting in a ring. We cast our eyes back down to the ring, set diagonally across the stage and superbly lit. *Definitely a good venue for a fight*, I thought, *this will be you soon*. I drifted off and started to do a Ron 'I'm No Nancy' Regan, wondering what music I'd have played as I walked like a gladiator down the steps to the stage.

Mehta brought me back to reality. 'What do you think of the boxing?' he asked casually, as if it were of only passing significance. I said I thought one of the fighters wasn't up to much. 'I don't know,' said Mehta. 'He's covering up well, tucking up. He knows how to look after himself.' There was more silence between us as we watched the boxing again. Then Mehta asked an unexpected question, to which I had no answer: 'Why do you think people watch this?' he said, gesturing to the audience, by now roused by some good shots thrown by both fighters. I shrugged my shoulders. 'Who knows?' was all I could think of saying.

Afterwards we had a beer in the bar. Mehta introduced me to a friend who seemed to be there in an official capacity, a tall man who, 'like me,' said Mehta, smiling as if at a guilty yet enjoyable secret, lived 'ahem, quite a glamorous life'. Strangely, he had small shoulders, too. Then Danny Mardell came over, pleased as punch to see Mehta. More introductions. Mardell had a swelling above his left eye. He came across as brutish and hard, an image bolstered by a press release issued on his behalf before the fight, in which he promised to destroy 'long-term rival' Miller, to 'silence the arrogant little man'. Later, having won the fight by a split decision, another press release would be released, this time praising his opponent, with Mardell saying: 'I came into the ring not liking this man at all, but I'll go for a pint with him now. He fought very well and took me all the way.' Both press releases spoke of how Mardell had recruited 'former schoolmate' Nigel 'The Dark Destroyer' Benn, one of Britain's most compelling middleweights of recent years, to knock him into shape and help him prevail, a year earlier, over Alex Leitch (a lawyer with City firm St Berwin) for the right to call himself British white-collar super-heavyweight champion.

I had heard that Mardell often fought for charity, and,

perhaps naively, had expected an affable, kindly man. But far from irradiating the Mermaid with his heart of gold, Mardell, in a slightly scruffy blue blazer and T-shirt, oozed surliness and menace. Of all the boxers I had thus far met or watched on the white-collar scene, he looked like a genuine, heavy-duty bruiser (later, it was no surprise to learn that he and Benn had a less than cordial relationship at school. Mardell avowed – and there was no reason to disbelieve him – that honours were even over four scraps that he and Benn had had.)

Standing there, intimidated by Mardell, I couldn't think of anything to say other than the anodyne 'you've been in a fight', a statement of the obvious intended to elicit a 'yeah, did you see it, bloody hell it was tough' kind of response. A big man, Mardell replied: 'Nah, I walked into a fuckin' lamppost, didn't I?' He didn't laugh as he said this, but Mehta did. Not because he found it funny, but because the situation was awkward and Mehta knew it was awkward. He had a lot more sensitivity than the occasionally hapless utterances from his mouth suggested. He asked Mardell how he had got on. 'I won, didn't I? Course I fuckin' won. I told ya I'd fuckin' do it, didn't I?'

Lacey rang to tell me that before he could match me with one of his boxers, he needed to have a look at me. 'I want to see what Umar and the Swindon crowd have done with you,' he said, suggesting that I join him for a Real Fight Club session at the Lennox Lewis Centre in Clapton. (It seemed that things had not worked out at the Kronk and The Real Fight Club had found a new home.) This was fair enough and I arranged to meet him on the evening of 27 May 2003. 'You'll do some sparring with one of my lads,' said Lacey.

'Don't worry, nothing to worry about. If you do all right I'll put you on the show on the 12th.' So that was the date: if I got through the sparring, my debut as a white-collar boxer would be just over two weeks away, on 12 June 2003.

Before arriving I met an old friend, Jules, for coffee at his flat in Hackney Wick. Jules is a jazz guitarist, *good with his hands*, as the American academic and boxing writer Carlo Rotella would say, but doesn't play anymore. Publicly, at least. His retreat from music has always frustrated me, and I have often yearned for him to have a Jonathan Phillips moment, something that tells him that *he has to play, that without music he is lost*. But Jules never has those moments or, if he does, he keeps them to himself. He does not seem to be lost; on the contrary, he has a self-sufficiency that I can only admire. I cannot believe he has no ego, and yet somehow, Siddartha-like, he has managed to lose it, still better, to sustain its loss. He works and lives alone and plays his guitar so well that his fellow apartment dwellers (he lives in a new block, with neighbours I have never seen, despite many visits) must, if they have any sense, or sensitivity, not to mention thin walls, believe that he is a professional musician, a session player or rhythm guitarist for pro bands working places like Ronnie Scott's and the 606 Club. So often I have envied Jules his talent, his steadiness. We are, in many ways, diametric opposites, and yet our friendship has survived since we met, aged thirteen. Jules helped me when the glass wasn't just half-empty, it was shattered and I was treading its shards into the soles of my bleeding feet. Now, as we sipped our coffee, Jules was worried.

'It'll be OK,' I said, of the impending session at the Lennox Lewis Centre. 'I think. The trouble is, I have no idea what level they're going to be, I have no idea what level

I am, after all this training with Umar and Agim and the lads at Walcot. And if I don't impress, that's it, no fight.'

Jules eyed me with concern as I articulated differing fears. Was my fitness good enough? How many rounds would I have to do? What would the fighter I was due to spar with be like? Would Lacey tell him to take it easy or to throw everything at me? *Would I get hurt?*

I always end up talking forever, and Jules always listens, patiently. This time, when I had finished, he said something very simple, but impossible.

'Don't go. No one's making you. You don't have to. Just forget it. You don't owe anyone anything.'

I smiled. Maybe that moment summed up why we're different. 'Nah, I can't do that,' I said. 'I have to go. I'll give you a shout later.'

At the gym there were a couple of likely lads hanging around outside. I drove past in my too-posh car and wondered whether it would get stolen if I left it for a couple of hours. The answer was to park it right outside the gym, but the same self-consciousness as at Walcot gnawed away at me and I ended up driving up and down the surrounding roads pointlessly for about ten minutes, trying to figure out what to do. I'd never been to this part of London and had no idea whether it was safe or not. It didn't look dodgy, but you never know. It struck me that I was supposed to be attending a white-collar boxing training session, and so presumably there would be other nice middle-class pugilists rolling up in cars that you need a university-educated engineer to fix, however good with your hands you might be. Instead, though, there were rusting Fiestas and tired VWs and a variety of other knackered, has-been cars. And the bunch of blokes waiting outside the gym, which had grown by the time of my third drive past (had they seen me? Would they recognise me in the gym and say to themselves: 'That's the idiot who was driving back and forth for twenty minutes?' before laying into me with powerful and unstoppable blows?), did not look very white-collar. They all looked like boxers, in hooded sweatshirts and tracksuits; there wasn't a pinstripe suit or pair of slacks and blazer to be seen.

Eventually, cursing myself for my ludicrous and time-wasting manoeuvres, I parked reasonably near to the gym but not so close that anyone could definitively say 'see that car there? It belongs to one of the boxers. One of the white-collar boxers.' I got out and walked towards the gym, pleased that I had had the foresight to change into shorts and sweatshirt before leaving Jules's place, only to feel a compulsive urge to double back and check that the car was locked. This I did another two times before finally telling myself to stop being so *useless* and get on into the gym.

Inside, there was a strangely quiet, almost subdued atmosphere as a handful of boxers jumped rope and warmed up. I'd expected it to be teeming, but there can't have been more than about ten fighters present. There was a woman, Ann, with short dark hair and a toned body, hitting a bag with good technique and speed. She looked like she'd been boxing all her life. In the changing room I swapped introductions with a balding man in his forties, who asked if I'd boxed before. 'A little,' I said, telling him that I was writing a column for the *IoS* about taking up boxing. 'Yeah? So you're a journalist?' I nodded and mumbled with barely any conviction, for I still didn't know how to describe myself. Answering his question with so lacklustre an affirmation must have made him think that it's true, journalists really are a bunch of cynical, world-weary old bastards. He told me he had boxed in his youth, and had taken it up again to get fit, but he wasn't sure if he would get in the ring and have a fight. He seemed impressed when I told him I had one coming up – if I did OK tonight. 'Good on yer, mate,' he said, 'fair play.'

Back in the gym, Alan Lacey was talking to a blond and lean man who was tying wraps. He broke into a smile when he saw me and clapped me on the back. 'All set? Feeling good? Ready?' he said, making to throw one punch to my chest, followed by a bodyshot to my kidneys. 'Not really,' I replied, shaking my head, sweat already breaking out in my curly hair, which I had grown long by way of a bizarre decoy: all fighters have shaven or close-cropped hair, I reasoned, and so, if I grew my hair long, they would be lured into thinking that I was an inept clown rather than a tough old boxer who was more than a match for them. 'You'll be fine,' said Lacey. 'How's Umar?' I told him he was well, and then Lacey set off to work the gym, talking to various boxers.

The blond man had tied his wraps and was pulling on some gloves that he had brought with him. I was about to say 'Do you come here often?' but realised that this was not quite the right question. 'Been boxing long?' I said, as nonchalantly as I could. Like the balding man, he had boxed as a schoolboy. He told me, in a London accent, that he had had some amateur fights, and fancied getting back into boxing 'for the fitness'. He seemed like a decent, likeable sort, but it struck me that, so far, I had detected only Cockney and Estuary English; there wasn't a white-collar voice to be heard.

A black man with short dreadlocks called everyone into the ring. He was one of Lacey's trainers, an amateur of 'total class, I mean really fuckin' hot' according to Lacey, called

Andy Wallace, whom I recalled also trained Alex Mehta. He had us shuffling around the edge of the ring one way, then the other, sometimes with our hands on our heads, others with them pushed out in front, in fighting stance. I felt desperately inelegant, aware of my body and its dissonance, and was reminded of a version of Samuel Beckett's *Square Dance*, which I had seen on television when I was about thirteen. I had stayed up late (my parents were out at some function or other) and I had chanced upon what I recall as a mute, increasingly frenetic vignette in which four or five hooded figures walked, shuffled, nearly ran back and forth along the edges of a square. I felt like one of those figures, in the squared circle of the boxing ring, just as peripheral and no better a dancer.

The warm-up over, Lacey had a word with Wallace, who proceeded to take sparring. Some of the other fighters skipped or worked out on the bags, but I watched, intent on getting an idea of what level I was dealing with. The blond man was first up. Wallace didn't seem to hit him but after a couple of rounds he had had enough. 'Shoulder's gone,' he said, grimacing as he walked past me. Lacey had a word with a slim twentysomething Asian who had, I fancied, been giving me the eye a little since I'd arrived. I'd clocked him as my prospective sparring partner, and I was right. Wallace vacated the ring and I climbed in to spar with Rajiv 'Batta Bing' Bhattacharya, who was (unbeknown to me) the British welterweight white-collar title holder.

Had I learnt enough, by that night, not to take anything for granted? I don't think so. I looked at Bhattacharya as he stood in his corner and fancied my chances. He had to be giving away at least a stone to me. Surely the bigger man will always prevail? Eventually?

I sparred for perhaps four or five rounds with the southpaw Bhattacharya. The pace was quick and no quarter was given. Not by me, anyway; he might say that he took it easy, on Lacey's orders. Who knows? Boxing can be the least certain of encounters. But what is certain is that he hit me hard on the nose, midway through; blood poured on to my white T-shirt, so profusely that I had to keep wiping it with the back of my gloved hand. To no avail, the blood kept flowing. This was the first time I'd bled during sparring. It didn't hurt, but it was irritating: how could I concentrate, with all this blood cascading down over my mouth and chin, on to my T-shirt? I charged into Bhattacharya a couple of times, another first: Umar had worked on holding and clinching techniques as a way of wearing the other fighter down, and now I remembered the message. *Use your weight, tire him out.* In boxing, a game fighter can get himself badly hurt by going in too deep against a capable opponent. Luckily, either Bhattacharya wasn't that good, or he had indeed been told to take it easy, but when I steamed into him, tagging him with one decent right and a left hook off the jab, but mostly just bashing into him with my greater size and weight, he looked worried, as if he were afraid I might squash him, and did not land the kind of head-snapping uppercuts that good fighters dispense to clumsy fools like me when they dare to step inside. He did, a couple of times, roll his left arm in a bolo motion, *à la* Muhammad Ali, a flash habit more irksome than it was effective, but after the four or five rounds I felt that honours – if not even – were only marginally weighted in his favour. (But, of course, he had probably been told to take it easy, and could have annihilated me if only he had been allowed to; there is no doubt that as well as a bleeding nose, he gave me a whopping headache.) I thought that would be it, but Lacey gestured to me to stay in the ring. In came Wallace, who took me through another two rounds. He popped head and body shots at me, studiously avoiding my nose (because, as he said afterwards, 'I could see that you were hurt, and didn't want to make it worse'), until finally that was it, I could heave my lungs in one corner to hear Lacey say, 'OK, that'll do ya, well done.'

The balding man was due to spar. He hadn't heard Lacey call time on my session and he thought he was going to be against me. I climbed out of the ring and walked towards him. 'Not you, is it? Bloody 'ell,' he said. 'Nah, I'm finished, mate,' I replied, and as I headed to the changing rooms and towelled down, I said to myself: 'Not bad, not bad at all.'

Outside, my car was where I'd left it, in one piece. It had been a good evening. Lacey had been as engaging as ever, showing me how to deliver more power in my straight rights, how to slip and block, and throwing in a 'Go on, son!' or two just for good measure. As I drove home to the Cotswolds, my head and nose hurting, I felt glad that I'd taken up boxing. I felt fit and healthy, together and strong. I felt ready for a fight.

7

CARNAGE IN CASA

My fists were numb. I was sure I had broken at least two of the knuckles on my right hand, already badly scarred and swollen, and my left was barely in any better shape. My feet hurt, too, especially my right foot, but worst of all was the blood, gushing down my face from a deep vertical cut high on my forehead.

Still, I kept going. I ignored the pain and the crowd of people and their cries and imprecations and anger. I didn't care whether I had broken my knuckles or hands. I didn't mind the blood on my face. It was, far from being discomforting, a relief. At last, the total absorption in the physicality of violence, the bliss of pain and annihilation, the end of everything. I didn't think of the effect of what was happening on anyone who cared for me, didn't remotely register the fear on the faces of the four or five people standing nearby, didn't once think of the consequences of what I was doing. I just kept head-butting the whitewashed stone wall, again and again, as hard as I could.

Soon enough, I felt concussion sweep into my brain like a chill wind in a derelict, graffiti-stricken warehouse. I felt as if I were bouncing around, inside myself, unable to stop ricocheting from one cold wall to the next. I tasted the blood on my lips and stared ahead, trying to focus. My head was pounding but gradually the white wall reestablished itself, a few inches in front of me, marked with my blood. The blood had oozed with its usual effortless trajectory down on to my chest, there to adorn my nice smart blue shirt. I looked around me, saw disbelief on the faces of everyone there, and said: 'That's it. It's over.'

I turned and walked past one man, who had long ago thought better of trying to restrain me. I went up the stairs and a man stood aside to let me pass. He gasped when he saw the blood everywhere. I left the restaurant and went back to the pointless bedsit that I had never called home. I opened a bottle of red wine and lit a cigarette. It was a long night and I barely slept.

Next morning, I went to the local hospital to check out my aching hands and feet. Lots of bruising, more scars on the knuckles, a broken bone in one of my feet and a highly disapproving doctor. I wandered out of the hospital in a daze, sleep-deprived and hungover, but somehow divorced from the catastrophic events of the previous evening. On the way back into town, I passed a church and contemplated sitting on a bench inside for the rest of the morning. There I could pray and turn over a new leaf, or hide. But I had already thrown up once, in the park next to the hospital, and feared that the wrath of the Almighty, let alone the local priest and his vergers, would know no bounds if I were to do so within hallowed walls. I stumbled on, away from the church, nauseous, my foot jarring with every step, but inexorably approaching the town, getting nearer and nearer to The Quadrangle, a squat and grey modern monstrosity of a building that blighted the Regency elegance of Cheltenham and housed the City-type practice I had joined some eighteen months earlier. Images of the previous night's mayhem darted around in my head like drunks in a funhouse. *What have you done? Why did you lose it so badly? What the hell will happen now?* And yet, for all that those thoughts jangled around in my head, it still didn't seem real, I couldn't make the connection between what had happened and the fact that I and I alone was responsible.

What happened was this: I had an argument with Suzi, the woman I had left my wife and children for, in Casa, a swish eaterie in Montpelier, one of Cheltenham's more elite locales. It was a work do; I can no longer recall the occasion and rarely are such events ever distinct in one's mind, but pretty much everyone from the office was there and it turned out to be an evening that few people present would have any difficulty remembering. I had drunk a lot before the argument began, and, as ever, the booze worked its disastrous magic. But it wasn't just the booze, it was also the past year's worth of duplicity and betrayal, the endless shuttling back and forth between two women, the impossibility of getting anything right, the inability to be a decent, regular guy, all this accumulated idiocy and regret that sent me over the edge. I followed Suzi downstairs, berating her for some nonexistent crime or other, getting nowhere, until she sought refuge in the toilets. I followed her in, to the forbidden, sweet-smelling realm of the ladies' toilets, so much more pleasing with their boxes of pink tissues and delicate mirrors and wallpaper with roses and air of restraint and dignity than the grey urine-drenched edifices used by men, and the argument continued. There was nothing to discuss, nothing to be gained, I was determined to push everything as far as I could because I was drunk and because I loathed myself. I started hitting one of the toilet doors as Suzi watched, appalled. I hit it continually with both my left and right fists. Then I kicked it a few times. It was a big, heavy door and it came off its hinges. Suzi left and I found her outside, in the hallway, surrounded by staff from Casa who had arrived to find out what all the commotion was. I added to their disquiet by launching my head against the white wall opposite the door to the ladies' toilets. No one tried to stop me, no one said anything: they all stood still, catatonic in the face of such madness.

I head-butted the wall repeatedly, as hard as I could, until I could taste the blood from my forehead on my lips, until my shirt was sodden with it, until my head pounded with pain as everyone *stopped, the noise stopped*, and they all stood in silence, watching, waiting. I hated myself for everything I had done, for everything I had become, for letting Karen down, for letting my boys down, for letting Suzi down, for failing so miserably to be a normal, decent, corporate type who would blossom or at least toe the line in the soft gentility of pretty Cheltenham with its racecourse and Regency houses and annual influx of Irish racegoers and limestone hills and company cars, petrol paid and a chauffeur thrown in, too. I hated my drinking, my smoking, my infidelity. I hated my failure to belong, and as a consequence of that night, I ensured that the tangential grip I had maintained on my supposed identity as a bright young successful lawyer, complete with wife, family and mortgage, was shattered.

I was stumbling along from the hospital, on autopilot, heading to The Quadrangle, when my phone (a work phone, designated mine, but not mine, merely loaned) went and it was my boss, Caroline. 'How are you?' was the first thing she said. 'Not too good' was all I could think of saying. She suggested we meet in a café for a coffee. 'Don't bother coming in to the office, Don and I will meet you.'

We met and she and Don Addler, who had recently been appointed the firm's managing partner, reiterated their concern. 'You need to get yourself straight, you've got a hell of a lot on your plate, and you need help,' said Don. 'The important thing is you,' said Caroline. 'What are you going to *do*?' I sat there, dumbly, in a daze, nausea deep within. 'I don't know,' I said, 'I just don't know.'

Caroline looked me intently in the eye. 'Alex,' she said, 'you know what we've got to tell you, don't you?'

Suddenly, it dawned on me. Why it hadn't occurred I do not understand. Did I really think we would meet for a coffee, shoot the breeze and then part with Caroline and Don saying, 'Look, old chap, we can't have you running around like that, smashing everything up, terrifying the staff of Casa and behaving like a lunatic, it's just not on, after all, you're a solicitor and solicitors don't go round creating mayhem, in fact come to think of it we are the keepers of order, the representatives of a higher force, namely, The Law, that which, with all due respect, you have flagrantly disregarded, and not for the first time either, for is it not the case that you have left a trail of debris in your wake for the past year, ever since you elected to leave your wife and family for reasons known only to yourself, or, perhaps, not known to yourself, and, if we were to enquire a little, to deputise a trainee to undertake some research into your former life, is it not true that we would find a history of illicit behaviour, of a nature that ill befits a solicitor, for remember, of all society's roles this is one of the most exalted, but rest assured that we have done no such thing, trainees have better things to do with their time, so suffice it to mention the glass frame of the picture that you put your fist through a few months ago, an incident that led to a visit to the hospital with two of the partners, as well as numerous rumours of disruptive and dangerous behaviour, and now, on top of all that, a period in which your fee-earning has far from exceeded expectations to the extent that one of our brethren has regularly called for your dismissal, you embark upon a mini-rampage in a swish local restaurant, embarrassing yourself and us, but nevertheless as compassionate individuals we recognise the immense strain to which you have been subject, albeit that it is all of your own making, so why don't you just take yourself off for a month, don't worry about a thing, get yourself straight and then when you feel right, come back. After all, you're one of us'?

No: I did not think that would happen. I did not think anything, had not thought anything, but soon was getting up, wobbling, walking away, trying to comprehend the news that I had been sacked.

Don came after me. He caught me up and put an arm around my shoulders. He was wearing a beige jacket with matching trousers, with nice smart shoes, and with his close-cropped, tidy hair looked every inch the successful, high-earning company man, the perfect managing partner. He lived in the real world, he was stable and he was normal. He did not have a drink problem. He was not adulterous. He did not hit inanimate objects and did not let everyone down. He had worked in the US and drove a big black car. He did not support a seldom successful west London football team like Queen's Park Rangers but instead was a proud Manchester United season ticket holder. His shirts were always well ironed, his many shoes polished, his arrivals were on time and his departures just right. 'Look, get away from everything and get yourself sorted,' he said. 'Get some help. If you got yourself straight, I'd give you a job.'

I told him that was nonsense.

'Yes, I would; if you came to me and told me what had happened, and could show you'd sorted yourself out, I'd give you a job.'

Don did not mean that he, personally, would ever give me a job again. I had more chance of turning into a giant insect. My days as a lawyer in Cheltenham, if not everywhere else, were numbered. He meant that if I emerged from what could only be described as an abject, self-engendered disaster *someone else* might just give me a job. 'I would,' he repeated, 'I would give you a job.'

'No, you wouldn't, and you know it.' I shrugged off his arm, and made my way towards my bedsit, kicking over a few of those large green council bins en route and swearing my head off.

Near the church at the bottom of Montpelier, the enormity of what I had done hit me. Suddenly, I made the connection: I, myself, that morning, hungover, tired, with aching limbs, was the same person who had caused a significant amount of damage at Casa the previous night, and who had just been sacked. My body sagged, as if an immense punch of unprecedented velocity had connected with my chin. I slumped down on a low wall, by the church, opposite Munchies, a sandwich bar run by two likeable lads who, it occurred to me, had seen me buy lunch there every day for weeks and would never in a thousand years suspect that now, as one of them waved a cheery 'hello', I had just wrecked my life once and for all. It was a sunny September day, and people were coming and going, quietly getting on with their lives, law-abiding lives of normality and calm, Sunday lunches and secrets, lives of sensible, well-practised guile and drama-free diplomacy. And I sat on that wall and thought: *You stupid fucking idiot, you stupid stupid stupid fucking prick. You have ruined everything. How the hell are you going to provide for Karen and the boys? What the fuck are you going to do?*

A few days later I met Don at the office on a bright Saturday afternoon to return the company car and clear out my office. I fiddled around packing up my gear and driving it home, while he worked in his office, directly opposite mine on the other side of The Quadrangle. The time passed quickly enough and I was grateful that this was being done on a weekend, not when everyone else was around. Soon, everything was done. I looked around my office and down at the park below, full of teenage thugs and drunks in the summer but otherwise a pretty enough place. Before everything had gone wrong, I would meet Karen there for lunches. We would go to the café and she would look after Elliot, our younger boy, in his pushchair, while our elder son, Harry, and I would run around on the grass, in circles or up and down the small hills. Why had I fucked it all up, why had I ruined a comfortable and lucrative existence that would have been the envy of any number of people? Why, that Saturday, wasn't I in the office doing a bit of extra work, like a diligent partner-to-be, with Karen and the boys arriving after going shopping as they used to and me giving them chocolate from the office supply, writing out the little slip of paper that was required on such occasions? Why had I proved so incapable of being a regular guy? Why wasn't I like Don? I cast my eyes around, looking down into the park for one last time. I felt weary and sad but caught sight of a file lying on my desk. It was some litigation that I had been lumbered with in which two wealthy Cotswold incumbents were suing each other in a boundary dispute. Headway could not seem to be made, costs were mounting, dog excrement was (allegedly) thrown on walls, settlement seemed impossible. I dreaded working on the case, which was worlds away from the kind of media law that I had practised in London. As I looked at the file, I thought to myself that maybe it's true, every cloud does have a silver lining, at least that file is no more a part of my life and then I thought, you do not have a job, you owe thousands of pounds run up on the never-never given that you were apparently a hotshot young lawyer with partnership prospects, your wife and children have no visible means of support, so perhaps a more apposite phrase is that it never rains, but it pours, but then again that didn't fit either because it condones an abnegation of responsibility, a sense of being borne passively along, at the mercy of a vengeful and malevolent universe, when what had happened was my fault and no one else's, so when all was said and done, at the end of the day, maybe there wasn't a cliché that would do the job.

It was time to walk round to Don's office and give him back the keys and the phone and all the other useless accoutrements of office life that were the firm's, not mine, though I did keep a few biros and Post-it Note pads because, let's face it, everyone does. A few days earlier I had heard from Karen that Don had been in touch, had been kind to her and had promised to see what he could do, to see if he could get the partners to agree to the payment of my notice monies. This was notwithstanding the fact that I had apparently caused £5000 worth of damage in Casa. I have always believed this figure to be an exaggeration, possibly even apocryphal, but I certainly caused some damage and what appears equally definite is that the firm settled Casa's qualms with tact and diplomacy. I was pleased that a dialogue existed between Karen and Don, and, indeed, the day before I had received a letter saying that two months' money would be paid, directly to her, not me, 'to alleviate the distress caused to your wife and family by your actions', or something like that. All this being the case, I felt that some words should pass between Don and me. I wanted to thank him, and I wanted to apologise, and I hoped, perhaps, that I would be able to look him in the eye and move on.

I knocked on his door and walked in. Don remained sitting at his desk and did not return my tentative smile. There would be no men-together, you'll-be-OK chat, no I'm-so-sorry catharsis, no all-the-best, look-after-the-kids homilies. He thanked me for returning everything and resisted my unspoken but obvious overture to talk. I thought, how strange: managing partners like Don say their doors are always open, that you can wander in and talk whenever you want, but this doesn't apply when you've been sacked for gross misconduct and, let's be honest, why should it? I went to shake his hand, and he half-rose and proffered a soft, limp wrist in return.

I felt like an unwashed tramp, whose flesh he had to suffer.

PART TWO

8

NICE BLONDES AND MEAN-LOOKING LADS

My legs buckled and I was staggering from side to side. Vince 'Dynamite' Dickson had caught me with a huge straight right to the face, landing it full on my chin. I saw a thin film of blood falling from my mouth, and memories of being dropped by Harold Scott in Swindon came rushing back. When Harold had hit me, I'd had no choice – my legs had gone without me even knowing about it, and down I went, on to the frayed, off-green carpet of Walcot's downstairs ring. This time, I was conscious of what was happening. My central nervous system had just been knocked out of kilter but I could see myself, as I if were a spectator on the balcony above the ring, wobbling from foot to foot, half dancing like a pathetic drunk among the debris of a party when everyone else has gone home, teetering on the edge of collapse. Is it normal for fighters to be conscious of how they look, aware of what is happening to their bodies, when they have just taken a shot that takes their legs away? Do the same thoughts go through their minds as went through mine, that night in York Hall, the spiritual home of British boxing, where I was making my white-collar debut in front of eight hundred people?

I thought: *If you're going to hit the canvas, you do not need to get up again. Nothing and no one can make you continue the fight. You have done enough. If you go down, paramedics and the doctor will jump into the ring. Who knows, you might be taken to hospital. There will be a commotion as people try to work out how bad the injury is, a round of applause as you stagger heroically to your feet. But it will be over.*

No more than five seconds could have elapsed between this near knockout blow and the referee, Simon White, taking my gloved hands and making me stand in a neutral corner. He asked me if I was all right. 'Remember,' he said, 'this is white-collar boxing. No one's going to get hurt.' There it was again, The Real Fight Club's politically correct mantra. This is *white-collar* fighting, it is different from other forms of fighting. In this arena, the likes of Vince Dickson smash hard right-hand punches into their opponents' faces but *no one gets hurt.* The truth, though, was that I was hurt. I hadn't gone down, but my legs felt like jelly, my arms were flaccid and useless, and if my brain had retained a strangely lucid understanding of what was happening to me, that very lucidity kept nagging away at me. *You can quit, no one can say you didn't try.* The urge to fight had left me, everything that I had steeled myself for had vanished as quickly as sunshine in the high Alps. I looked into Simon White's eyes. I wasn't up for it, I didn't feel all right. It looked like my debut as a white-collar boxer had been brought to a painful and premature end.

This was what I had been afraid of in the days leading up

to the fight. I had been edgy and aggressive, snapping at Karen and the boys, wholly preoccupied with how I would fare against Dynamite Dickson, then thirty-four, who I had heard worked for Schlumberger, an oil company whose website proclaims its commitment to 'empowering employees'. Dickson worked in IT for them – specifically, disaster recovery of systems in the event of, say, a terrorist attack or a fire – and I wondered whether his bosses felt that white-collar boxing was taking empowerment a little too far. Did they know of his pugilistic pastime? Later, Dickson told me that people in his office knew that he boxed, but that far from being accorded any special status – positive or otherwise – on account of this, his pugilism was regarded as merely another pastime. 'They see it just as the sport that I do, like some of them play football,' he said, with a modesty that many boxers have: if Dickson was a hero among his colleagues, if the girls in the office swooned at the presence of a real fighter in their midst, he wasn't going to tell me. What he did tell me was that, without boxing, he wouldn't know what to do with himself. 'It keeps my aggression at bay. It's not that I'm aggressive but more that I hate bullies. I'm quite highly strung and have got a short fuse,' said Dickson. I knew exactly where he was coming from. But back then, I still wasn't sure of what he subsequently declared: 'I'll always be involved in boxing, probably in coaching as I get older. Without boxing, I'd go nuts.'

Alan Lacey had matched me with him after my sparring with Rajiv Bhattacharya at the Lennox Lewis Centre, though he wasn't Lacey's first choice. I had been working as a lawyer at the *Independent* on the Isle of Dogs, clearing some copy, hoping that my evaluation of risk was still OK, when the mobile rang. I took the call and went outside, away from the newsroom floor.

'Is that Mr Champ?' said Lacey. Perhaps it was, in a manner of speaking. 'I've got just the fight for you!' said Lacey, ebullient as ever. At last, I would know who my opponent would be. 'Great, let's hear it,' I said. 'Well, actually, let me put it this way,' said Lacey. 'I'm *asking* if you'll fight him, not ordering you to. Well, I can't order you to do anything, anyway, can I? Might be nice if I could! But this is an ask, not an order.' I wanted to scream at Lacey to spit it out – what did he have in mind? But diplomacy seemed apposite. I laughed. 'Who is it?' I said. 'Not Raj?'

No, no, no, said Lacey, though he paid me a compliment: 'You did well against Raj, he's one of our best fighters, probably in the top six.' Lacey was about to digress into a discussion about Raj – like the narrator of *Tristram Shandy* he can never resist conversational byways. His mind dances from one topic to another with seeming incoherence, and yet unlike many similarly cursed, or blessed, people, there is always a thread, and he somehow reels himself back to it. But I was at work, there were stories to clear upstairs and I didn't have time to allow him to wander off on too many other detours. 'OK, put me out of my misery, who is it?'

Lacey started to laugh, the laugh of a man about to play a mildly disconcerting joke, who wonders whether it will work out. It dawned on me who he had in mind, and I wasn't wrong. 'How about "The Pink Pounder"?' said Lacey, barely restraining his mirth.

Charles 'The Pink Pounder' Jones is billed by The Real Fight Club as 'the world's first openly gay white-collar boxer'. Jones is an architect, and I knew of him from media interest in his first bout for The Real Fight Club in February 2003.

He was, by all accounts, a good boxer but with one fairly major flaw, as Lacey confirmed. 'He's got good technique,' said Lacey, 'but no power. He can't punch hard. I think he'd be a good match for your first fight.'

I too laughed when Lacey suggested the fight. The irony was irresistible. All this training, all the hammerings I had taken in London and Swindon, all the work by Umar and Harry, the blows taken from Agim, the bruises to my knuckles, my worn hands and aching wrists, my despairing wife, and Alan Lacey was suggesting that my first fight be against a gay, forty-three-year-old architect. Architects are cerebral creatures at the best of times, not known for their physicality. Somehow this was not the enactment of primeval gladiatorial theatre I had envisaged.

Was Jones's sexuality a problem for me? I am loath to protest too much, lest, as lawyers like to say, inferences be drawn. But if I am unable to list a coterie of gay friends, I don't think Charles Jones's being gay was the problem. Or rather, it was, but not because I objected to his sexuality. The problem was instead one of perception. Lacey was holding up the possibility of engaging in six minutes of brutal, exhausting and intimate conflict in front of an audience that, for all I knew, would want me to deliver a KO to The Pink Pounder and what they might regard as his pretensions to masculinity.

And so, when Lacey asked me if I would fight Jones, a conflicting array of instinctual responses went through my mind. I was reminded of some lines from Harry Sylvester's 1934 tale 'A Boxer: Old'. Describing the weariness of Coburn, the story's thirty-three-year-old protagonist, as he clinches his younger, stronger opponent, Sylvester writes: 'Coburn hung to the other wet body, his head bowed over

Machter's shoulder, as if in a gesture to hide, half-knowingly, his pain from some vague, critical body . . . A strange pair of lovers, they seemed, to one minded at that moment to note the grotesque.' Would Charles Jones and I enact a similar spectacle, as we tired in the third round? Would I be conscious of his sexuality in any clinches? Perhaps we would talk about double jabs and uppercuts in the bar afterwards, compare bruises and cuts like a couple of pro boxers. *Like a couple of regular guys.* What would my mates think? I thought of my uncle, gay, and the prejudice he had suffered in his life, from family and friends, and of the antipathy shown to his partner of many years, as if somehow it was all his fault. And as the banter continued with Lacey, the very notion of 'fault' seemed obscure, recondite even, nothing to do with the idea of fighting Charles Jones.

'OK, I'll do it,' I said. 'Go on, son!' said Lacey. 'It takes a lot of courage to fight him, what with all the issues that go with it. Good man!'

But no sooner had Lacey congratulated me than again I thought of my friends, some thirty or so of whom had promised to come to the fight. If decisions are not formally announced in novice white-collar bouts, there is always a winner in a boxing match, one fighter has always done better than the other in the eyes of the crowd. What would my friends make of it? If I won, in their eyes, in the eyes of everyone else there, I would have beaten a gay man. It wouldn't count. And if The Pink Pounder prevailed over me, it would be even worse. *All that training with tough guys and you couldn't even beat a queer* . . . My courage deserted me and I found myself asking Alan for time to think it over. 'Can I sleep on it and get back to you for sure tomorrow?' Lacey was relaxed. 'Go on, son!'

Back on the *Independent* newsroom floor, it took a few minutes before I could concentrate on the copy. The shift over, I drove home mulling over Lacey's proposition. To fight The Pink Pounder, or not? I asked myself time and again whether I had a problem with the fact that Charles Jones was gay, and each time it was not me who had the problem, but my friends and the world I moved in. I rang one of them to get a feel for a contest against a gay adversary. 'You're joking!' he said, dissolving into fits of laughter, then adding: 'How will you feel afterwards if you cane him? You're in a no-win situation. If you win, and beat the shit out of him, everyone will say it was easy and accuse you of being a homophobe. If you lose, we'll take the piss for the rest of your life.'

Next morning I thought some more, and then rang Lacey at midday. I told him I would fight Charles Jones, but not as my debut fight, not when I had thirty friends coming to watch who would be assessing the results of six months' worth of relatively monastic devotion to the noble art. I felt fairly regretful and started to mutter various apologies. 'No problem,' said Lacey. 'Say no more. I understand. I'll sort you with someone else. No problem at all.'

A few days later I learnt from Lacey that I would be fighting Vince 'Dynamite' Dickson, an 'ex-boxer' for whom this would be a second white-collar bout. An ex-boxer? Lacey reassured me that though Vince had boxed in his youth, he was in nowhere near the shape I was. 'Mind you, he's going to hit you,' said Lacey. 'You'll know you've had a fight.'

Lacey not only matched me with Dickson but also came up with my nickname. This had been causing me some angst. I couldn't think of anything, and everything that friends came up with either sounded too vainglorious, too humble or just unfunny. Neither Alex 'One Punch' Wade, nor Alex 'Wildman' Wade was quite the ticket. Someone insisted I walk out as Alex 'The Lawman' Wade and my oldest friend, Rich, suggested either of my childhood nicknames. These would have had me climbing through the ropes as Alex 'The Swindle' Wade or Alex 'Theo Thug' Wade. The former arose because of the chorus of The Sex Pistols' 'The Great Rock and Roll Swindle', whose refrain – 'Ronnie Biggs was doing time/until he done a bunk/now he says he's sold his soul/he's sold his soul to punk' – my friends used to delight in singing with my name replacing Biggs's, while the latter was invented by Rich to describe the character I became after a certain amount of alcohol. Neither was all that apposite, but at least Rich managed to think of something, including Alex 'Oxbridge Interview' Wade, based upon the foundering of my attempt to get into Oxford. The exams had gone well enough, but an eruption of truculence in the interview put paid to my chances. *We have considered your candidate*, the college wrote to my school, *but our doubts about him were confirmed following his interview performance. We do not feel he is the sort of person to fit into life at Oxford University.* But as soon as I mentioned my failure to find an appropriate name, Lacey had the answer. 'It's obvious, innit?' he said. 'You're Alex 'The Slugger' Wade. That's what the paper calls you, anyway. How can you be anything else?'

As the fight loomed, I began to wish I would be fighting Charles Jones instead. At least, according to Lacey, he didn't punch hard. My mood grew steadily worse as the days slipped away, and was at its worst after a session at Walcot two weeks before the fight. I had been next to useless, sparring against Ben Fitch, a Western Counties Schoolboys champion. He could have killed me if he'd had one hand behind his back and his eyes closed. Thank God the Mehta fight wasn't first up. I could see in Harry Scott's eyes that he was worried. 'You need a lot more work,' he said. 'When are you here next?' There was hardly any time left before the fight. 'I'll get down as much as I can,' I said. I called Umar and told him I'd spar with the Swindon lads for the build-up to the fight. I thought he might take offence but he was fine. 'Good enough,' he said. 'I'll see you on the night.'

On the days I wasn't in the gym I ran between four and six miles, sprinting between trees, slowing to a jog, sprinting again, trying to get my body used to the rhythm of a fight. Often Jonathan Phillips ran with me, by now emboldened by a successful performance with the Trinity Orchestra of the Rachmaninov Piano Concerto No. 3. He sounded more confident about life, about who he was, what he wanted to do, and yet I worried for him. *Slow down*, I wanted to say, *Don't make the mistake I have made so many times. Don't get carried away. Keep your feet on the ground.* And yet I couldn't give Jonathan this advice, just as my friends could never give me any advice – or rather, none that I would heed. Perhaps none of us ever really wants advice; what we crave is merely understanding, recognition. Only lawyers' clients and doctors' patients actively seek and act upon the advice they are given; in our personal lives, advice is evanescent, action inconsequential.

What Jonathan made of the boxing I never really knew. He was interested in the fact that I was doing it, but I doubted if he had any real sympathy for pugilism, whether white-collar or otherwise. I asked him once if he would come and watch the fight. He shook his head a little too quickly to enable him to backtrack and humour me with 'I'd love to but . . .' comments, and out came a throwaway line about not being able to stand the blood. Jonathan was at home with the sounds of his Steinway, but would be as ill at ease in a boxing environment as I would at a ballet. Why should it be otherwise? There is no reason why anyone should enjoy the spectacle of two men beating the hell out of each other.

The sparring got harder and harder in Swindon as the fight approached, and each time as I drove away I thought of Jonathan and his Rachmaninov, Jonathan and his Steinway, his total commitment to music, as selfish as any obsession and yet surely one of beauty, albeit intangible, that enhanced the lives of those around it. What effect did boxing have on its practitioners, their friends and families, onlookers, fight fans, TV audiences around the world? Did it enhance their lives? Did it *ennoble* those who saw it? Or did it brutalise them as much as Vitali Klitschko's face was brutalised by a fortunate, and out-of-shape, Lennox Lewis nine days after my fight, at the Staples Center in Los Angeles? Klitschko's face required sixty stitches, and the gash beneath his left eye was one of the worst seen in modern boxing. Klitschko should have won the fight, was, according to those in the know, the better fighter, the more gallant. Had Lewis used the tools of a science that was *sweet* to inflict that kind of damage? Was the art deployed really a noble one?

But if I couldn't blame Jonathan for his reluctance to attend a fight (my own or anyone else's), and if there were times in the sparring leading up to York Hall on 12 June that hurt me, that made me feel like quitting, there was a moment on the Sunday before the fight that touched me to the core.

I arrived at Walcot a little early and was greeted, typically, with a faintly perceptible nod from Harry Scott rather than too many words. Soon the club filled up, young lads upstairs, the rest of us below. Harry told me to climb into the ring at the back of the club. As I did so a couple of the youngsters also got in. We stood there, milling around, as Harry called for everyone above to come downstairs. I caught sight of Amy, Walcot's only female boxer, looking as fit and athletic as ever. When everyone was crammed into the downstairs hall, next to all the bags, Harry told the young lads to get out of the ring. I was left on my own, with everyone looking at me.

'Now then,' said Harry, taking up a position in front of the ropes. 'You all know Alec. He's been training with us and he's got his first fight coming up.' Harry paused, but apart from lapsing into calling me Alec, so far, so good. 'It's not easy for Alex. He hasn't been boxing long. He hasn't got the skills and has to rely on his natural ability.' So I had no skill? This was a bit of a blow, but if Harry Scott is one thing, he's a realist. And another: he's a man who knows boxing. 'Anyway, he's been good to us. It's not easy getting the papers interested in this club, here in the Western Counties. But I know Alex will always stand by us.' There was another pause before Harry went on. 'Now, he's got his first fight this Thursday, against someone we hope is at his level. But even if he is, Alec's still got to be careful and hope he doesn't get caught. With his fight coming up, I want you to put your hands together and wish Alex all the best.'

There I stood, in the ring, Alec or Alex, the object of all this attention. Everyone clapped and I caught Amy's eye, then that of Mark, aka 'Beano', the big, burly bouncer. They were smiling. I suspect they all thought I was barking mad, but still, these people whom I barely knew were applauding me, wishing me luck for an event that had increasingly been terrifying me and which I suspect they regarded as not quite the real thing. Nevertheless, where once I would have felt undeserving, I was content to take their applause, to feel the camaraderie of boxing and enjoy the surge of confidence it gave me.

That confidence did not, though, last long. I took such a hammering from Ben – even though he was holding back – that I could barely open my mouth afterwards. The pain reminded me of the time my jaw had been broken, when a right hook sent me to the ground in a Sunday League football match in south London with a clean fracture of my right jaw. All I had done was win the ball from the opposition's centre-half, a solid man about six foot two. I turned away from him on the halfway line, and bang, he whacked me in the face from behind. I hit the dry earth so hard that I grazed a knee. It took a minute or so before I knew where I was. I sat up groggily on the parched early season grass, and a team-mate rushed over with the magic sponge. Water dripped all over me, down my sweat-soaked nylon shirt, down my shorts, on to my socks. The deluge made no difference to my jaw. Like a fool, I carried on playing, even confronting my assailant later in the game. 'You'd better hope my jaw isn't broken,' I said to him, a sneaky, fractured lawyer to the last. This mixture of bravado and incipient legal threat didn't intimidate him. 'Want some more?' he yelled furiously, stomping towards me. No, I did not, not being able to open my mouth was enough, not being able to chew the steak Karen had cooked that evening was sufficient punishment. I felt rather pathetic as I stood my ground, staring at him, praying that he wouldn't hit me again.

That had been eight years ago, but back home after that Sunday morning session at Walcot it felt like yesterday. Once again, I couldn't chew meat. Again, there was a numbing pain down the right side of my face, stretching up my jaw and deep into my right ear. Even the left side my face hurt, too.

But where eight years ago Karen was sympathetic, this time she was annoyed. The more I boxed, the more she shook her head with what seemed dangerously close to disdain. When I had had my jaw broken, it had been through no fault of my own, and Karen had been happy to accompany me to hospital. For all my later known and manifest sins, the absence of intent absolved me: all I had done was go off to play a game of football. I did not ask to get thumped, and did nothing to deserve it (as players in my team would subsequently testify in a trial that went horribly, excruciatingly wrong). But now, as a thirty-seven-year-old who should know better, I was voluntarily sparring with tough young lads at a well-regarded boxing club, by way of preparation for a boxing match, albeit a white-collar one, where no one would get hurt. Karen took the view that I was stupid and, I think, disliked the obsession that boxing had become. What had at first seemed romantic had become merely tawdry and violent. Even if it was keeping me from the booze and fags, perhaps she saw it as yet another avoidance of our marriage, perhaps she feared it would unlock rather than contain all those demons of aggression and angst. Whatever the case, there was little by way of condolence when I returned with a badly messed up jaw, and this time I went to casualty on my own.

At Cirencester Hospital I was asked how it had happened. Boxing, I replied. A street fight? queried the nurse. No, boxing, I said. She eyed me with amused suspicion. 'You don't look like a boxer,' she said.

I laughed. I had to, even though it hurt my jaw. Here I was, on a Sunday afternoon, in Cirencester Hospital, the only patient in casualty, with what felt like a broken jaw. How had it happened? Sparring with an amateur fighter who was no more than seventeen. Trying to explain the *raison d'être* of the whole thing would have been futile. 'I'm a writer,' I said. 'Ah,' she nodded, as if all was clear now, as if writers have a licence to do stupid things and acquire injuries that normal people don't. But still, I was a writer who did not look like a boxer. It must have been the hair – long and curly then, so often the butt of criticism from Umar. Not a boxer's shaven head or crew cut. I would have to do something about it for the fight. If there was going to be a fight, and the way my jaw felt that seemed very unlikely.

But the fates were with me (or was it against me?). The jaw was not broken; it was badly bruised and swollen, a condition common to boxers that has a Latin name, I forget what. I would be fine for the looming fight. 'Keep your guard up!' said the young male doctor as I left, clenching his fists and rolling his body as if to slip a punch. I laughed with him and winced with a fresh delivery of pain from my jaw.

I slept well the night before and felt relaxed in the morning. After taking the boys to school I drove into Cirencester and had a haircut. Grade two at the back and sides, all the curls lopped off. 'Are you sure?' asked the hairdresser. 'Yep, sure. I've got a fight tonight and I've got to look the part, even if I'm not.' The hairdresser glanced at me in the mirror, then turned the radio on and finished cutting my hair in silence.

Back home, I had some work to do which kept me busy until lunchtime, but then, with little to preoccupy me until a friend arrived to give me a lift to London, the nerves set in. I did a bit of light exercise, some shadow-boxing and jogging to try to dissipate the tension. It made no difference. I had a bath and my arms were shaking. I was terrified, just as I had been at the end of the show at the Mermaid on 20 March. All

I needed was for Rob Pickles to appear from nowhere and tell me how scared I looked.

Karen did her best to be understanding, but how can anyone who does not box, or who has not watched a boxing match, ever really understand? The fact was that at York Hall that night I would be climbing into the ring to do and suffer violence. Despite somehow putting up with me for all the years we have been together, this was the first time there was *intent* on my part, deliberate, calculated intent preceded by months of training. Maybe not enough training, but still, I was in better shape than I had been for years, and was about to kiss my wife farewell to go and box in the East End of London. Again the dissonance between what we fondly imagine as the past and the stark truth was evident. For as long as I had known her, Karen had spoken wistfully of her family's pedigree as East End boxers. Her father and his two brothers had all been able to look after themselves, back in the era of the Krays, boxing as schoolboys. As did – so it seemed – every male from those years. And yet the more I trained, the more I inhabited the mental space that the males in her family had done, as *boxers*, the less enamoured of the world of boxing she became. And as with Jonathan Phillips, what seemed to be Karen's own essence was flowering exponentially just as I delved further into boxing. When we met, well over a decade before, I had fallen in love with a strong, capable woman who loved art and literature. We had had children and enacted society's archetype, not so much by design but more unthinkingly, as if there were no other fate for us. Perhaps there wasn't, given the way she is, the way I am, or rather, the way we were. She stayed at home and mothered the boys while I carried on wearing the suit and earning the cash. Our roles became ever more polarised, until soon I could no longer see the strength, and all she could see was the twice-weekly drunkard who either lurched home at all hours or was stressed and wound up when he was sober. But after the carnage, Karen found herself again; she started to paint, as she had always wanted to do and had done before we met and yet never, somehow, had the time to do when we were together. She paints abstracts born of her childhood in Cornwall. Hers is a very different canvas from mine.

After Vince 'Dynamite' Dickson smashed that hard right on to my chin, as I wobbled around on the canvas, among the myriad thoughts in my richly disorientated mind was a fleeting image of some photographs Karen had had enlarged and framed. They were black and white images of her mother and father from the 1950s, taken on holiday on Selsey beach. Her father looks raffish in a black suit, with his mop of curly black hair, while her mother looks pretty, selfless, delicate. There is an extraordinary stillness to the images, as if this were not really a busy day at the beach in high summer, but a posed series of shots in which everything has stopped, the boats of the fishermen, the shrieks of children, the imprecations of the ice-cream sellers, the hum of traffic, even the waves, tide and currents of the English Channel. Why did those images jumble around in my mind, when I could hardly stand?

Dickson's punch seemed about to ruin everything, but at least I had survived the first round. This was the limit of my inner ambition: not to go the way of Paul 'Mad Manx' Beckett and suffer a humiliating first-round KO. Standing in the neutral corner, with Simon White uttering words that seemed hopelessly redundant ('Are you all right? This is white-collar boxing – no one is going to get hurt'), it dawned on me that I had got through that first round, that mine had not been the fate of Mad Manx Beckett. *I can quit*, I thought to myself. At this juncture, having taken that kind of punch, *You can quit, and no one can hold it against you.*

Was this really the case, though? I had driven to London with Ian Smith, who at the time was working as a lawyer in Bristol. Ian is an émigré South African, a writer and painter as much as he is a lawyer, and far more sensitive than the stereotype of his countrymen. But reflective and cerebral though he can be, Ian has a masculine essence shaped by years of being a good athlete. He was a surfer for a South African province, sent on its behalf to compete in California as a teenager, and has run sub-three-hour marathons. He knows his rugby, his cricket and his motor racing as authoritatively as a seasoned sports writer. He is a superb swimmer, a lot quicker over 1500m than me or anyone else I could mention. In sum, Ian is a man who has standards of performance, by dint of having achieved as a competitive sportsman. If those standards are not expressly articulated, they are nevertheless there. On the way to London we talked little of the fight, as if it were of no real importance (of course, it was not of any real importance; in the great scheme of things, it was as meaningless as anything else), but behind the façade of a digressive conversation about law, music, women and sport, my nerves were jangling away, gnawing at me with increasing vigour. Each time I ventured an observation about my feelings of fear, that was all it could ever be, a mere observation, inchoate, undeveloped, given the parameters of male discourse established by Ian and me on the journey. Could I then have said 'No, I'm not all right, I want to stop' in front of Ian and other friends, in front of all the people who I didn't know and who had paid between £20 and £30 to watch the fight? Was this really an option?

Certainly so far as Umar was concerned, it wasn't. He arrived at York Hall on time, at 6.00 p.m., while Ian and I got there an hour later. Umar was in typically good spirits. 'How're you feeling?' he said, wrapping an arm around my shoulders. 'Fine,' I said. 'Nervous, but fine.' 'Good enough,' said Umar. He did a double take and noticed that I had had a haircut. 'At last, you've got rid of that bloody choirboy hairstyle,' he said. I shook hands with Agim, and Umar introduced me to a friend of his called Ali, who would also work my corner. We went immediately to the red-corner dressing room, a square the size of the average garden shed, and with its dilapidated shower cubicle, a few scattered chairs and tables and slow-flushing toilet, little more accommodating. It seemed barely possible that only a week or so before a fighter of Audley Harrison's earning power and celebrity might have used so primitive a space for his prefight preparation. But its shabbiness is part of York Hall's mystique. Opened in 1929 by the Duke and Duchess of York, the arena is the only traditional boxing venue left in London and can hold an audience of 1200. Tower Hamlets Council has been considering plans to demolish the building, leading to outrage in the boxing world, for whom York Hall's disrepair lends an extra rawness to the scenes of violence that have been witnessed from the rows of chairs placed around the ring, as if for a parish council meeting, and from the balcony that runs around the interior of the building, in places no more than ten feet above the ring. 'Ringside' at York Hall really does mean ringside, and even elsewhere in the hall there is not a bad view anywhere: you are so close to the action that there is no better place to understand just how exhausting and perilous the activity of fighting is.

I shared the room with two other debutants, Darren 'Wallop' Sieler and 'Smokin'' Adam Owen. Both were composed, able to sit still and conserve their energy. This I found impossible. For all the advice given by Umar, Agim and Ali to sit down and relax, I was seated for no more than a minute before I would get up and pace up and down. Umar kept up a flow of chatter but none of it registered in my mind, and the closer the fight came the more I just wanted to get out there and get on with it. My nerves decreased to the point that when I weighed in on the stage I felt calm and even reasonably unfazed by my first sight of Vince Dickson. He was a bull of a man, who looked almost a stone heavier than me, with massive biceps and shoulders but also a protruding gut. As we stood next to each other waiting to go on stage for the weigh-in, neither of us said a word. I had half-expected some desultory prefight conversation, along the lines of 'Good luck, mate' and 'Let's have a beer afterwards' but instead, nothing. Even if it was white-collar boxing, this was serious. Neither of us wanted to be humiliated in front of eight hundred people, and both of us would give our best on the night. As Barry McGuigan, 'The Clones Cyclone' and former World Boxing Association featherweight champion, says: 'A boxer *knows* when an opponent is hurt and, like a dog sensing a badger's desperation, he turns up the heat. So disguising the pain is imperative. It becomes instinctive. Boxing *is* the acceptance of pain – and you have to accept more and more of it as you go up in class and you get hit harder. You're driven not by fear of pain but of humiliation.' McGuigan had won his title in 1985 in a fight against Portuguese boxer Eusebio Pedroza, the contest staged in front of 25,000 fans at Loftus Road, QPR's ground. Standing on the stage before the weigh-in, about to box at a level worlds removed from that of The Clones Cyclone, I knew what McGuigan meant. At all costs, *humiliation* had to be avoided. But unlike McGuigan, the fear of pain was a factor, too. McGuigan has talked of how boxers build up a tolerance to pain – 'in fact,' he says, 'your immune system learns how to cope with it'. This, though, is a comment that holds true for professionals and seasoned amateurs. For me, not much more than six months into a crash course in boxing, the sight of Dickson was worrying not just because of the fear of being humiliated by him but also because, quite simply, he was so well built that taking a punch from him would be very painful indeed. This was the kind of man who you don't pick a fight with (as if to pick a fight with anyone is acceptable?), but that was precisely what I would shortly be doing.

After the weigh-in I saw the doctor. My blood pressure was fine, whatever else it is that doctors investigate before a fight was fine, and someone produced a piece of paper in which I agreed that everything I was doing was at my own risk. I would not, if I signed this document, hold The Real Fight Club responsible for any injury that befell me. I signed it without even reading it properly, half-remembered scraps of law telling me that surely it is not legally permissible to contract out of liability for death or personal injury . . . What thoughts there are in lawyers' minds.

Back in the dressing room the whip arrived. He was a slightly camp individual who had apparently boxed on one of The Real Fight Club's shows, whose job it was to make sure the fighters were ready when called for their bouts. I was ready: my gloves were on and taped, my boots laced, I had climbed into a pair of shiny red shorts that, with the foul guard underneath, felt like they were riding up to my chest, and I had donned a white singlet emblazoned with The Real Fight Club logo. I looked the part and so, perhaps, I was ready. The whip joked about this and that but, as with so much said to me before the fight, none of it went in. Charles Jones, he of Pink Pounder fame, was floating around, tall and lean. I had introduced myself earlier and now watched him moving around backstage. Surely a fight against The Pink Pounder would not be difficult, but as it was, I was up against the squat and heavyset Vince 'Dynamite' Dickson, an ex-boxer. Umar, though, said he had found out about Dickson. 'He's rubbish,' he announced, conspiratorially lowering his voice. 'I've spoken to one of The Real Fight Club blokes. They say he's fat and useless.' But wasn't he an ex-boxer? 'Nah,' said Umar, 'that's all bollocks. He's had one white-collar fight and that's it. I'm telling you, you're going to do him. It ain't gonna be a duckwalk, but you'll do him, man, you'll do him. Just think, *think*, remember what you've been told, everything I've been doing with you, the sparring with Agim, the training with that lot in Swindon, just *think* and remember it all.'

I knew what Umar was trying to do – to bolster my confidence and psyche me up for the fight – but the problem was that I didn't believe him. I had heard from Lacey that Dickson was an ex-boxer, and why would he have lied? Umar's version of Dickson's credentials beggared belief. According to Umar, he was a fat slob who had somehow blundered through one white-collar bout, out of condition and not even technically proficient. But I had stood next to Dickson before the weigh-in, and I knew that he was far from out of shape. He was carrying too much weight, yes, but for all Umar's motivational 'He's rubbish' speeches, I knew that

I was giving away a few pounds to a man who looked useful and whom I had been told was an ex-boxer.

I didn't watch any of the fights before mine. I didn't want to watch other boxers being hit, being dropped, wincing in pain, looking scared. I knew that if I did it would affect how I was feeling. And the nearer the fight came, away from the action, the better I felt. I worked out on pads with Ali and felt sharp, though when he started throwing jabs back at me I failed to slip or block properly and got caught. *Typical,* I thought, *Your bloody defence lets you down again.* With five minutes to go until I was on, I asked for a minute on my own in the dressing room.

I had thought about this minute for months, from the very inception of the idea of the fight against Alex Mehta, throughout the training with Umar and Agim, the sparring with the lads at Walcot, and latterly from the moment I knew it would be some time before I would fight Mehta, that a humbler opponent such as Vince Dickson would be first up. I had imagined myself thinking of all the things that had made me mad, anything from racism and child abuse to poor manners and selfishness, all culminating in an image of a tidy, inoffensive managing partner who was certainly free from all of these save perhaps for selfishness and yet whom I could not forgive, not because he had sacked me but for something else; and on the other hand I had seen myself thinking *You deserve this, because of what you have done; if you get hit, it's the way it should be.* As neat a blend of mental S&M as you could find, and either way, certain to get me fired up. And on the night, alone, at last, in the dressing room, none of these thoughts was with me. My mind was blank, save for one thing, more urgent than any other: I must have a puff of my asthma inhaler. I asked for a minute alone so that I could be free of the barrage of motivational bluster that I didn't believe, and so that I could inhale some Ventolin in private, so that neither Umar, Agim and Ali, nor the other fighters, cornermen and whips who were back and forth from the dressing room, would see that for all the ripped and toned muscles of my upper body, I was fundamentally *weak*, the kind of child whose father once said: 'Perhaps you should sit this one out, it's too difficult for you', when around him other boys were engaged in some testosterone-heavy activity.

I had my minute, and my blast of Ventolin. What a drug it is, how it has transformed the lives of thousands of *weak* asthmatics around the world. Ali returned. He was a good-looking man in his late twenties or early thirties, who seemed sincere and decent. 'Time to go, man, you OK?' he said. 'I'm fine,' I said. 'Let's go.' There I was, standing behind the curtain at the edge of the stage, waiting for the announcer to call my name.

Umar asked if I wanted to walk out first. I told him to go ahead; I knew he would like the attention. I was aware vaguely of the words 'Alex "The Slugger" Wade' booming through the hall and then the opening riffs of the music I'd chosen, The Stranglers' 'Hanging Around', began. Suitably menacing, I felt, better than my other contender, Tom Waits' 'Step Right Up'. I noticed some men clapping to Jean-Jacques Burnel's heavy bass line and smacked my gloves together. This was it.

Vince 'Dynamite' Dickson popped a jab at me before I got one in on him. This wasn't in my game plan. I wanted to be the first to connect with a jab, so that Dickson, experienced as I believed him to be, would know that I was *there*, that I wasn't going to be just a slowly moving punchbag. Getting the first jab in and surviving the first round were the high points of my strategy; in fact, come to think of it, they *were* my strategy. And within a couple of seconds, Dickson had disrupted even this most rudimentary example of pugilistic planning.

I came straight back at him, throwing my own jab, fairly stiff and straight after all the lectures from Umar over the past five months. Indeed, from the first few seconds I could hear Umar screaming 'Jab! Jab! Come on, Alex, jab!' as if that were the only punch I had. And as things turned out, apart from a few straight rights, it was. By the midway point of the first round I was so tired that throwing anything more complicated than a one-two was going to be a miracle. Undoubtedly the exhaustion came from the nervous tension of boxing in front of a large crowd, but as much as that it was because of one fundamental error that I fell into at once: I was not breathing out as I threw punches. How many times had Harry Scott and the Walcot trainers told me to breathe out when throwing shots? How many times had Umar and Agim given the same basic boxing lesson? So often that I had lost count. And on the night, not once in all the punches I delivered and tried to deliver did I breathe out. I jabbed away and banged in some rights, every time with a mouthful of oxygen, never with an energy-preserving exhalation of breath. When a flurry was over I would tuck up and catch some air. So simple a thing, and yet so difficult to get right.

The first round was fairly even, with Dickson catching me with one solid jab and a right that rocked me a little. But I caught him too, and sat down after those first gruelling two minutes feeling that, yes, I had survived, and that I could *do this*. I recalled something Harry Scott had said about letting my limbs go limp on the stool between rounds, and so dropped my arms to my side and stretched out my legs as if I was drunk. Later one of my friends said I looked finished. I wasn't – I was tired, more tired than I had ever expected to be – but I was following orders. I can't remember a thing Umar said to me other than more exhortations to jab, but I do remember thinking that I had achieved at least the second part of the strategy. I had survived the first round. Mine was not to be the fate of Paul 'Mad Manx' Beckett, humiliated in front of everyone.

The bell went for round two and Dickson was up and ready about five seconds ahead of me. I padded towards him and straight away we had reversed positions, so that he was boxing out of my corner and I had my back to his. What a view his corner must have had as he unleashed a vicious straight right, one that I did not see coming and which penetrated my lax guard like dry sand through a sieve. I felt my neck snap back as the blow landed full on my mouth, just above the chin, just below the nose. What a punch. It took my legs away and I swayed and staggered and yet somehow caught my balance without hitting the deck like Mad Manx. I saw blood arching down towards the canvas and wondered if my nose had opened up or my gums. Back and forth I tottered, slipping first to the ropes then stumbling forwards again, until at last the disorientation had gone and my body had recovered, if not my mind. This much was probably obvious to the referee as he took me to the neutral corner to my right. Those words – *Are you all right?* – and then, after looking me in the eyes intently, he went to the ropes and leant down to speak to – who? Alan Lacey? The ringside doctor? The judge? His girlfriend? I had no idea but back he came, and then I heard those other unforgettable words:

'Remember, this is white-collar boxing, no one is going to get hurt.' Again I was asked if I was all right. This time I nodded, as a strange collage of 1950s photographs assembled itself in my mind's eye. I was not all right, but then, compared with the feeling of that punch when it landed, I was much better. I was *able to continue*.

When the fight resumed I knew I had to hit Dickson as soon as possible. I had not consciously decided this, but it was obvious. If I did not come back at him with as much vigour as I could muster, this bull of a man was going to finish me, and it was going to hurt, as much as and maybe more than that huge right at the beginning of the second round. And so no sooner had we squared up than I jabbed him and went in with a number of one-twos, forcing him around the ring as blow after blow landed. Most he avoided with good defence work but at least Vince 'Dynamite' Dickson knew his opponent was still in the fight.

But if he thought I wasn't scared, he would have been well off the mark. I looked at Dickson and felt petrified. I was so scared that forcing myself forward to jab at him was a monumental act of will. This man had just hit me so hard that my legs had gone, my entire nervous system could have been reprogrammed for all I knew, and I was terrified that by engaging with him close up I was laying myself open to the same thing all over again. And sure enough, in that round, though I was by far the busier fighter, one other right got through, not too hard but enough to snap at the vertebrae at the top of my neck again.

The bell went and there was the sanctuary of Umar and my corner. I had a vague impression that Umar would congratulate me for coming back into the fight, when I could have gone down. Nothing of the sort was on the cards. I sat there, this time my body limp from sheer exhaustion, only to hear Umar lay into me with a verbal assault almost as painful as Dickson's punches. 'Jab! Jab at him! Fucking get out there and jab and keep your guard up! You're not tired, you're going out there to win this! Come on! I haven't put all this work into you for nothing! Get out there and finish him off! Jab! Double jab and hook off the jab! Come on!' On and on came Umar's words, and there was nothing I could do to stop them.

Through the haze I saw a friend, Darren Mulloy, sitting near-ringside. He, with two other old friends, Rich and Elliot, were the only people I noticed on the night, once in the ring. Standing there waiting for the fight to begin, I had seen Rich and Elliot, whom I had known since the age of five, up on the balcony. I had raised my right arm to them not merely in salutation, but also as a kind of *Here I am, lads, isn't it ridiculous?* acknowledgement. And now, in between rounds two and three, there was Darren, a solicitor-turned-academic, a contemplative, highly intelligent man, with a look of deep concern on brows that were as knitted as any cartoon cliché could have them. And as my gaze somehow caught his, one of the two card girls for the evening swept across my view, her straight blonde hair and lithe physique obscuring everything as she strode on high heels around the ring. I started to follow her body, to think of her curves and admire the ripple of her thighs in her skimpy dress, but stopped myself as I perceived the unparalleled absurdity of thinking of a woman, women, sex, anything else, at that juncture. Later, one of my friends, suitably impressed by her, asked me if she had distracted me. I told him the truth. Yes, but not that much. Or maybe too much. As lawyers say, it all depends.

The third round proved a reprise of the first, a little less tentative but with both of us looking evenly matched. I landed one good, hard right, to cheers from the contingent of the crowd rooting for me, but so too did Dickson. It seemed that every time I found a way through, he just banged a shot back at me, even finding the energy and technique to throw a couple of uppercuts. By now, though, I could see that he was exhausted, too. Again I heard Umar's shouts of 'Jab!' and then he added: 'Come on, hook off the jab, do it!' I wanted to, I desperately wanted to land a hook off the jab, a neat surprise punch that I could throw in sparring, followed by a straight right, left hook, straight right combination, but on the night I dared not. I heard Umar's words, and I sized Dickson up, and I thought about it, but I concluded (all in the space of perhaps one or two seconds) that to try a hook off the jab and any of the move's natural sequential combinations was a risk too far. In doing so, I would be too exposed, too fragile; Dickson was good enough to seize the opportunity to blast me with another hard right, and by this stage just his jabs were hurting. Beyond that, I was too tired, could not even double jab, let alone jab and find the momentum to twist my arm into a left hook at the midway point of the jab's retreat. Discretion was by now, literally, the better part of valour.

I took one punch at around one minute twenty seconds that caused Simon White to usher me into the neutral corner again. It wasn't too hard, but I was grateful for the chance to ask him how long was left. 'Thirty seconds,' he said. 'Are you all right?' I nodded. Just thirty seconds left to get through, thirty seconds in which to avoid being hit. I nearly didn't make it, as Dickson hit me in the last seconds, causing a minor stumble. But then the bell went. The fight was over.

Dickson and I smacked gloves. 'Cheers, mate,' I said. 'Well done,' said Dickson. 'Good one.'

Before Vince and I had our photograph taken, Alan Lacey climbed into the ring, grinning from ear to ear. He gave me a trophy and shook my gloved right hand. 'Well done!' he said. 'Well done. You're a fighter now! Go on, son!'

Back in the dressing room, Umar, Agim and Ali were elated. 'You won that fight!' they chorused. 'Man, that was fantastic,' said Umar. 'You did me proud. And I tell you what, you won it. You won that fight.'

'No way,' I said, slumped in a chair, drenched in sweat. But Umar and my other cornermen were convinced. It didn't matter that Vince Dickson had nearly knocked me out at the beginning of the second round; according to amateur boxing rules, I had thrown and landed more scoring punches, and given that I had survived that big right, I was the winner. I didn't believe them, whatever they said, even when Umar insisted I had hit Dickson with a punch that had taken his legs away, albeit not quite so spectacularly as mine had gone. Nor when Umar said I had hit him with a punch that had cut his nose. I had seen none of this, and none of it seemed believable. It was as incredible as Umar's prefight protestations as to Dickson's incompetence. And yet there in the dressing room was a friend, Simon, himself not a bad boxer, who was agreeing with everything Umar, Agim and Ali were saying.

Whatever: I had survived the three rounds, and it felt like the hardest thing I had ever done. It felt so hard that I was due a few pints and some cigarettes. As soon as I had showered, I made my way to the bar. The congratulations of my friends followed, so too those of people I didn't know, there to watch the boxing, wishing me well in thick East London accents.

After about half an hour, Umar rushed over with the judge, there to score a British heavyweight title bout. 'If you don't believe me, ask him!' said Umar. The judge nodded, rather as a kindly uncle at a wedding. 'Yes,' he said, 'I thought you would be interested to know how you got on, even though, as you know, only title fights are formally scored at this level of boxing. So yes, I scored your fight, and yes, you won. Not by much, but you did just enough. Well done.'

I was flabbergasted. Not only had I survived the three rounds, coming back from a punch that could easily have floored me, I had – albeit unofficially – won. The relief and elation were, suddenly, immense.

As last orders were called, I walked out into the hall to find Alan Lacey. I hadn't watched a single one of the other bouts, though I had heard that Charles Jones had not fared well. By this point I had downed four or five pints, apologising to Umar when he had seen me lighting a cigarette with the third post-fight lager. 'None of my business,' he had said, with a slight shake of his head. Still, it was nothing too major, and hadn't I earned it? I found Lacey, surrounded by lingering fight fans and a Cockney who was telling him how useful he was, how he wanted to join The Real Fight Club and have a fight. Over in the bar the usual stragglers were still drinking. There were people sitting on chairs and a few up on the balcony. I noticed all these people – the audience – for the first time that evening. I thanked Lacey and found my friends. There was talk of a few beers in a nearby restaurant.

As we walked down the steps from the large wooden doors of York Hall into the warm, humid night, I asked one of my friends what he had made of the evening.

'Nice blondes and mean-looking lads,' he said. 'Exactly as it should be.'

9

GIRLS ON TOP

Cathy 'The Bitch' Brown was not impressed. 'He's a brawler,' she said, as we sat ringside and watched Vince 'Dynamite' Dickson batter his opponent in the last fight on the card, a Real Fight Club event entitled '21st-Century Corinthians', held at the Grange City Hotel near the Tower of London.

'Look at him, he's just steaming in to have a tear-up,' said the diminutive Cathy, an attractive woman, no more than five feet tall, with long dark hair and slender as a model save for powerful biceps and inescapably perfect breasts. It was difficult not to agree as I sat next to her, watching Dickson going furiously about his business, and yet I was a little miffed by Cathy's lack of admiration for Dickson the boxer. I had seen Vince earlier, before his fight, and had felt a camaraderie that took me by surprise. It was just two weeks after my own fight with him, and there we were, standing in the corridor adjoining the room in the hotel in which a ring had been set up. Vince was due on soon but we found time for a quick chat. I told him that my fight against him had been tough, almost the hardest thing I'd ever done, and that I couldn't believe it when the judge had said I'd won; after all, Vince had all but knocked me out in the second round. Vince was modest and self-effacing, and then said, almost as a parent gently reprimands a child: 'You *are* going to have a fight again, aren't you, Alex?'

'Yep, sometime,' I replied. 'But not with you. Good luck for your fight.'

When Vince climbed into the ring, I gave him a cheer and took a drag on my cigarette. I turned to Cathy and said: 'This is the bloke I had my fight against.' She nodded, disinterestedly, and we settled down to watch what was indeed a riotous affair rather than an elegant exposition of the noble art. I was drunk, and I cheered Vince on with commensurate abandon. I wanted Cathy 'The Bitch' Brown – a professional boxer and holder of the British women's bantamweight title – to take me seriously, to see Vince Dickson up above us in the ring boxing and say to herself 'Well, that bloke who's been sitting next to me all night getting more and more drunk, smoking away, must have something if he could have a fight against that tough lad there', but instead Cathy saw, with her professional eyes, only the technical deficiencies of the two men in front of her, their recourse to the ways of the street brawl rather than fidelity to the science of boxing. Still, she knew what was on my mind. 'I can see why you're pleased you beat him,' she said, as Dickson smashed his right fist hard into his opponent's body.

I nodded, as if indifferent to whether I had ever had a fight with Dickson, let alone beat him. Watching him fight, I found it impossible to believe that just two weeks before he had nearly knocked me out at York Hall. Not because he looked clumsy, or ineffective – far from it. He looked tough and muscular, anchored to the ground, immovable. I could not believe that I had had a fight against him. How had this happened, how had I found the courage to climb into the ring and take him on, how on earth had I survived? Minutes before Dickson's fight had begun, I had turned my chair away from my fellow guests, who included Boxing Hall of Fame inductee Mickey Duff, so that I could see every shot thrown and taken. I roared Vince on when he seemed to be gaining the upper hand, and waved my arms in exasperation when his opponent was prevailing. Because I had fought Vince, I felt a strange bond between us, almost as if we were partners in crime. Meeting him by chance before his fight, I had felt embarrassed by the cigarette in my hand, as if to smoke was to let the pair of us down, to ignore the code of health and fitness that is integral to a boxer's welfare. 'I'm just smoking and boozing a bit tonight,' I'd said, 'but soon I'll get back into the boxing and quit again.'

But I was drunk by the time Vince was fighting, and it was as if the booze and the fags had never gone away. In the two weeks since our fight, I had trained just twice at Walcot, and had spent a lot of the rest of the time in the pub. Celebrating, initially, then filling the hours when the high had faded. Or sometimes I hadn't even got as far as the pub, instead opening a bottle of red wine at home, then another, and, throughout, smoking. The first time back at Walcot, after the fight with Dickson, I felt fine, but the next occasion was dreadful. There is not a boxer in the world who can fight when he is drinking and smoking, and just one session is enough to take the edge off months of training. This applies to the world of white-collar boxing as much as it does to any other. The night before the Real Fight Club's '21st-Century Corinthians' show I had trained at Walcot, but the night before that I had got drunk. The session at Walcot was a shambles; I had left with Harry Scott shaking his head, decidedly unimpressed.

Still, I was at the Grange City Hotel on the back of a fight at York Hall and however useless I'd been the night before at Walcot, at least I'd made the effort and *been* there. I was entitled to call myself *a boxer*, of sorts. But driving to the 'Corinthians' event, the familiar urge to drink until oblivion became yet more insistent the closer I got to London, and once there I lost little time in availing myself of the endless free booze in a way that left everyone on my table convinced that when I told them that yes, I too had had a boxing match, just two weeks earlier, at York Hall in Bethnal Green, in front of eight hundred people, a match that I had miraculously won after surviving a near-KO in the second round (and that yes, only last night I had been training in a tough old amateur club in Swindon), I was a delusional lunatic.

Along with Mickey Duff, Cathy 'The Bitch' Brown and a veteran cuts man with magic hands that he held poised above Cathy's, to cure a recalcitrant ache, there was a doctor present, a bald, tanned and highly articulate man whom I asked whether he shared the standard British Medical Association line on boxing, that it is dangerous and should be banned. 'These guys don't seem to be hurting each other,' he said, looking at the boxers on show, 'they seem to be enjoying themselves.' I couldn't resist telling him that I, too, was a boxer, and he looked at me with disbelief. 'You? You had a fight?' Yes, I said, telling him all, saying that I was treating myself to some booze and fags in celebration of months of training and a successful debut but that yes, soon,

I would get back to it and have another fight. He didn't smile and it was clear that, as a doctor and as a man, he had a far greater dislike of my evident ability to down glasses of red wine and smoke than he did for boxing, white-collar or otherwise. If I hadn't been so drunk I might have felt sad, but as it was I quaffed another free glass and turned to watch the action.

The day after my fight against Vince 'Dynamite' Dickson I woke up at about 5.30 in Jules's flat in Hackney Wick. Not an hour of the day that suits me at the best of times, let alone after a fight, but Ian Smith and I had to hit the road early to catch a ferry at Portsmouth. We were going to Le Mans – my first trip to one of the world's most romantic motor-racing events. Ian had contacts with one of the dark-horse teams, Riley & Scott Racing, and had got us access to the pits. It seemed too good an opportunity to miss, but that morning, waking up at some ungodly hour, and later, in France, amid the deafening noise and pervasive petrol fumes of Le Mans, I felt that going to the race was a mistake. I wanted to be with Karen, Harry and Elliot. I needed to have the comfort of my family after such an extreme experience; I wanted to hold the boys and take them to the park and watch videos with them, talk to Karen, open a bottle of red wine and cuddle up on the sofa. I wanted to listen to Jonathan Phillips play his cherished Rachmaninov Piano Concerto No. 3, which he would be performing at a local church on the Saturday of Le Mans. None of this would be happening. Going to Le Mans was a dream come true, but straight after my debut fight at York Hall it was coming true at the wrong time. This didn't turn it into a nightmare, but it meant that on top of the massive adrenalin rush of fighting, coupled with the release of having put in the hard work and survived, my brain and body were being overloaded when they were not capable of taking much more.

We stayed away from the track, in a pretty town called Nogent-le-Rotrou. I couldn't get the fight out of my mind, and wanted to talk about it continually, but we were in France to watch the motor racing, and anyway, there had already been a debrief straight afterwards, when Ian and I and a few other friends had a meal in a Greek restaurant round the corner from York Hall. Chris, an old friend from my days with Richard Desmond, had a video clip of the fight on a digital camera and I'd watched intently, seeing for the first time Dickson's heavy, disorientating blow to my chin and my own counterattack once my head had cleared. It looked all right, not the best boxing in the world but not the worst. Later, at Jules's flat, we'd watched a video recorded by Steve Holdsworth, a former professional boxer who records every bout held by The Real Fight Club and then sells the tapes to boxers at the end of the night. Holdsworth, an amiable character who likes a fag or two, had been floating around backstage before the fights, encouraging boxers and joking with cornermen and whips. He provided the commentary for the bouts and had said I looked 'tidy' and had given a 'gutsy performance'. He also said, at the end of the tape, that I had proved to be anything but The Slugger. I winced when I heard this, sitting there with Jules and some friends, watching the tape Holdsworth had put together. Those three two-minute rounds had felt so intense, so visceral, and I'd felt so elated to have survived Dickson's punch, and yet they were nothing to Holdsworth as a former professional boxer. And on the tape, however tidy I looked, however gutsy I had proved to be, I also looked flat-footed and leaden. I may have hit Dickson plenty of times, but it was he who deserved his soubriquet, not me.

Alone in my hotel room in Nogent-le-Rotrou a couple of days later, I was rummaging for some clean clothes when I found my boxing gloves and the red wraps Umar had given me. Ian and I had returned to the hotel mid-afternoon to catch up on some sleep, but when I saw the gloves, I felt the urge to box. I looked around the small room, and before long had upended the bed and pushed it up against the wall. I moved a table and a chair and did some stretches, then press-ups and sit-ups. I did loads, I can't recall how many, but I have always been able to do both easily so it was probably about two hundred press-ups and four hundred sit-ups. I tied my wraps, then put the gloves on, and I shadow-boxed around the cramped room. It was a sweltering hot day at the beginning of a heatwave that would last in Europe throughout the summer, and within minutes I was drenched in sweat. I kept going, jabbing, hooking and throwing uppercuts, slipping and blocking, feinting, hooking off the jab, launching powerful straight rights that I imagined connecting hard enough against an opponent to leave Steve Holdsworth or whoever else might be doing the commentary with no alternative but to say, at the end of a tape of my next fight, 'Well, if ever a fighter deserved his nickname, it's The Slugger!'

An hour or two later I was drinking a beer and smoking from a crumpled packet of Marlboro Lights in Riley & Scott's corporate hospitality suite. Ian had introduced me to a friend, an English ex-pat who lived outside Paris, like Ian a motor-racing fanatic. We sat and talked and watched the drivers and mechanics of Riley & Scott wandering in, calm and unhurried, grabbing coffees and snacks, and the topic of my fight came up. Ian's friend greeted the news that I had fought the previous night in a boxing match with perplexity. He was a peaceable man who, I would wager my last centime, had never had a fight in his life. He looked at me quizzically, and then asked whether I would do it again.

'I don't know,' I said. 'It was pretty much the hardest thing I've ever done. But there are tangible benefits to boxing, to the whole process of getting fit and having a fight.'

I wanted to tell him what they were, to ramble on for the next hour about courage and camaraderie and commitment, respect and discipline, but his attention seemed to drift, and Ian suggested we go to the stands and watch the cars flying down the start-finish straight, so I said 'sounds good' and drank my beer, before lighting another cigarette to help me on my way.

Estelle 'Model T' Ford was getting the better of her opponent, Ann 'Sweet P' Parisio. A twenty-five-year-old actuarial assistant, she was lean and fit, and knew how to punch. So too did her opponent, herself a thirty-eight-year-old freelance television documentary maker whom I had seen training the same night that I'd attended the Lennox Lewis Centre. But if Ann Parisio had looked the part at the Lennox Lewis Centre, barely breaking sweat as she slung fine straight punches at the bags, she was having trouble dealing with Estelle Ford. She was tentative and nervous, and couldn't seem to settle into any kind of rhythm. Perhaps the hype had got to her: this was the highlight of the '21st-Century Corinthians' show, The Real Fight Club's first-ever female white-collar boxing contest. Alan Lacey had dubbed it the 'Girls On Top' show.

Both women appeared relaxed before their fight and were

greeted raucously by the suits packing the Grange City Hotel room set aside for the evening's white-collar boxing. Their bout was towards the end of the show, and, by then, a lot of people had drunk a lot of booze, with the notable exception of Spencer Fearon, who was in the middle of training for a comeback fight. 'I'm gonna do the business,' he told me, when I reminded him that we'd met with Umar, at the Mermaid Theatre in March. 'You wait and watch, man, I'm feeling good.'

Fearon was accompanied by a ravishingly beautiful woman, the kind you see with boxers in the movies, who I took to be his partner. Aside from her, there weren't too many other women in the audience, which as a collective couldn't wait to see two women have a tear-up. But Mickey Duff wasn't convinced. 'Women boxing is wrong, all wrong,' he said, ponderously, as if a lifetime of thought had gone into research on the subject. 'I just don't hold with it.'

If Duff was old-school, Alan Lacey espoused a more modern, perhaps even politically correct, view. 'The girls are fit, and they're going to put the men on the undercard to shame,' he'd told me. Taking one look at Parisio and Ford as they climbed into the ring, Lacey's optimism was well founded. The two women were in great shape. I stole a glance at Cathy Brown, marvelling again at her superb physique, and found myself thinking of Amy Wharton, twenty-four, Walcot's only female boxer. By day, Amy worked as a stable lass, but outside work she found the time to study to be a beauty therapist as well as train as a boxer. She had wonderful technique, quick reflexes and bags of stamina. One Sunday at Walcot, Harold had spotted me lifting my head as I threw punches at a bag ('like a weather vane', as Umar had also noted). He found a golf ball from God knows where and made me tuck it under my neck. I then had to hit the bag, keeping the golf ball in position, with a penalty of twenty press-ups every time I let it drop. I lost count of how many press-ups I had to do. Then it was Amy's turn. She didn't drop the golf ball once.

'The girls are motivated and talented natural athletes,' Lacey had said. 'This is not a gimmick.'

The crowd shared his enthusiasm. Men leapt up as every punch was thrown, and seemed to side with Estelle 'Model T' Ford midway through the first round. Perhaps Estelle had more friends there than Ann, or maybe it was her feisty looks that captivated the crowd. Possibly Ann's occupation was a little too creative, maybe the suits preferred their women to be grounded in the reality of facts and figures. I felt sorry for Parisio as I heard one of many drunken males near me bellowing encouragement to Ford, at her rival's expense: 'Go on, Estelle! Go on! Kill her! She's fuckin' useless!' I felt like telling him where to go, but there would have been no point. He was not alone in being braying, drunk and obnoxious, and for the first time, looking at the contorted rage on the face of this man and those near him, listening to their demented howls, I witnessed how ugly a boxing event can be. I doubted that they even knew Estelle Ford but something had made them plump for her, the booze fuelling the derision they heaped upon Parisio. Where was their 'Corinthian spirit' that night at the Grange City Hotel? I doubted they knew what the words meant. Where was the nobility in screaming at Ann, telling her she was 'a useless cow'? How did this benefit Estelle 'Model T' Ford? Moreover, their sentiment wasn't even grounded in reality. After a hesitant opening Parisio settled in to the fight and defended herself admirably, tucking up and taking Ford's shots, and throwing a few of her own, too. By the end of the three two-minute rounds she had done well against her former kick-boxing adversary, a woman more than ten years her junior who didn't lack for fitness, ability or confidence. 'I train at least four times a week, very hard,' Ford told me a few days before the fight. 'I feel good and I'm really looking forward to it. There's loads that girls can do better than men, and we're gonna show up the guys on the night.'

Ann 'Sweet P' Parisio was filming in Scotland in the days leading up to the fight, and trying not to think about it. She had sparred with Ford, and knew what she was up against. 'Estelle's very good,' she told me. 'But my day job is intense and I don't have the time to think about fighting her every minute.'

Parisio was in love with boxing. She had been training for two years, through The Real Fight Club, and adored the 'power and beauty' of boxing. 'It's something that just hits you,' she said. 'Can you think of anything more beautiful than watching a boxer shadow-boxing?' A vision of my own inelegance struck me, and I thought that maybe if Ann Parisio saw me shadow-boxing, she might revise this view, but she went on to explain what boxing meant for her, as a woman: 'Since I've been boxing, I see my body as more functional, more of an efficient machine. All women suffer a pressure to be thin and conform to the fashion industry's view of beauty. It's rubbish, but it still gets to you. Through boxing I can get away from all that, I can say to myself "who gives a shit?"' For Parisio, boxing was not just a healthy way to relieve stress (another point she made in its favour), but an escape from what society expected of her. Naturally enough, she had no problems with pugilism, and would not, I suspect, warm to the Mickey Duff line on women in boxing. 'If men can fight, women should be able to as well,' said the sensitive-looking, crop-haired brunette. 'Why not? Fighting is a basic human instinct.'

Parisio and Ford had one common desire for their fight, beyond those of every boxer leading up to every fight (not to get hurt, not to be humiliated, not to be embarrassed; to win, to destroy the opponent, to throw good clean shots throughout; to touch gloves and embrace at the end, mutual respect assured). They wanted a card man. 'Why not?' said Ford, while Parisio, more emphatic, wondered whether one of The Real Fight Club's boxers might take on the role of strutting around the ring between rounds. On the night, their wish was granted as Lacey hauled in a giant of a man, presumably a model, striking with blue eyes, a greasy hairless chest and bald head. The women might have been pleased but as the card man strode around the squared circle the dismay of the audience was palpable, a marked contrast to the whoops of delight that had earlier greeted the arrival of a brunette card girl, one of the two who had been working on the night of my fight, whose feline equanimity I was far better placed to observe from my seat next to Cathy 'The Bitch' Brown than I had been at York Hall.

By the end of the fight I had Estelle Ford and Ann Parisio even, but seconds after the bell a tall blond man in a bedraggled grey suit cupped his hand to his mouth and hollered: 'Bollocks! Lacey called it early! She was fuckin' all over her! Well done, Estelle, you had her!' Whether he was right would remain in the realm of the subjective: this might have been a fight between two women, but it was white-collar boxing, and the taking part was a victory in itself. A formal winner would not be declared. Instead, Cathy 'The Bitch' Brown climbed through the ropes and presented Ford and Parisio with trophies commemorating their contest, as Alan Lacey looked on, beaming like a proud father.

I was drunk by the end of the fights, but though I hadn't spoken to him all evening something possessed me to have a chat with Mickey Duff. He was seated at the other side of the table for much of the night, too far away to talk to, but a few people had disappeared and he had moved round to my side. Duff is a legend, one of those men who has been in boxing all his life, who has done and seen it all (including, as of that evening, white-collar boxing), a man who has been promoter, manager, matchmaker, cornerman and boxer. Born in 1929 in Krakow, Poland, Duff's real name was Monek Prager. His father, a rabbi, moved to England in the 1930s to escape the growing Nazi menace. Duff, whose name has entered the lexicon of Cockney rhyming slang (a 'Mickey Duff' is a 'puff' of marijuana), took up boxing during the war and fought more than a hundred amateur fights before turning pro illegally at fifteen. He went on to win sixty-one of sixty-nine professional contests as a lightweight and welterweight, and retired at the grand old age of nineteen. In the late 1940s Duff abandoned a career as a sewing-machine salesman and returned to boxing, where he emerged as a dominant force for the next few decades. He was involved, one way or another, with a series of successful British fighters, including John Conteh, Jim Watt, Alan Minter, Terry Downes and Howard Winstone, and also worked with champions Maurice Hope, John 'The Beast' Mugabi and Cornelius Boza Edwards.

As Duff sat next to me, it struck me that he was a dead ringer for my former boss, Richard Desmond. Both had large, capable hands, broad shoulders and huge chests, and stood about five foot ten. Both were Jewish and had the same glint in their eyes, a sparkle that signified threat and discomfort as readily as it promised laughter and one-liners. Then, as I heard Duff speaking, his accent settled into the London matrix not simply of Desmond and Lacey but also of Karen's father, John. I asked him what he thought about the women fighting, and then, struck again by his East End intonation, wondered if he might even have known John. 'I know it might sound daft,' I said, 'but did you know a gym in Canning Town above a pub called the Royal Oak?'

Duff didn't hesitate. 'Course I do,' he said, 'bloody 'ell, I remember it well. It's not there any more but yes, certainly I remember it.'

I couldn't believe it. Karen had told me about this gym – where her father and his brothers had boxed as teenagers – since we'd known each other, and had often talked of trying to find at least its site, even if, as she had heard, it no longer existed. We had never got round to doing anything about it, and probably never would. But here was Mickey Duff telling me he knew the place, and just that fact, I knew, would touch Karen. It was late, too late to call, but I thanked Duff and got up to ring Karen there and then. It was probably the only late-night booze-inspired call I have ever made to her that went down well.

Making my way unsteadily out of the near-deserted hotel room, alongside the ring, I ran into Rajiv 'Batta Bing' Bhattacharya. He had been working for the evening as a cornerman, and often helped Lacey out if he wasn't fighting on a show. Not for the first time, he was in a surly mood, moaning about having to wait around to be paid. We were joined by Simon White, who had been refereeing the Corinthians show. He didn't seem to believe me when I reminded him he had refereed my fight against Vince 'Dynamite' Dickson, at York Hall, but then, all smiles, exclaimed: 'Yeah! You took that big shot in the second round! I remember you! Good on yer for coming back so well.'

Batta Bing muttered some more about money, and I chanced a comment about how hard he'd been when we had sparred. 'The thing is,' I slurred, 'are you as good as Alex Mehta? I mean, he's a legend, isn't he?' Batta Bing didn't look happy. 'Nah, man, he's not that good.' He mentioned money again, and scoured the room for Alan Lacey.

Lacey duly appeared, a little flustered. He is not a man who bears stress well, but he had, once again, put on another well-run and entertaining show. The punters had got their money's worth. The only gripe anyone could have (assuming they did not hate boxing in the first place) was the uncouth comments made by a small section of the crowd towards Ann Parisio, who herself had probably not heard them and exuded elation as she said her farewells to Lacey and other Real Fight Club friends. Even Batta Bing got his cash and went away happy.

'Pleased with the night?' I asked Lacey.

'Damn right,' he said. 'And I'll tell you what, the girls were the best boxers on show. Fuckin' tremendous, really tremendous.'

Lacey said there was more wine if I wanted some, though he'd be heading off. That seemed like the best option for me, too. And so I said 'thanks for a great evening' and staggered out into the night, drunk, asthmatic from twenty-plus cigarettes, the very antithesis of the men Duff had trained, men like Karen's father and his brothers, men whom he might even have known and whom it was highly unlikely he would recognise in me. Outside, it was warm and humid. I walked through the deserted streets of the City, until I got to Shoreditch High Street, where I stood waiting for a cab next to the phone boxes outside The Light Bar.

On the floor, there were the same old tart cards, trodden into the ground. A homeless man sat begging by the nearby garage. Some drunken suits shambled along, their inebriated voices deadened by the occasional cars until finally they were out of sight and lost in the still night. One of my shoes felt sticky – chewing gum, to which a card depicting a near-naked brunette with legs splayed and a smile on her face had got stuck, its accompanying text promising 'Anything goes' in a 'discreet apartment, two minutes from City'. I got the card off my shoe and scraped away the chewing gum as best I could. I squinted unsteadily at the card and noted that 'kissing' was also on offer, as if in the category of illicit thrills *à la* 'O' and 'A' levels. Once it was in my hand, I didn't know what to do with the card. To let it fall back on the floor was to add to the indignity its model had already suffered; to throw it in a bin was worse, as if to cast it deliberately among the detritus of London. So I put it in my pocket, just as a cab turned up.

'Good night, mate?' said the driver.

'Yeah, top.'

'What you been doin'?'

I told him I'd been to a white-collar boxing event at the Grange City Hotel, in which two women had had a fight.

'White-collar boxing? I've heard about that. That's boxing for City folk, innit? What, are girls at it as well, then?'

'Yep, and they were good. Put most of the men to shame.'

'Good on 'em,' said the cabbie. 'Were they lookers?'

I caught his eye in the rear-view mirror, and felt the tart card in my pocket.

'They were very attractive,' I said. 'But you should have seen the card girls. Stunners.'

'I can believe it, mate, them ring girls are gorgeous, they always are. Love it when they have to squeeze through the ropes, with their little bikinis or split skirts. What they wearing tonight, skirts or bikinis?'

I told him they were wearing nice black dresses with a split that led up to the crotch. He liked that. 'Fantastic! Bet you had a good look when they were climbing through the ropes, eh!'

I wanted to duck the question, but mumbled something about how I'd done my best.

'Too right! I woulda done, no doubt about it. Anyway, who won between the two birds?'

I explained that in white-collar boxing there are no formal winners, save for title fights. 'The theory is that just taking part is enough, given how hard boxing is.'

'Yeah, I can go with that. But, mate, there's always a winner, you always know who was the better fighter, doncha? The crowd always knows. So come on, who won?'

I looked out of the window at the streets of Hackney and for some reason drifted off into imagining meeting Mickey Duff with Karen, at the Royal Oak in Canning Town. He would put his strong boxer's arm around her and clasp her shoulder with one of his old boxer's hands, and as the two of them looked up at the derelict shell that was once the Royal Oak Duff would say that yes, he knew her father and his brothers, they were good men, decent boxers, he could see their faces now, what were they doing, were they well, it was different in those days of course, women didn't box though now they do, not something he approved of, women had a different role in life, theirs was not to fight, best leave that to the boys who want to fight, because some of them do, that's the reality, some do, and if they do you have to accept it.

The cabbie disturbed this reverie. 'Come on, mate, who won? There's always a winner, in every fight, I don't care what anyone says.'

We exchanged looks again in the mirror.

'It was a draw,' I said.

10

WHITE-COLLAR WARRIORS

The hands of the man who had studied the bruised flesh of Dave 'Boy' McAuley's face and moulded it into a monumental lump of bronze were large and white. They did not look like boxers' hands, but they were good hands, hands of strength and sensitivity that had left their mark on the world. They were hands that clasped mine warmly as I arrived with Karen at Belfast City Airport, and they were hands that drove a car smoothly around the Falls and Shankhill Roads, hands that pointed out the loyalist and Catholic murals, hands that showed us the desperate graffiti of war-torn Belfast, hands that indicated the peace wall, hands that gestured as if in passing at an army bomb disposal unit at work, and hands that ushered me swiftly back into the car when I held my camera too obviously and too long in the false stillness of a summer afternoon on the bunting-bedecked Shankhill Road. They were hands that had crafted a series of bronze heads of celebrated Irish people, from the loquacious Reverend Ian Paisley and former Taoiseach Charles Haughey, to politician John Hume and the poet Seamus Heaney. They were hands that had immortalised Irish champion boxer Dave 'Boy' McAuley's head in bronze, hands whose owner said of McAuley: 'He was like a Hellenistic bronze of a boxer. I could really feel the bruised flesh of his battered, scarred face. His head had taken a hammering but was like an unexploded grenade. You could feel the tension and controlled aggression.'

The hands belonged to sculptor-turned-abstract-artist Philip Flanagan, who we were visiting at his home in Lough Erne, County Fermanagh, in July, a month or so after my fight. I would be interviewing him for the Review section of the *IoS*; Karen was accompanying me because she and Flanagan had got on when they'd met a couple of months earlier. They shared similar artistic concerns, and I was pleased that, for once, Karen was with me on a work trip. Flanagan had a shock of curly black hair, not dissimilar to mine before I had most of it cut off, but there the comparisons – physically, sartorially – stopped. He was large with a cherubic face, and favoured corduroy jackets and jeans, rather like a hippie squire. He was courteous and charming, unerringly generous, the perfect host.

He had put together a debut collection of paintings entitled 'Bullersten', a Scandinavian term meaning 'a large stone that makes a noise when it is moved', which we had seen on show in England. Rocks and stones fascinated Flanagan, whether rubble left after a riot in Belfast or the stones found on the shore of Lough Erne. 'I can remember being fascinated by boulders as a child,' he told me. 'In Belfast, depending on where you lived, they would be painted red, white and blue, or green, white and orange, and placed a short distance away from buildings to stop car bombers detonating bombs. There was always a sense of *after-energy* in Belfast, an amazing feeling of tension after a battle or fight. And here in Fermanagh, it's the same, it's as if something has *happened* in the landscape. I try and get across that feeling in my work.' Flanagan's work sought to capture the *after-energy* of Belfast but also that which he sensed in the landscape of stone circles, cairns and monasteries around his home on the shore of Lough Erne. It is an ancient place, where the Flanagan family has its roots. Flanagan's paintings have a spiritual serenity informed by their creator's feeling that he has returned home: 'These islands fascinate me. They're full of ghosts. I'm happy here and feel secure.'

One afternoon we rowed across the slate-grey water of Lough Erne, from Flanagan's home, to the island of Inishmacsaint. It was an almost still, intermittently blue-skied day, and on Inishmacsaint an ancient high cross was just visible through the trees. Flanagan loved the tiny, uninhabited island. 'I just feel, looking out over the fields, that there's something more to the whole thing than is first visible. I can sense people walking along the shoreline, and can feel that it's a happy place. So for my paintings of this area I mix the oils very carefully, so that you can see the brush strokes, because I want to create a carapace of light and texture that vibrates, that gets across the spirituality of the Fermanagh landscape.'

Karen, herself an abstract painter, needed no convincing. As much as Flanagan and his partner, Maria, she adored the landscape of Lough Erne and County Fermanagh, with its lush, deserted lanes and endlessly changeable Atlantic weather, and talked of upping and moving there. *The urge to escape and start again where no one knows anything...*

We drank a lot in the evenings, and in the mornings I was as *slightly rough* as ever. As I lay in bed, trying to recover, trying to escape the sun that was pouring through the bedroom window, which for some reason had not been blessed with a curtain, the familiar unholy alliance of despair and sexual compulsion seemed to crush me, while along the corridor, Flanagan, Maria and Karen bustled around, getting on with it, as if they were free. I had had my fight, but nothing had changed. Rancid from the booze, I went for six- to eight-mile runs along the lanes, looking, as Flanagan said to Karen, 'like a marine'. I thought of Dave 'Boy' McAuley and wondered if Northern Ireland was the answer.

On the way to Flanagan's Lough Erne home, we had stopped in Enniskillen for a pint or two at Blakes of 'The Hollow', one of Ireland's most celebrated pubs. A Victorian bar in the same family since 1887, with an exterior still of black and red painted stripes (painted originally for the illiterate – red and white stripes signified a barber's shop, red and black, a pub), inside there were nooks and snugs and old upended beer barrels. It was cosy and unthreatening and easier than ever to down a Guinness. I lit up a cigarette and felt happy, glad that it was all going well with Flanagan, whom I would be interviewing. On the wall of Blakes, opposite the bar, I was surprised to see a QPR programme, hanging as if in pride of place. 'I don't believe it,' I said to Flanagan. 'Is this a QPR pub?' This wasn't so ludicrous a question, given the Irish contingent in Hammersmith and Shepherd's Bush, but Flanagan put me straight. 'No, that'll be for the boxing.' I looked at the programme again: it was for that Barry

McGuigan 1985 title fight against Eusebio Pedroza, the contest staged in front of 25,000 fans at Loftus Road.

Leaving Blakes, Flanagan pointed out a few more of Enniskillen's landmarks. Every road in Fermanagh seemed to converge on the town, itself slotted between the Upper and Lower lakes of the Erne. There was a rather grandiose castle dating back to the fifteenth century, and, near the waterside, the forbidding gates to Enniskillen Royal School, attended by Oscar Wilde between 1864 and 1871.

'Oscar's school,' said Flanagan, as we drove past the gates.

Wilde, a Dubliner, was sent to the school by his eminent father, Sir William Wilde, whose intention was no doubt to groom his son for the military, judicial or religious establishment not merely of Ireland but the British Empire. The school had pedigree, with the majority of its pupils being boarders, sons of judges, solicitors, army officers, the gentry and its servants of God, while local boys (for this was, of course, a single-sex school) from Enniskillen's merchant class made up the rest of its intake. There was, according to John Cunningham, author of *Oscar Wilde's Enniskillen*, tension between those whose parents paid for their education, and those whose did not. 'Sometimes this manifested itself in fights between individual boys or in mass snowballing contests,' says Cunningham, having exhaustively researched memoirs and records from the time. One pupil's account of life at the school 'includes fistfights over the use of the fives ball courts and one of the Masters organising and refereeing the subsequent fight between himself and another boy in the courtyard of Portora Castle. The Master's theory was that if the boys gave each other a good hiding they would become friends afterwards.'

My schooling in Devon was at more progressive

establishments which had long since ceased to condone boxing or any other kind of fighting among pupils. I too went to relatively prestigious schools, and my father similarly intended that I would be moulded into a lawyer, or an army officer, perhaps even a diplomat with guile and élan, but at any rate a man of distinction, able to prosper by dint of my fine education and well-rounded mien. I did indeed become a lawyer, despite having first completed a literature degree and done my utmost to evade my fate. But it was futile. The Law drew me to its well-upholstered breast, and, as many sons are wont to do, I followed in the footsteps of my father, a solicitor who had served his time in the London of the Krays before moving to south-east Devon for a quieter life. (My mother tells a story about when we lived on the Chiswick High Road, a mile or two from Umar's home. She took a phone call in the middle of the night, to be met with silence. Later another phone call was made. This time a voice abused her. Then another call was made, and this time the voice said: 'Tell your husband to lay off.' This happened at the time Dad was acting for a nightclub owner who had been firebombed by the Krays for refusing to pay protection money. Who knows who was on the end of the line? And where was Dad? He, though, never seemed worried by incidents of this kind, and in my teens I recall that once, when Mum was terrified at the prospect of his impending visit to a female client whose violent husband had promised to be on the scene, he shrugged off her fears with the words: 'Don't be so silly, it'll be fine. Remember, I used to box.') Like Dad, I had worked in London as a young solicitor, in libel cases at Peter Carter-Ruck and Partners and then as Richard Desmond's in-house lawyer, before quitting for a stress-free life beyond the city walls. Unlike my father, who blossomed in Devon and has run a successful practice for the past forty years, my move to the country did not reap dividends.

On the day that I was sacked for my night of madness in Casa, my father rang, having been told the news by my mother. I was walking along Cheltenham High Street, full of shame and self-disgust. 'You're scum!' screamed Dad into the firm's mobile phone. 'You're scum and you always have been! Your mother's told me what's happened and I think it's a disgrace! I wouldn't give you a job, never! You're scum, do you understand! S-C-U-M, SCUM *SCUM SCUM*! You'll never earn any decent money again and now you're in the gutter, where you've always belonged, because you're *SCUM*!'

He would have continued but Karen grabbed the phone and cut him dead. 'How dare you speak to your son like that!' she shouted, heedless of the shoppers in the centre of Cheltenham. 'How dare you! Leave him alone!'

I can't remember how that conversation ended, but after everything I had put her through, Karen – whom I'd met to discuss the previous evening's disaster – had the humanity to stand up for me when I was exactly where Dad correctly said I was. We held each other, and for a few seconds it seemed we were lovers of old, that nothing had happened, that the previous night had been just another night, a quiet evening in watching television while the children slept upstairs. And then I remembered what Dad had said. *You're scum, you belong in the gutter. You're scum. Scum scum scum.* Soon, too, Karen remembered what I had done, what I had been doing, the duplicity and betrayal, and it was not long before she also felt that I was as my father described me.

I recalled that moment and those words as we drove past the Royal Enniskillen School, and wondered if Oscar Wilde's father ever uttered them of his son. Had he known of Oscar's homosexuality, did it infuriate him, did it make him want to call him 'scum' as my failings had driven my father so to designate me? Or had he taken comfort in his son's status as one the most fêted wits of his day? Perhaps any disappointment in Oscar's election to join 'the people on the other bus', as Umar would describe them, was ameliorated by the knowledge that at least his education had served him well.

One man who did not tolerate Oscar's homosexuality was the founder of modern pugilism, John Sholto Douglas, a British aristocrat better known as the Marquess of Queensberry. Born in 1844, by the age of twenty-three Queensberry had already codified the rules that to this day form the basis of boxing. Save, in the marquess's day, for there being no limit on the number of rounds, modern boxing contests are fought largely in accordance with the noble-minded young Queensberry's sense of fair play. Wrestling was banned, rounds were to be of no more than three minutes with a minute's rest in between, and 'the gloves were to be fair-sized boxing gloves of the best quality and new'. The overriding objective of the rules was to allow 'a fair stand-up boxing match in a twenty-four-foot ring or as near that size as practicable'.

The marquess had little doubt that an affair was underway between Wilde and his third son, Lord Alfred 'Bosie' Douglas, who was sixteen years Wilde's junior. He wrote to Bosie exhorting him to mend his ways, to no avail, and just as fruitlessly engaged in not one but two *ménages à trois* at the Café Royal, where he joined Wilde and Bosie for lunch and, on both occasions, found himself mollified by Wilde's charm. But the affair continued ('It is a marvel that those red-roseleaf lips of yours should be made no less for the madness of music and song than for the madness of kissing,' Wilde wrote to Bosie in 1893. 'Your slim gilt soul walks between passion and poetry.') and the marquess, an evil-tempered, leathery old soul, grew ever more exasperated. In 1894, some twenty-five years or so after the Queensberry Rules had been introduced, he turned up at Wilde's house with a prizefighter, promising to have someone else beat the living daylights out of Wilde rather than do it himself if the relationship continued. Wilde met this threat with characteristic ebullience, saying: 'I do not know what the Queensberry Rules are, but the Oscar Wilde rule is to shoot on sight.'

The affair went on, evidently unbeknown to Wilde's wife, Constance, but all too obviously for the marquess's tastes. Eventually, when he could stand it no more, he left a calling card at Wilde's club. 'To Oscar Wilde posing as somdomite [sic],' said the card. So alien was the homosexual act that the straight-shooting marquess could not even spell it; modern-day tart cards, with their offers of 'A' levels, are better written. Wilde, seeking to spare Bosie's blushes rather than his own, sued for libel. Given that he was, in fact, homosexual, this was an error.

The marquess's solicitors instructed Edward Carson QC to defend him against Wilde's suit for criminal libel. Carson initially blanched at the retainer, having met Wilde at Trinity College, Dublin. But he warmed to his task, as rent boy after rent boy was discovered. Carson's own brother had been seduced by a homosexual, and Carson perhaps saw the trial as an opportunity to avenge this family skeleton battering the walls of his tidy legal conscience. The transcript of the trial, published by Wilde's grandson Merlin Holland in *Irish Peacock and Scarlet Marquess*, shows that Carson pulverised

Wilde in cross-examination; that he set him up from the outset, before getting him on the ropes and hammering in blow after blow, sucker punch after sucker punch. He made Wilde feel secure enough in the witness box to indulge in his famed wit, and then, slowly but surely, chipped away at it, at first gently, with a series of apparently meaningless questions, and then ever more insistently, until finally Carson's cross-examination resembled nothing so much as brutal assault by a seasoned heavyweight on a dilettante from the slick yet insubstantial world of the strawweights. There would only ever be one result: the humiliation of Oscar Wilde and the vindication of the Marquess of Queensberry (who, during the trial, refused a chair, and stood, arms folded, muttering and staring at Wilde).

Subsequently, Wilde was himself criminally prosecuted for immoral acts, described by the presiding judge as 'the worst I have ever tried'. He was sentenced by Mr Justice Wills to two years' hard labour. As John Mortimer notes in his introduction to Holland's book, the verdict was greeted by London's prostitutes with glee. They danced and drank in the streets round the Old Bailey, 'celebrating this triumph for heterosexuality'. Wilde's life was ruined and a glittering career brought to a cataclysmic end.

It was brought to an end by his own fatal self-destructiveness, the tenacity of the marquess and the brilliance of Carson as an advocate. Wilde, in effect, suffered a KO from the combined might of the legal profession and the father of modern boxing. How did Carson feel, later, when his old friend was in Reading gaol? Was he proud of his merciless cross-examination, praised subsequently by the judge, Mr Justice Collins ('Dear Carson, I have never heard a more powerful speech nor a more searching crossXam. I congratulate you on having escaped most of the filth. Yrs ever, R. Henn Collins.')? Did he, as I have heard barristers in the Royal Courts do, delight in the discomfort of his witness, as he set him up time and again, to land at will the stinging jabs and looming overhand rights of the British advocate's armoury?

'You were like Tyson in there!' I once heard an enthusiastic young solicitor say to his barrister. 'You were savage! You hit him so hard he was gasping for air!' This, of a witness cross-examined in the dusty confines of Court 13 in the Royal Courts of Justice, during a libel trial. Throughout the Western world, newspaper headlines and journalists regularly make the same links, deploying the metaphor of boxing as often as a heavyweight lisps. In the build-up to the US presidential elections of 2004, Gerard Baker, reporting for *The Times* from Wisconsin, introduced his copy with a reference to Muhammad Ali and expressly compared presidential debates to prizefights: 'Two men at the top of their profession squaring off in a ring before a worldwide television audience for the title of the world number one. The political candidates prepare for their debate in much the same way as boxers get ready for their bout: secluding themselves for days with managers and trainers and undergoing a tight diet and fitness regimen to keep them in fighting trim when they take the stage.' The piece was headlined: 'Presidential Fighters Square Up To Deliver Knock-Out Punch'. Similarly, Andrew Buncombe in the *Independent* of 26 October 2004, again on the US elections: 'Like an old champion fighter on the comeback trail, Bill Clinton returned to the fray of the US election campaign yesterday . . .' Another *Independent* writer, Jeremy Warner, utilised the romance of the ring to describe events in litigation involving Collins Stewart in his column of 15 October 2004. 'Two down, one to go,' began Warner, before writing that 'Little over a year ago, Terry Smith, the combative chief executive of the City securities house Collins Stewart, seemed to be on the ropes if not laid out on the canvas after a series of damaging allegations by a former employee went public.' Explaining how Mr Smith had made a comeback from this apparently unhappy position, Warner wrote that nevertheless, though times were rosier, 'there is one heavyweight elephant that Mr Smith is still hunting – the *Financial Times*'. Indeed, the libel action brought by Mr Smith and Collins Stewart against the *FT* acquired a degree of notoriety, given that a special damages claim of over £250 million was sought from the newspaper. Warner perspicaciously wrote that 'Nobody believes [Smith] can win such a sum' a few days before the High Court struck out this element of the libel claim. But as Warner wrote: 'The financial penalty may not, in the end, be very large, but I wouldn't fancy being in the *FT*'s corner right now.'

The mythology of codified pugilism illumines the grey and ambivalent worlds of business, politics and law so often that sometimes it seems that boxing was invented solely to serve as a kind of visceral, no-notes-necessary decoding device. Even Claudio Ranieri, former manager of Chelsea FC, found himself ineluctably drawn to images from the noble art in an account of his last days at the club, when all manner of Machiavellian goings-on appeared to be transparent to all but the dignified Italian himself. *The Times* serialised Ranieri's Chelsea diary, *Proud Man Walking* – whose very title somehow alludes to the upright position of a battered but victorious boxer – and, inevitably given its author's own description of his meeting with the club's new chief executive, Peter Kenyon, one extract was headlined: 'Shadow-boxing with the man to decide my fate'. Ranieri wrote of his first private meeting with Kenyon at an Italian restaurant that it was, 'an opportunity for us to make one another's acquaintance and talk about the present and perhaps the future'. But in the end the meeting proved to be inconclusive, nothing but 'the most exploratory of dialogues, with one studying the other, almost. This is an appropriate description of the atmosphere, albeit an odd one, as it suggests the attitude of boxers in a ring, sizing each other up during the first round. Is this what we were doing, metaphorically?'

What Ranieri certainly was doing was invoking the ubiquitous metaphor of boxing. In this, he is far from alone. 'Heavyweight QCs go toe-to-toe', said *The Times*, in the final stages of the Hutton enquiry, while in the US, 'Lawyers spar in early rounds of Stewart trial', said the press, before Martha Stewart took the stand. Again: 'Two Government lawyers strike blows for consumers', said the *Washington Post*, while elsewhere in the most litigation-friendly country in the world lawyers were 'sparring over subpoenas in Rowland investigation'. Jeremy Warner found the imagery of pugilism congenial again on 9 November 2004, in writing about a potential conflict between two colossi of the media and business worlds, News Corporation-owner Rupert Murdoch and his one-time ally John Malone of Liberty Media. Of a possible battle between the two, arising from a rights issue if Mr Malone exercised an option to acquire additional News Corp shares (which, in turn, would lead to the dilution of his shareholding), Warner had this to say: 'If we are to be treated to a stand-up fight between two of the world's greatest media tycoons, it may be worth hanging around just for the ringside seat. As we speak, Mr Malone will be consulting his lawyers. The ensuing fight won't be pretty.'

Boxing appears to be a fertile arena for subeditors searching for pithy headlines, but especially when the headline describes a legal story. It is almost as if boxing *is* law, as it is practised in the courts of England and Wales. For The Law, like boxing, is aggressive, confrontational, adversarial; it is not the quaintly investigative 'search for truth' favoured by the French judiciary, but an exercise in testing a witness's promise to tell the truth and nothing but by putting him under the most excruciating linguistic pressure. As in boxing, an audience – the jury – watches for any sign of weakness, as skilled white-collar warriors in the mould of Edward Carson QC deftly tease errors and omissions from a witness, just as a good boxer takes it easy in the opening rounds, swapping jabs, looking for openings, slipping and feinting, before unleashing his best combinations, a jab, straight right, left hook, jab again, then right uppercut, followed by more jabs, then more of the same, again and again, until his opponent collapses under the battery, until the witness can maintain his lies no more.

'I am a confirmed believer in the contribution of adrenalin to advocacy,' says Michael Beloff QC, one of the most successful and well-known of contemporary barristers. Beloff continues: 'Those moments when the Judge is about to appear in Court, and, in the traditional deference to the Queen's justice, one rises to one's feet, remain for me moments of unrefined anxiety – akin to those experienced by the sportsman about to enter the arena.' Beloff, speaking of the way in which the craft of advocacy is under threat from a variety of quarters, is compulsively, knowingly drawn to the imagery of conflict, the language of violence, precisely because this is his world, as much as the quotidian reality of cuts and bruises is the boxer's. Of the way in which innovations in civil procedure were introduced to facilitate pretrial settlement – to produce, in effect, a shift away from 'the unconfined adversarial culture of the former civil justice system' in favour of written, rather than oral, advocacy – Beloff says: 'The aim was to still the clash of advocates' arms, to prevent indeed the forensic gladiators from even entering the arena.' To Beloff's chagrin, for the work of the *forensic gladiator* is key to justice, and thus, in the adversary system, 'traditional oral advocacy is a plant to be cherished, not pruned'.

For Beloff, and other aficionados of the adversarial system, only once a witness has been exposed to the 'clash of advocates' arms' does the truth emerge. I was subjected to this clash when I appeared in court following the occasion my jaw was broken in that Sunday football match. I mulled over the incident after Karen and I had returned home from hospital, eying in the bathroom mirror my grotesquely swollen jaw, unable to eat the steak to which she had treated us, and it occurred that it wasn't on, you couldn't have some character playing local amateur football going round breaking people's jaws for no reason other than that they had won the ball from him. So I went to the police and reported it. Three months later they rang to say that they had interviewed the alleged assailant, and, lo and behold, he had confessed.

The months trundled on and then another call came through. The case would come on for trial in Kingston Crown Court, about a year and a half from the date of the original incident. There was just one problem: identification was an issue. I would have to attend a football match in which my assailant would be playing, and formally identify him. I duly arrived at a south London park early one Sunday morning no less than a year after the original incident, and identified my assailant.

The night before the trial, I went out on the town with a new colleague. I had left Peter Carter-Ruck and Partners to join Richard Desmond in his Isle of Dogs HQ, consisting then largely of porn but also lower-shelf magazines such as *OK!* and *Chic*, all housed in a modern building with bizarre metallic emanations on its roof. My colleague, Ed, was Desmond's first in-house legal appointee. He was a strange individual, who announced, within a day or so of my arrival, that we did not need to purchase the White Book (then the bible of civil procedure, now amended and of a darker hue) for the legal department because, as he put it, 'I know it inside out'. I wondered how this was possible – even lawyers of thirty years' standing would hesitate to make such a claim. But Ed was a man of rare self-belief. I spent the first six weeks working for him trying to fathom whether he was as good a barrister as he said he was, or whether he was an inveterate chancer who'd got a break. He had no doubts, that much was clear, but on the night we went out together (a belated gesture of welcome on his part; we had been too busy to have a drink up until then) he chose to demonstrate not his skills as an advocate but instead those as a streetfighter. It had been a long night and we had been taken to a posh gentleman's club, full of men who took their white collars for granted, and then outside, in the cold February night, a drunken argument about whether rally drivers were more skilful than Formula 1 drivers (as I passionately maintained, with nothing other than inebriation as my evidence) degenerated until suddenly I was on the receiving end of a major kicking. It was a kicking that I asked for: I made the first move, wound up by six weeks of protestations of legal brilliance (which, perhaps, riled my arrogant belief that, in fact, I was the better lawyer) and four hours of heavy drinking. I made to grab his tie, with what ultimate aim I know not (perhaps I hoped to still the clash of advocates' arms?), which prompted him to snap instantaneously into a fine impersonation of the Robert De Niro bad guy in *Cape Fear*. He screamed a speech the gist of which was: 'You motherfucker! No one fucks with me, you fucking motherfucker! I'll fucking kill you!' He then kicked me in the balls and hit me in the face and eyes with a punch or two, before kicking my head as I hit the deck. It was swift and well-executed, and not, when all was said and done, within the Queensberry Rules. I fell unconscious to the floor, and when I woke up I was in an ambulance, with Ed hovering benignly over me.

'Don't worry,' he said. 'You're going to be all right.' Then he said to the ambulance officer: 'He walked into a lamppost. Never seen anything like it. Incredible. Just shows what the booze can do.'

We got to the hospital and I was examined by a doctor and nurse. Nothing was broken, I was merely concussed and my right eye had closed up. Alone in the room with me, the nurse told me she didn't believe a word of this story about walking into a lamppost. She asked me what had really happened. I closed my eyes and said I couldn't tell her. She said: 'Look, it's none of my business, but if it was me I would press charges.'

Just then Ed entered. 'Don't worry, mate,' he said. 'I've rung your wife. She was worried but I've told her it's OK, you're with me.'

Next day I woke up with the sensation of having taken a beating both physically and from the booze. It is a familiar feeling but no less aggravating for that. I thought about ringing the court and saying I was ill, but thought no, I had to appear. After all, I said to Karen, who had applied some make-up to my eye to try and disguise its condition, 'the truth would out'. With that, I made my way groggily to Kingston Crown Court.

As is the way of things an anodyne opening examination took place, with the Crown Prosecution Service barrister ably enough if rather unenthusiastically taking me through what had happened. Then the defendant's barrister stood up to cross-examine me.

'Mr Wade, no one disputes that on the day of the football match you broke your jaw.' He paused and looked at the jury, before adding: 'And we're all very sorry about that.'

The jury looked at me, in my blue pinstripe suit, with a black right eye the lids of which were closed tightly shut. They did not look especially sorry. The barrister continued.

'But I say to you that what happened that day was that the defendant accidentally elbowed you. There was no punch: to say that there was is a lie, is it not?'

I didn't like this. I felt *slightly rough* and bruised and battered and was being called a liar. Before I could say anything else, though, he moved quickly on.

'Mr Wade, you're a solicitor, are you not?'

'Yes, that's right.'

'I see. Can I ask, you appear to have a rather large mark under your eye, did someone hit you?'

'Yes, I regret to say that's true.'

'Oh dear. Who was it, a fellow solicitor?'

'I'd rather not talk about it.'

'Well, Mr Wade, you can tell us whether it was a fellow solicitor.'

'It was a barrister, actually.'

Cue mirth among the jury. The barristers grinned and even the judge smiled. 'Was it after a conference?' asked the barrister, the term used for discussions between barristers and solicitors in the midst of litigation, and again, just at the most opportune moment, continuing with his cross-examination. He repeated his suggestion that I was lying, and this time I spluttered like a pompous, outraged lawyer that I would never mislead any court, least of all this one in circumstances such as this. Quite true, but, with my black eye, it was less than convincing.

Predictably enough, despite a barrage of evidence incriminating him, the defendant was acquitted. I walked forlornly from the court, thinking that the truth had not prevailed. Or perhaps, in a way, it had.

Beloff, in positing the view that only advocacy can determine the truthfulness of a witness, queries whether the advocate is better described as 'an actor or analyst'. Inevitably, the truth lies in between, as Beloff enumerates the 'many qualities' evident in a good advocate, almost all of which could as easily be applied to a good boxer: 'Fluency is one; a sense of rhythm is another, the slow to mix with the quick, the light to soften the dark, humour to mitigate passion. A fidelity to reason, the marshalling of fact, the dissection of law; a feeling for structure, the architecture of the submissions – are yet others too.' Beyond these, the master practitioner has two further qualities. 'Sensitivity to relevance is one – the capacity to identify what is central to a case, to focus on it and in consequence to discard what is peripheral,' says Beloff, himself a passionate sports fan whose collegiate affability is fixed in time in a series of photographs in his Trinity College home, in many of which he is beaming in the company of a famous athlete, boxer or other sportsperson. The other main quality is 'adaptability to one's tribunal. Advocates seduced, it may be by the sound of their own voices, may be tempted to put the performance above the result; but in the end, like it or not, advocacy is ineffective if, however dramatic, however powerful, however erudite, it fails to persuade the decision-maker.'

Following my Casa-related demise, I wrote a long and eloquent letter pleading with the firm to suspend rather than sack me. I made no excuses for my actions but gave one or two reasons. It was no good. Conduct such as mine could not be permitted: my written plea had failed to persuade the decision-makers.

Not, though, that there was any alternative. They were hardly likely to grant me a hearing in which I could muster such verbal erudition as I possessed and present my case. Who knows, perhaps I would have arrived, sheepishly carrying a briefcase full of papers, only to lose my marbles and smash up the office. Besides, there was nothing to be gained from staying, albeit on a temporarily suspended basis. I had had it with The Law. Joining the profession had been a mistake, motivated by an obscure urge to please my father, to be the son he had wanted. The truth, as easily said as written, was that I hated being a lawyer. Not because of The Law *per se*, but rather because of *the way it is*, its habitual annihilation of integrity in favour of billable hours and client development and marketing initiatives, rules and regulations and restrictions, policy directives from on high and local community legal association circulars, so that in today's world, simply helping a client is nigh on impossible. For that reason, the only law I have ever enjoyed has been newspaper law, when as a night lawyer one sits invisibly amidst journalists, advising them of defamation or contempt of court or other risks, saying something only when necessary and otherwise leaving the journalists to get on with the creation of words that will be read and savoured by devotees of whatever newspaper it happens to be that one is lawyering. Law, then, is helpful; it is even creative. In every other instance of my life, it has been negative, the very antithesis of creativity, nothing but a profession of decorum and respect and civility and prevarication and rules and pomposity and protocol and words, always more words, but words whose life has been annihilated by an insuperable weight of emotionless legalese that has, in turn, crippled most of those who wield the words of The Law . . .

What did the Marquess of Queensberry come to think of The Law and its operatives? Ironically, his successful defence of Wilde's libel charges meant that he had to acknowledge, once and for all, his son's homosexuality. He may have felt vindicated by the trial, and doubtless shared a glass or two with Carson and his legal team, but what, when the adrenalin of the trial had subsided, did he think? Did he ever regret writing to Bosie, saying, 'You reptile, you are no son of mine and I never thought you were'? Did he ever think *Perhaps I shouldn't have been so hard on him, maybe if I'd been kinder things would have turned out differently*? And what of his love of boxing? Did he perceive in the manliness of his boxers a reminder that he was right to do as he did, to persecute Wilde in the same way that there are those who would wish to vilify the man who boxed at York Hall on the same night as my first fight, Charles 'The Pink Pounder' Jones?

Sitting on the boat rowed by Philip Flanagan across to Inishmacsaint, listening to him and Karen talking about abstract art, I realised that getting sacked hadn't turned out to be such a bad thing. I was, at last, free of the legal profession. And yet I had hurt Karen, I had hurt other people, and I had lived a disreputable life in which the more I felt the divide between my supposed identity as a lawyer and my real self, the more I behaved badly. As Karen said, during our visit to County Fermanagh: 'Scars last forever.'

I sat in the boat, borne along by Flanagan's hands, on the listless, still-grey water, as the ancient high cross came into view. No, I said to myself, Northern Ireland isn't the answer. But boxing might be. I couldn't wait to get back to Walcot.

11

A LEGAL LIFE

Dad was not happy. He shouted up to my bedroom and summoned me downstairs. I was about twelve or thirteen, and earlier on a dull seaside Sunday afternoon had been amusing myself by ringing on various neighbours' doorbells, then running off. A time-honoured and relatively harmless occupation enjoyed by many young boys, and not one that will worry me unduly come the day my sons follow in my footsteps. In fact I'll probably join them. But my father saw things differently. He was a well-known local solicitor and could ill afford to have his offspring behave in so disreputable a manner. So when a retired colonel's wife rang my parents to complain about the continual ringing of her doorbell, which each time yielded nothingness save for the last couple of occasions when, rather cleverly, instead of opening the door she posted herself in a discreet spot from which she could determine exactly who the culprit was, Dad lost no time in reading the riot act.

'What is the meaning of this?' he bellowed, and neither for the first nor the last time, I stood before him, small and petrified.

'I don't know' was all I could think of saying.

'What do you mean, you "don't know"? What does "don't know" mean?'

He was very angry, fists clenched and lips pursed. I wanted to say 'I don't know' again but thought better of it. I stood silently as he continued shouting. Finally, he concluded with the words: 'Are you intending to start your criminal career now? Are you? Well, you had better think again. Now get up to your room.'

A few years later, when I was seventeen, Dad stood up in court and made a plea in mitigation whose words I have never forgotten. His voice trembled as he made the plea, and it was clear that making it was not easy for him, not because he did not believe in what he was saying, nor because he disliked his client, still less because he had arrived slightly late and was, perhaps, a little flustered, but because, quite simply, he would rather have been anywhere else in the world than in court, that day, making that plea. Of all the plans he had for his life, my mother's life, my life, the lives of his children, my father had not envisaged having to turn up in court and put his advocacy skills to use on behalf of his eldest son.

Pete came running towards me like a bear. 'Fuck you!' he screamed, gathering up his squat and overweight rugby prop forward's body and charging forward. As he was about to smash into me, I stepped lightly to my left and he careered on past me, skidding drunkenly to a halt like a cartoon character. 'You cunt!' he shouted, and turned to charge me again. For the second time I slipped him and told him to forget it, or else. He ignored me and came flying at me for the third and final time.

It had been a long night, and for Pete, an even longer day. We were the joint best men for Steve the Swift, whose stag night was coming to its predictably messy end. Steve the Swift and Pete had met with everyone else in central London at lunchtime, and had got swiftly on with the business of getting hammered. I was living in Leicester at the time, where I was studying a law conversion course, and had managed to convince Steve that I couldn't join the party until early evening. I knew that if we all started drinking at lunchtime things would go wrong, and figured that if I deferred my own arrival the mayhem might have a chance of being contained. At least I would be marginally more sober than the other lads, who themselves knew that when drunk I was liable to cause problems, not because I deliberately sought them out but because I seemed unable to do anything other than respond to the problematic behaviour of others. As my father used to say: 'You can smell a fight ten miles away. And then you go and join it.' It was not so much the likelihood of a fight that worried me – after all, Steve and his friends were all decent and fairly well-behaved people – as the inevitability of the drunken male antics that define the British stag night. Despite my lifelong love of booze, I have never felt comfortable when drinking in a group of other men. Stupid things are always said and done. And so, I decided to arrive late, to try to keep a sober head. I told Steve I had an exam on criminal law on the Monday, which was true, and that I had to read up on a few cases for the day.

As soon as I made my entrée into a West End boozer whose name I have long since forgotten I was subjected to some abuse from Pete. 'Call yourself a best man! What time do you call this?' I apologised and moaned about the demands of The Law. Pete had little truck with this, and still less for the idea of my becoming a lawyer in the first place. I knew him from university, where we'd both met Steve, and where I'd studied literature.

'You? A lawyer? No way!' said Pete. 'You won't be able to wear your favourite jacket any more and you won't be able to ponce about all day reading books.'

I laughed it off but there was an edge to what Pete was saying, inspired not merely by the booze he had consumed all afternoon but by the simple fact that we had never liked each other. I disliked, in him, what I felt was insensitivity and a Manichean view of the world, while he seemed hostile to my book-reading tendencies and affiliation with ambiguity. I played football, he was a rugby player. The enmity we felt had never been expressed in anything other than mild mickey-taking, but that evening it exploded.

We meandered around the West End before ending up in Shoreditch. The area not only houses Alan Lacey and The Real Fight Club – now, at least – but has always been known for its dodgy pubs in whose semi-discreet rooms strippers writhe around while men watch. All good harmless fun if you can ignore the ubiquitous absurdity. We did the requisite amount of futile watching before leaving for another bar, which turned out to be a transvestite haunt. I was twenty-three at the time and had never seen a transvestite before, and found the sight of them rather arresting. I couldn't believe that men would make such an effort to look like women and couldn't take my eyes off them. One especially was attractive enough to look, even on a second glance, like a real woman, and who knows, on another night maybe I would have had a chat and we'd have kissed and my hands would have wandered and suddenly I'd have thought *Jesus Christ I'm kissing a bloke!* but as it was I looked and wondered and thought *Jesus Christ, it takes all sorts*, and then when we left that bar to go in search of yet another, I said outside: 'Bloody hell, they were amazing. I've never seen anything like that before' but this was a comment that did not go down well with Pete.

'What's your problem with them?' he snarled.

'Nothing,' I said. 'I've just never seen blokes dressed as women. I thought it was amazing, that's all.'

Pete wouldn't let it go.

'But so what? What's the fucking problem?'

'There's no problem. None at all. I just thought it was incredible. Come on, you've got to admit they looked amazing. I mean, would you go to all that effort?'

'You're fucking insulting them, that's what you're doing, you fucking twat. You're fucking out of order.'

I said that I wasn't, and that we should leave it. The group had become stretched out by now, as we walked blearily along the street, and the nearest person to us was about twenty feet ahead. I walked on from Pete and tried to catch him up.

I heard Pete swearing at me, but didn't look round. Suddenly he was level with me. 'You cunt. You're a fucking cunt,' he said, with an intense, alcohol-fuelled determination, and with that he grabbed me around the neck and pushed me against a wall. 'I'll fucking have you! I'll fucking have you, you cunt!'

We stood poised like that for a second or two, two drunken fools arguing over nothing on the streets of London, helping to blight the city. I shoved him away from me and told him to leave me alone. Then he attacked me and I smacked him with a decent right in the face. It was a good punch and he fell to the ground. I walked on to join the others. One or two had realised that something was going on and had stopped to look.

'Fuck off, Pete,' I said. 'Just fuck off.'

And then came the charges. Not once, not twice, but three attempts to nail me with a rugby tackle. Each time I told him to forget it, but then, when he wouldn't, when I saw him hurtling at me for the third time, I slipped him and tripped him as he came past. He lost his balance and stood awkwardly in the warm summer night, waiting to be hit.

Next morning I got a phone call from Pete. I had stayed at Steve the Swift's place in Walthamstow and Pete lived round the corner.

Pete sounded rough. 'You need therapy, Alex, you need help. You really need help. As for the wedding, I'm not going. I wouldn't trust myself to be anywhere near you without killing you. You can tell Steve.'

I felt bad about what had happened and apologised. 'Look, Pete, I'm sorry. But I lost my temper with you after you kept provoking me. You kept on and on and on, I told you to leave it, and when you didn't, I lost it. What was I supposed to do?'

'Alex, you beat the shit out of me. I'm sitting here with two black eyes and bruises everywhere. I can't move. You need help. Goodbye.'

I told Steve, and told him to have Pete at his wedding, not me. I'd lost it, yes, and I didn't deserve to be there. Pete was an oaf of a man, but I should have turned the other cheek. Again and again, that's what I should have done, and that's what I wish I'd done.

Steve decided we were both as bad as each other, and, come the day, neither of us was at his wedding. I don't know what Pete did, but I went to see QPR lose 4-1 at Sheffield Wednesday, and in the evening revised a few criminal law precedents. The ones about assault and GBH gave me the shivers.

It was late on a Friday night and Oscar's was heaving with its usual crowd. Small-town hooligans, soldiers from the local army base and summer tourists mingled uneasily, united by the twin aims of drinking themselves into oblivion and finding a girl. I was talented at the former but not, at the age of eighteen, much cop at the latter. Not in nightclubs, anyway. I could never think of the right words and none of the girls I fancied showed any interest in me. The solution to this impasse lay at the bar, where I would stand and try and look cool and, convinced even then of the transformatory and metamorphic potential of alcohol, down as many pints of lager as I could, while around me the testosterone flowed and my mates did their best and more often than not we all ended up back at Rich's dad's flat, drinking yet more having vandalised a few things on the way home. This was life in Exmouth, a nice enough seaside town in south-east Devon where I was working on one of the local papers. I no longer lived at home, having been kicked out by my father who objected to my arriving home drunk one night and burning my preparatory school sign on the fire. I don't think Dad knew it was the school sign – that which proclaimed the existence of one of the schools to which he had sent me at great expense – but somehow I had acquired it and used it as firewood as I settled down to watch, for the first time, Marlon Brando in *On The Waterfront*, a great film whose Budd

Shulberg script spawned the immortal line 'I coulda been a contender!'.

Dad woke up and came downstairs to find me lying next to the blazing fire. An electric fire was also on and the room must have stunk of booze. The irresponsibility of my lighting a wood fire next to an electric fire infuriated my father. 'Useless' was his nickname for me in those days, but that night he left what was always a semi-ironic appellation behind in a tirade about my worthlessness that was far from unconvincing. I responded with drunken belligerence and before we knew what we were doing we were fighting, him in his pyjamas and me fully clothed.

A few years earlier, when I was about fourteen, I had stayed up with Mum and Dad in the same room that later saw the immolation of the school sign, watching Jane Fonda in *They Shoot Horses, Don't They?*. It was a late-night Sunday film, preceded by a ritual Sunday dinner, after which I was supposed to have washed up. I didn't, but as soon as the film ended I set off to the kitchen to do my chore. Dad found me a minute or so into my scrubbing of plates and was not pleased.

'What do you think you're doing?' he said.

I looked at him with genuine surprise. I couldn't see what the problem was. 'I'm doing the washing-up,' I said.

'Get upstairs. You should have washed up hours ago and don't you dare think you can do it now.'

I stood facing Dad, amazed at his anger. I couldn't understand what difference it made when I washed up, so long as it got done.

We must have stood frozen for a minute, staring into each other's eyes. And then Dad whacked me with a left hook to the jaw. I went to bed and cried myself to sleep.

A year or two later, there was another incident. I was drunk, out of control, misbehaving somehow or other, and in the end Dad and my brother (two years younger than me and now a highly successful corporate lawyer) carried me up to bed, Dad saying 'Baby's going to bed' as I flailed around, trying to escape their clutches. Finally I did, and stood on the stairs, shouting at Dad, promising him that when I was sixteen, the next time he laid a finger on me, I'd get him back.

So there we were, three or four years later, hurling each other around the living room as the school sign smouldered in the fireplace. No one got hurt but it was hardly the kind of behaviour that could be tolerated, and next morning Dad told me to get out. I went and lived with my grandparents in Exmouth, just five minutes' walk from the local paper. At the paper the following Monday, the senior news reporter told me to ring up the headmaster of my old school. My heart sank. It turned out that the head had been on the phone, telling the paper of the disappearance of the school sign. I had to ring him up and write the story.

'Well, it's just appalling,' he said in a pristine upper-middle-class accent. 'Some thugs stole the sign and damaged the structure supporting it. It's just disgraceful. Who would do such a thing?'

I agreed that it was terrible and took my notes.

'I mean,' he continued, incredulity rising, 'the people who took it must be morons. Total and utter morons.'

They were, and one of them, perhaps the most moronic, got his just deserts outside Oscar's a couple of months later. I was there with all the lads and a French friend whose sister I had coveted ever since I had laid eyes on her. As usual in or anywhere near Oscar's, my luck was out and I wasn't too dispirited when the last song was over and it was time to head off. It was a relief to be shot of the place. As we were leaving, Laurent was hassled by a few locals. 'Nancy-boy frog!' 'Fuckin' French queer!' The words were thrown around with happy abandon, animated by envy of Laurent's good looks, but I didn't like hearing them. Laurent was a mate and hadn't done anything to anyone, and now, after an uncontroversial night, he was being picked on. Some fired-up locals were looking for a fight because Laurent was French and *different*.

I told Laurent I'd deal with it, and told the locals I'd see them outside.

Only one of them was there, standing about ten feet to the right of the entrance in a darkened part of the path below Madeira Walk. 'Come on then! Fancy it, do ya?'

I walked towards him saying 'yeah', with a cocky grin on my face and both my hands in my jeans pockets. Before I knew what had happened he had dropped me, and I didn't even get my hands out to break my fall. I got up and got a punch in, but I was drunk and, so I heard, he was pumped up with speed. He took me out effortlessly and proceeded to kick me in the head. It was only when he picked up a rock and started to hit me on the head with it that a friend's sister saw what was going on and started to scream. He legged it and the ambulance came.

The following day, I revisited Oscar's with my father. He took photographs of the pool of blood on the path as evidence for criminal proceedings that would be brought against my assailant. That morning, he had picked me up from hospital, and looked shaken to the core when he saw me. I couldn't open my right eye and had stitches in its lid. Both eyes were black and blue, as were my face and head. My left thumb was broken and my left arm was in plaster. One of my ribs was broken, plenty of others bruised. My chin had been cut open and stitches were hanging off it like fish-hooks.

Whatever I had done, this was not the fate Dad wanted for his eldest son. The evidence he assembled didn't persuade Exmouth's magistrates, who took the view that I'd been up for a fight and had got what I deserved. My assailant was bound over to keep the peace, a result that all good criminal lawyers will agree was as good as it gets. Still, Laurent's sister was beautiful, and being tended by her in the ambulance was a treat. She was about the only girl I ever spoke to following a night at Oscar's.

It was a windy day towards the end of summer. I'd gone out for lunch with Marc (in whose flat I would, years later, interview Umar), who was then my fellow lawyer at Richard Desmond's publishing company, Northern & Shell. It had been a tough few weeks and we'd cleared the decks for a session. We ate at Bank, a swish French restaurant on Kingsway, in the company of a lawyer called Paul, a fine technical exponent of his craft but not quite as keen on revelry as Marc and me.

Paul headed back to his office and Marc and I moved outside and drank a few pints. London was dusty and noisy that day. There was some building work going on nearby, men with jackhammers pounding away. Fairly far gone, we moved on to the Coal Hole on the Strand. More lagers followed, and we were met by Marc's girlfriend at the time, Lisa, a fine-looking woman. Lisa is more than capable of holding her own on the drinking front but Marc and I were well on our way and she had a fair bit of catching up to do. It was crowded in the pub so we moved outside. It was a warm evening, we managed another pint or two and then decided to call it quits. After all, we'd been drinking all afternoon and I had a third and final interview with a well-regarded 'City-type' law firm in the Cotswolds the following day.

Just as we were going Lisa noticed a tall, fair-haired man standing near the door, talking to a small, fat, white-haired man who looked like a professor. Both of them had lots of hair, a good thing in men of their age. I think the fat one was a professor and I'm pretty sure he was Welsh. Of the tall one, Lisa said: 'Isn't that Richard Harris?' Marc, aka 'The Best-Looking Man In London' (so-called by a client of mine who knew him), looked over, I looked over, we all looked over, and, sure enough, it was.

With the Dutch courage of about eight pints of Stella I walked up to Richard Harris, whose shoulders were as broad as his hair was wild, and told him that I thought *A Man Called Horse* was a great film. Richard Harris was a decent bloke and, despite the foolishness of this comment, said 'thanks'. Encouraged by this I asked him if I could buy him a drink. Maybe he looked into my eyes and felt sympathy for one so inebriated as to say stupid things about a film he'd appeared in years ago, and which I'd only seen the once, when I was about fourteen, and which subsequently I have found unwatchable, but anyway, Richard Harris said: 'No, let me buy you a drink, what would you like?' The Best-Looking Man In London and Lisa had joined me and Richard Harris bought us all drinks. He introduced us to his white-haired Welsh friend and told us he was staying at the Savoy. He was huge and had unbelievable physical presence. We talked about the Rugby World Cup. I attempted to schmooze him in a pathetic attempt to make him remember me if I got my job at the firm. What a client he would be! For one so young and full of promise . . . But he already had lawyers, plenty of them. He'd been involved in a libel action too, many years ago (libel was my field; sometimes I even called myself a libel lawyer). He said he knew Kevin Bays, an acquaintance of mine from Davenport Lyons. 'A good man,' said Harris, 'knows his law.'

We downed three or four pints with him before he announced he had to leave. I think he got a prompt from his Welsh friend, who was something of a minder. But he wasn't gone for long. About ten minutes later he came back and told us he'd enjoyed our company so much he had to have another drink with us.

If the truth be known I think he wanted to have another drink with Lisa.

The night ended and off we all went. I seem to recall that Marc and I were optimistic that we'd get invited up to his room for more drinks. We weren't.

I got home to my house in Kingston, completely off my head, at about 2.00 in the morning. Karen, bless her, went crazy. By this stage she was sick of London and increasingly fed up with what I was making of my legal life. It seemed to involve more stress than I could handle and far too many nights out at functions that, as I would maintain, I really ought to attend. Karen wanted me to get the job with the reputable Cotswolds firm, and an all-day drinking session wasn't the best preparation for an important interview.

I slept in the next morning. I don't think this was the night Karen came downstairs in the middle of the night to find the front door open and me nowhere in sight (that particular night, I am told, she went to close the front door and found me naked in the street, wandering about. I have no memory of this incident.).

Karen eventually succeeded in waking me up. About an hour behind schedule we set off for Cheltenham, the home of the firm whose ranks I aspired to join. The traffic didn't help and I was about an hour and a half late. I was interviewed by Caroline, a leading defamation lawyer, and Tim, a large bear of a man who was then the firm's managing partner. He wasn't impressed with my being so late but the road works on London Road (Cheltenham) did play their part.

Tim was one of those difficult interviewers. I think he'd have been prickly even if I'd arrived ten minutes early. I can't remember anything he said though I know he did say something. 'Why are you so late?', perhaps, or, 'Are you always this late?' I'd already had a couple of interviews with Caroline and had got on with her. We talked about this and that, the usual formulaic stuff of interviews, and I did my best to lean back in my chair so that they wouldn't smell my breath. They sat opposite me, the impressive boardroom table was my shield and my sword, at once the barrier separating them from my rancid breath and the tool upon which I banged my fist to show my mettle.

A lie – the table was a shield, no more. If I banged my fist it was when they both left the room for a few minutes (important calls from important clients have to be taken; this is the way of things).

Maybe I looked impressive, I certainly looked pale, shattered from the night before, jittery and flushed. I suffer dreadfully from hangovers, even the light ones make me feel *slightly rough* and paranoid. Still, they didn't seem to notice. I left out the details of my session with The Best-Looking Man In London, told them how great I was and how I would do this and that to enhance their status, their image, their reputation, their profitability, even more. The mad fools believed me and gave me the job.

Mind you, I believed myself. I may even have asked them if they knew who did Richard Harris's legal work.

The world was my oyster.

'The world was my oyster, but I used the wrong fork.' So quipped Oscar Wilde, but at least he was at the table and, presumably, liked oysters. Unfortunately I detest anything from the sea. Fish and sharks; crabs and lobsters; mussels, shrimps and prawns – they all make me retch. Perhaps my childhood has something to do with this. At the age of six, I was force-fed some cod by my father's mother. No matter that I was turning green with revulsion, and had to run to the bathroom to vomit, she kept making me eat the cod that she had prepared for a Sunday lunch when Mum and Dad were away. To my delight, my own children love fish, of all kinds, especially tuna, which, I am told, is very good for them.

But I hate seafood. And the world, in Cheltenham, did not prove to be my oyster. Or if it was, it was an oyster that I took a hammer to, and smashed to smithereens.

Were there any pearls among the debris? It was difficult to believe so as I scuttled back to London and got work on the newspapers as a night lawyer. During the first few jobless days I made some calls and a contact, Louise, gave me work as a night lawyer at the *Independent*. My sacking in Cheltenham coincided with some space on the rota and Louise, though she didn't know me that well, was prepared to give me a chance, given that I'd previously worked as a night lawyer for the *Daily Mirror* and the *Independent*. My tenure then had briefly overlapped with Louise's arrival as head of legal for the *Independent*, and, for a while, I had moonlighted at the newspapers for the experience and, alone of all the jobs as a lawyer I have had, the pleasure. If it had not been for Louise, I am not sure what would have happened, but as it was within a very short time of being sacked I had at least some shift work to do. I also managed to get on to the night lawyers' rota at *The Times* and the *Sun*.

I lived with a friend for a while, working during the week and returning to Cheltenham to see Karen and the children on weekends. Sometimes I would get the train, putting my bike on it and cycling everywhere I went in London to save money; other times I would borrow friends' cars. I was hopelessly confused, unable to make sense of what had happened and yet desperate to get some money coming in so that Karen and the boys would be OK. Soon enough my abject self-absorption began to pall and my friend suggested I find lodgings of my own. I took a bedsit in Wandsworth, a nice light room in a quiet road, and got a temporary job as a compliance lawyer with BT. This was fine so far as it went, which was not very far. But in March 2000, six months after I had been sacked, I got a break, with an offer of a job at City law firm Theodore Goddard, now, in this world of mergers and syngery, Addleshaw Goddard. I had been out of full-time work for about six months, and now here was an offer to join – if only for a six-month contract – a heavyweight City firm. I jumped at it and agreed with my boss, an excellent man called Paul (who was prepared to gamble that my peripatetic legal career and indeterminate marital status were not necessarily indicative of a shoddy legal brain), that I could continue to work as a night lawyer.

I would cycle in from Wandsworth, work for a day in the City, then go to the *Independent* or *The Times* two or three evenings a week. I would get drunk every other night, because I couldn't bear being on my own and there was little else to do. I had given up karate and no longer felt any aggression towards anyone or anything. I saw a psychotherapist whose manner saddened me and, for all his deliberate silences (cultivated so that I might blunder into the odd epiphany by virtue of my compulsive need to fill the void), before long we fell out over money, of which I had very little and which he, naturally enough, required for services rendered. Suzi – the woman with whom I had fallen in love in Cheltenham – was my Trojan horse, he said. I remained obsessed by her, unable to let her go despite all the evidence to suggest that severing contact was not only what she most earnestly desired but also best for all concerned. I decided that I had to be wholly honest with Karen, and so, although we were trying to rebuild our relationship, I told her that I was still in love with Suzi. I didn't want to live any lies any more and thought that being straight like this was the right thing to do.

Unsurprisingly, Karen found my new-found honesty difficult to bear. As the months drifted by she became ever more alienated from me. As I would plough my furrow of self-pity, booze and confusion in London, she got her life together and found herself being courted. I had no idea of this and was hoping that Karen and I could work things out and get back together. Just a couple of days into my new job at Theodore Goddard (a job of which I could justly be proud, said my parents, for this was a law firm of real history and pedigree; my father even remembered them from his days as a solicitor in London), I was cycling home and stopped to call Karen from a phone box. I had a new mobile phone but it was a pay-as-you-go thing and the card had run out. The line was engaged for well over an hour. I found a shop still open and bought a new card, and eventually got through to Karen late that night from my bedsit.

'You've been engaged for ages, what's going on?'

'Oh nothing, just talking to a friend.'

'That was a long call. Who'd you talk to for so long?'

'Just a friend.'

'Well, look, I wanted to say that I've been thinking about everything, and I really want us to try and make it work. I really want us to get back together. I know I've let you down terribly and I've been awful, truly awful, but we've got the boys and each other and I really want us to make it work. I love you, you're the centre of my world, and always have been. I don't know why I did what I did, but I want to change and get things right.'

'It's because you fell in love, so you told me.'

'I know, and I did, but it's over now, please can we try to work things out, surely it's worth trying?'

I went on like this at length. I'd felt more and more anxious in the days leading up to this plea, and, now that I was making it, had a terrible feeling it was falling on deaf ears. Silence was not Karen's style, but there was a lot of it in response.

'Are you still there?'

There was a pause, and then she said: 'Alex, I've met someone.'

I gasped, but thought to myself, 'Well, I can't blame her, it was only a matter of time.' Indeed, we had talked about how – if I continued to oscillate in my emotions between her and Suzi – she would inevitably meet someone else, and had even joked about the kind of man I could handle her being with if this happened. Rugby-playing macho type, not great; sensitive, non-sporty bloke, OK, because at least

I'd be able to do vital things like swim the 1500 metres faster than him.

'OK. It had to happen. Who is it?'

'I can't tell you. Alex, please understand, I just can't tell you.'

'Come on, you owe me his name, at least. I'm not going to go mental, I promise; I just want to know.'

Still she wouldn't tell me, but I persisted. 'Come on, just tell me, after everything that's happened what difference can it make?'

Then she told me it was Don Addler, the man who had sacked me, and, to break yet another promise, I did indeed go mental.

The police officers were called two days later to the Wandsworth bedsit. They were called by my parents, whom I had phoned in the middle of the night after drinking copiously and taking a few sleeping pills. Not enough to kill myself, but enough to make me slur my words and for them to be worried when I had called them and blathered on meaninglessly in the depths of the night. The officers, a man and a woman, tidied up the bedsit and the remaining pills and gave me a glass of water. They talked to me for about an hour and sobered me up as much as was possible. I told them I'd rung up Don and threatened to kill him. They rang his mobile and left him a message saying that I knew what I'd said was stupid, and that I was sorry. They made sure I was OK before leaving and told me things would work out. They were so kind that for a moment I believed them, and, with the amount of booze and pills I'd consumed, for once I fell asleep easily.

The night before, after Karen had told me she was seeing

Don, I had gone AWOL from Theodore Goddard and driven to Cheltenham in a second-hand VW Golf I'd bought a few weeks earlier. It broke down on the way and the AA towed me to Cheltenham. I told the AA man the whole story and he said he hoped Don wasn't at the house. He wasn't. I spent the day pleading with Karen. By the end, I thought I'd succeeded and returned to London. But that evening she rang me to say she had changed her mind. She wanted a chance of happiness with Don. There was nothing I could do. I got drunk, smoked about fifty cigarettes and took enough pills to indulge the fantasy of suicide.

The morning after, looking around the bedsit, I realised that it was 11.30. I had taken the previous day off, and now, barely a week into my new job, I was set to arrive half a day late. I threw up, showered, got my suit on and set off to Balham Tube station. I couldn't walk straight and had to stop myself from being sick in front of a collection of school kids. I made it to the Tube, only to feel nausea rising unstoppably. I moved away from the entrance, leant into the road, and vomited into the gutter, feeling my body cracking and heaving, my head pounding, knowing that I would be sick again before I reached the City. I went down on one knee and the sickness continued, stinking puke joining the concrete amidst the litter of London, crisp packets and cigarette ends and a crumpled lager can and chewing gum, all now with the added lustre of my nausea. Opposite was a pub, with a mottled yellow sign, its doors open. I thought: *you can go back to the bedsit, sleep, and go to the pub in the evening. You can get drunk, and do the same thing all week.* And I knew that if I didn't get on the Tube and go to work, that was what I would do. I thought of my boys, and I thought of Karen, and I said to myself that whatever happened, I had to keep going, I had to avoid being the dad who threw up in the gutter and stayed there, because that was all he was fit for. I hauled myself into work and talked to Paul, who knew that things weren't right but told me to keep my head down and do the best I could.

Getting the Tube that day took more willpower than anything else I have ever done in my life.

'My son acknowledges that he acted stupidly, that he behaved deplorably, and that his actions were wrong. They were wrong, pure and simple. But he is not a bad person. He has a lot going for him, with the prospect of a place at Oxford and his 'A' levels approaching, and I would ask for leniency. Above all, he regrets profoundly what happened, but underneath it all he is a good man with a lot of potential.'

So spoke my father in Honiton Magistrates' Court when I was seventeen. He was making a plea in mitigation after I had pleaded guilty to the theft of a £1.65 bottle of cider from an off-licence. I was drunk when it happened. Someone else smashed the window, and, it being the end of the evening and all the booze having been consumed, I put my hand through the newly naked shop front and pilfered a bottle of Strongbow. I don't even like cider and had more cause than mere distaste to regret my actions when, hours later, the police arrested me and a friend, the incriminating and half-consumed bottle of cider underneath the bus-shelter bench on which we had slept the night. Charges were pressed and there was no option but to hold my hands up.

Years later, I had to declare the existence of this criminal conviction, albeit that it was technically spent and wiped from my record, to the Law Society. They made me attend an interview at their HQ in Chancery Lane, where I sat at one end of a large oak table while three senior committee members sat at the other. They were served tea and biscuits; I sat with nothing in front of me but the expanse of the long oak table. I expressed my regret for such stupidity and told them it was the result of youthful overexuberance. They barely said a word but a few weeks later sent me a letter saying that they had decided I was fit to join the profession, to become a *Solicitor of the Supreme Court*, but that I should consider myself 'admonished'.

Perhaps if they had told me I was *unfit, not the sort of person to join The Law, not a PLU*, things might have been a little different.

12

A WELTER OF BLOWS

Simon 'Rough Justice' Dowson-Collins, otherwise known as Simon 'Two Names' Dowson-Collins, climbed through the ropes and into the ring at York Hall with the look of a man about to exact terrifying revenge on an enemy whose crimes were too horrific to describe. Sweat ran from the shaven head of the forty-year-old lawyer, whose fitness was as astounding as his eagerness to experience the thrill of his first white-collar fight. I knew Dowson-Collins from my days as a media lawyer in London, and, in the old days, there were times when we would enjoy long and liquid lunches and roam the bars of the West End into the early hours. Unlike me, Dowson-Collins had somehow survived the demands of his lifestyle and worked successively in various accomplished legal roles until landing a job as in-house lawyer for the publishers HarperCollins in the UK. It was a job we had both applied for, and though I made it on to the shortlist, I have a feeling that (all else being equal, which may, or may not, have been the case) my rather chequered CV did not inspire confidence in my reliability as a lawyer for so prestigious an organisation.

Simon had prospered, and as head of legal for HarperCollins fitted the bill perfectly for a profile for *The Lawyer* magazine. So one sunny spring day, three months into training with Umar, I turned up at HarperCollins' swish Hammersmith offices – the same to which I had trooped in the hope of landing Simon's job some two years earlier – and sat down to talk to him about his job.

'I love it, it's been a wonderful opportunity and it's a great job,' said Simon. 'There's no way I'd consider going anywhere else.'

We chatted about the role and what it entailed – contractual negotiations with authors and advising on the legal risks in a manuscript – and Simon smiled wryly when I told him I was jealous, having been in the frame for the job myself. 'I was aware that you'd applied,' he said, a subtle smile playing on his lips. The topic moved on to a common passion – QPR Football Club – and then I mentioned that I was into boxing, and had a white-collar fight coming up.

Simon's eyes lit up. There was a tangible sense of *eureka* as he got up and walked over to a filing cabinet. 'Look,' he said, opening the bottom drawer. And he held up a pair of bag mitts. 'I love boxing,' he said. 'I've been kickboxing about eighteen months. It's fantastic, brilliant for the fitness and a good way of working off the aggro. Why don't we do some sparring together?'

So a few days later we were at the Energise Centre in Hammersmith, and I introduced Simon to Umar. 'He'd like to join us for training, is that OK?' I asked. 'Good enough,' said Umar, who had moved training sessions to the Energise

Centre so that we could work out on the bags and have more room for sparring. He spent the next hour pushing us through various exercises before sparring with us. Simon looked useful, very quick with superb technique. He continued training with Umar for a few weeks and then joined an amateur club near his home in Staines. He contacted Alan Lacey and went along to a Real Fight Club session, and was matched against Phil 'The Bomb' Boyce, a City broker, on the night of my mother's birthday, 16 October 2003.

Meanwhile, Simon had come to watch my fight in June against Vince 'Dynamite' Dickson and was the first to congratulate me after I'd survived this in one piece. He agreed with Umar, Agim and Ali that I had won the fight. 'Fucking fantastic, mate!' he said, slapping me on the back in the changing room, as I collapsed on to a chair and refused to believe a word any of them were saying. 'You landed a load of shots on him! Great effort, absolutely great.'

I wished I had some of Simon's unconscious absorption in the moment on the night that I watched him fight at York Hall. Instead, though, I stood alone at one edge of the hall and couldn't get my head round the whole thing. What on earth was 'The Real Fight Club'? Who *were* these people? What were the fighters on the card – from names new to me such as Pat 'Monsta' Cleary, Richard 'Tricky Dicky' Clarke and Steve 'Old' Ford to old hands such as 'Sugar' Jimmy Rogers, Tom 'The Marauder' Lloyd-Edwards and my own adversary, Vince 'Dynamite' Dickson – getting out of it? Why were they there? Why was David 'The Thrilla' Villa-Clarke – who, as The Real Fight Club proudly proclaimed, 'made history' in being its first black fighter – making his debut as a boxer that night? And what was anyone getting out of watching these men hit each other?

In Villa-Clarke's case, it turned out that he was fighting for charity. His church, unnamed on the fight card, was raising funds to equip a newly built hospital in Labolabo, Ghana. His bout would be preceded by a charity raffle draw. Similarly, Lacey's 'Girls On Top' night had raised funds for The Daisy Fund, set up to help to pay for the hospital treatment of Daisy Lloyd, a four-year-old born with a rare form of cancer of the eye. Charity is a recurring drive in many white-collar events. Hard-man Danny Mardell has raised funds in each of his fights, for his own charity, which he created after his son, Danny, was born with Down's syndrome. 'I rejected him when he was born,' Mardell told me. 'I'm ashamed to say it, but that's the truth.' For all that he had achieved in his life – the Bentley, the business empire, the mansion in Chingford, Essex – Mardell could not accept that his first son was less than perfect. But after nine difficult months, the turning point came.

'I realised that Dan needed me,' says Mardell. 'He's a wonderful boy who never ceases to light up the room. I fell in love with him, and wanted to do something to help him and other Down's syndrome children.' He attended a white-collar boxing event and resolved to win a British title. He was almost twenty-stone. He called the project 'Danny's Challenge', and set about raising as much sponsorship money as he could for Mencap. With the help of Nigel Benn, he met his challenge successfully. Mardell, down to fifteen-stone, beat Alex Leitch, and won his title. He also raised over £100,000 for Danny's Challenge. Many would have called time on the boxing, but Mardell keeps climbing back into the ring. He told me that he was putting together a 'Spank the Yank' bout in New York in which he and other white-collar boxers would fight the finest of their peers across the Atlantic.

As I sipped a lager-shandy, determined not to get drunk and to be able to drive home rather than have to stay in London, charity seemed as far away as the pugilists of Gleason's Gym, NY. I felt out of place among the crowd at the bar, fight fans all, a quixotic blend of East End hard-men who had wandered off the streets of Bethnal Green and City types – male and female – there to watch their colleagues do battle, all lapsing into a patois of inanity that was surely not the way in which they normally spoke. Alan Lacey looked as harassed as ever, and I told myself that it would be better to leave him to get on with his work for the evening, but the reality was that something had turned inside, something meant that I couldn't talk to him because to do so would have been profoundly false, for on that night I looked at the aggression of the crowd and heard their deranged imprecations and witnessed a string of inelegant boxers and it seemed to me that boxing whether of this level or any other was just about the most stupid pursuit on earth.

And then on came Rajiv 'Batta Bing' Bhattacharya, introduced as the holder of the British welterweight white-collar title, to take on James 'Golden Boy' Bolton, a property developer. The speed and power of Bolton's punches was breathtaking. He blasted into Batta Bing mercilessly for the first two rounds, with shots so hard that people in the crowd were wincing. He was fit, strong and athletic, and Batta Bing could do nothing but cover up and absorb his blows. Until the third round, that is, when he came back at Bolton so well that I wondered whether taking all those punches at the beginning was actually part of a *strategy*, something not always evident at white-collar level. The southpaw Batta Bing found his range and started landing some shattering punches of his own, but he couldn't resist showing the crowd how pleased he was with himself by dropping his hands as if to say 'come on then' and even swinging a bolo move as well. The crowd did not like this display of arrogance and loud boos were interspersed with cries of 'kill the cunt!' from those who were particularly fond of humility. Batta Bing didn't care. As ever, the fight ended without an official victor, and, just as predictably, everyone had their own idea of who had really won.

'The boy Bolton won it,' said a couple of lads next to me when I asked them who they had ahead. 'No doubt about it. He was a right hard bastard.'

'Nah,' said an older man in rich East End tones, out for a night of boxing on his own. 'That was one of the best displays of defensive boxing I've ever seen. The Asian lad was the winner.'

Things were a little clearer, if less distinguished, in Dowson-Collins' fight against Phil 'The Bomb' Boyce. The Bomb bombed. Maybe he was psyched out by Dowson-Collins' prefight evil eye. He had apparently been boxing for six months, fewer than the eighteen months or so that Dowson-Collins could claim through kickboxing and, latterly, boxing, but he looked ill at ease from the moment he climbed through the ropes. Who knows what got to him, but one thing was for sure: it was not Dowson-Collins' ability as a boxer that won him the fight (for again, albeit unofficially, there was no question that there was a winner). Dowson-Collins did not take a backward step, but chose to throw almost every punch with his head so low (as if to avoid counterpunches) that it was almost at waist level. Haymakers flew from both hands, some landed, some whirled harmlessly around The Bomb's headgear, few were thrown with anything that could be called control and still less were from an art that was noble or a science that was sweet. Dowson-Collins was relentless – relentlessly inelegant, relentlessly aggressive and relentlessly less impressive than he was when we had sparred with Umar. Then, he had had poise and fluency; now, he was like a dervish, unleashed and unaware of the futility of his actions. The blows rained in on (and as often around) Phil Boyce, who gamely soldiered on with just the occasional look of terror despite no doubt wondering what the hell he had got himself into.

'It was The Bomb's first fight but he acquitted himself well, staying on his feet under a welter of blows, landing several punches and always going back for more.' So said Patrick Sawer in the next day's *Evening Standard*, before wrapping up his piece with a quote from Charles 'The Pink Pounder' Jones, who that night fought Steve 'Fountain' Penn: 'That was bloody hard work. All the sparring and the training can't prepare you for that. It was the closest I've got to a near death experience.' (These words were rather more famously uttered by Muhammad Ali after the astonishing 'Thrilla in Manila' fight against Joe Frazier in 1975.) Jones went on to say that when you're in the ring, 'it's just you, on your own. Nobody is going to help you.'

I drove home after congratulating Simon and politely declining his invitation for post-fight beers. I wondered whether he would have another fight, and put my money on 'no'. As for me, for all that I was less than enthused by some of the crowd and more perplexed than ever by boxing – not least, in its white collar guise – I drove home along the empty M40, away from London and into the heart of the sleepy Cotswolds, and recalled the intensity of the fight between

Batta Bing and James Bolton and the sheer madness of that
between Dowson-Collins and Phil Boyce, and I felt bizarrely
inspired.

Just as in Fermanagh, I couldn't wait to get back to the
gym.

When I'm training, whacking the bags or pads or sparring,
I very rarely work myself up and imagine wreaking
violence. Instead, I am absorbed in the moment, in the
physicality of what I am doing. In my Wandsworth bedsit,
in the days when I got used to the fact that the man who
had sacked me was now seeing my wife, sitting on the sofa
which she and I had bought, while my children slept
upstairs, charming her in our charming Cheltenham cottage
with his normalcy, money and sensitive side, I felt like
wreaking a lot of violence, and all of it on him. These urges
were intensified by his total refusal to engage with me, on
any level. I sent a couple of emails, imploring him not to get
involved; I may have left another message, subsequent to
the one in which I threatened to kill him. My
communications after that on the night of my drunken
stupor were polite but pointless, for Don Addler had not
climbed to the top of the legal tree without learning a trick
or two. He knew that to do nothing – to *prefer not to*, as
Melville's Bartleby has it – was, in these no doubt unique
circumstances, to win, to take the sting out of my anger and
leave me to fulminate into the void.

Only once did I hear of any comment that he had made.
Karen conveyed to me that he had told her I could do what
I liked, but he was not scared of me. This I doubt. I think
Don Addler would have jumped out of his skin if he had seen
me. He would have had every reason to, for the truth is that

though I know I deserved everything I got, that he and Caroline and their cohorts had little choice but to sack me, I loathed the man for courting my wife once he had rendered me unemployed, for his ability to impress her with his endless money when I had none, and my emotional volatility on this subject was such that if I had seen him I would have been unable to guarantee that I would not have smashed the hardest straight right of my life into his bland and inoffensive face. This, Don Addler knew, and unless he was all along made of a very different stock to that which I encountered, he is not the fighting kind and would not have relished such a confrontation.

And why should he? There is no reason. It is better to prefer not to. Nor was there any reason for me to feel any anger towards him (and yet I did, I did). What could I expect, after a lifetime of lunacy and philandering the principal surprise of which was that I had lasted as long in The Law as I had? Could I expect Don Addler to abide by some quaint code of honour that says *you don't kick a man when he's down*, so that when I was down, in the gutter in Wandsworth, albeit because of a disaster of my own making, he should have stepped back and said, 'Hmm, this is a tricky one, I'm attracted to his wife and she's attracted to me, and the bastard brought his fate upon himself, but when all is said and done I'd better leave well alone'? No, I had no entitlement to that kind of thinking, I had forfeited my place at the table, and codes, quaint or otherwise, did not apply to me. I was simply a wrecking machine, that was it, that was all I'd ever been, carnage and destruction were my *métier* and I was so good in my chosen field that I'd even managed to destroy the veneer that had allowed access to the doors of The Law, that which had enabled people to make the same mistake as Marlow in

Lord Jim, seeing the renegade Jim for the first time: 'I liked his appearance; he came from the right place; he was one of us.'

One of us. The right place.

Phil 'The Judge' Maier didn't sound too tough. He had a slightly high voice allied to an equable manner and, to boot, was just a little too good looking for a boxer. But he was a veteran of more than fifty white-collar fights in his home town of New York, including one against the luminary of British white-collar boxing, Alex Mehta.

'He hit like a truck,' said Mehta, who had fought Maier to win the world white-collar light-middleweight title.

Maier, a former Marine, qualified as an attorney in 1981 and became a New York administrative law judge in 1993. US administrative law is analogous to UK employment law, and so Maier fields disputes between employer and employee, arbitrating on conflicts that he sees as similar to those in boxing, albeit that 'in boxing I am one of the combatants, while as a judge I am neutral'. He took up boxing in 1997, as much as anything to work off the frustrations of a marriage that was ending in divorce, and was hooked: 'It is just a great way of releasing tension in people's work and personal lives,' said the judge, one of whose fights was against a performance artist who filmed their fight by means of a camera strapped to his head. 'He kept telling me to hit him hard,' said Maier, 'but I wouldn't. White-collar boxing is about fun, not hurting people.'

There it was, the familiar, soothing mantra of the white-collar boxer: his – or her – pursuit is *fun*, it is *not* about hurting people.

In October 2003, around the time that I watched Simon

Dowson-Collins at York Hall, preparations were well underway for a Real Fight Club event that would give me a chance of finding out just how much fun fighting Phil 'The Judge' Maier would be. Alan Lacey had come up with the idea of a lawyers-only evening of boxing, to be held at the Marriott Hotel, Grosvenor Square, in late November. Lacey always comes up with names for his shows, and this one was to be called 'A Legal Minefield'. The press release pulled no punches:

'The first annual lawyer white-collar boxing fundraising gala – lawyers, barristers, judges (& defendants) in the ring – starring white-collar warriors learning the noble art who work in the legal profession for leading institutions such as: the State of NY, Davis Polk & Wardell, Allen & Overy, Skadden Arps Slate Meagher & Flom, SJ Berwin, Linklaters, CMS Cameron McKenna, Richards Butler, Goldman Sachs, JP Morgan, Chase Bank, Cleary Gottlieb Steen & Hamilton, Judicium & many more in 3 x 2-minute non-decision bouts regulated by the IWCBA.'

Heavyweights all, and then a line from The Clash: 'I fought the law, and the law won.'

It was an event that I couldn't miss. It would give me focus and ensure that I kept going down to Walcot and got back in touch with Umar again. Not least, because a few weeks earlier I had had to abandon a planned fight against The Pink Pounder; young Basher at Walcot had damaged the muscle around the sternum and I had also cracked a rib, necessitating another trip to Cirencester Hospital, where I was told I couldn't fight for a while. Lacey had matched me against Charles Jones but didn't like taking risks with his fighters, and so as soon as I told him of this latest injury, the match was cancelled. Frustrated by this and compelled by the legal theme, I unhesitatingly signed up to fight on the 'Legal Minefield' card – to lots of 'Go on sons!' from Lacey and as many requests that I try and pull in the punters from among my learned brethren, past and present.

Lacey considered matching me against Simon Dowson-Collins, but as time went by changed his mind and decided that a bout between myself and Phil Maier would be on the card. One night, as I drove home from a shift at one of the papers, I rang up Alex Mehta to ask whether he agreed with this choice of opponent.

'Phil's good, but from what I've heard, you're not bad,' he answered. Then he giggled a bit. 'Raw and, er, untutored, but Alan says you've got a lot of promise. I think you'll be all right.'

As soon as the idea of the fight was mooted, I started going back to Walcot in earnest. Harry Scott and Dave Veysey were not convinced that fighting a man who had had more than fifty contests was a good idea. 'It's too much,' said Harry. 'You'll get yourself hurt.' Dave nodded. 'Does sound a bit heavy,' he said, in his laconic way. I smiled and thought: but he's a *white-collar* boxer, he's not in the same league as you two or the lads down here. The fights he's had have, by and large, been within the confines of Gleason's Gym in New York, before audiences nowhere near as large as that which saw me fight at York Hall, and aren't I, by continuing to train here, learning the craft in a way that will see me through an encounter with him?

'Forget it,' said Harry. 'Take your time and get in shape before you have another fight.' Again, Dave – who had had thirteen amateur fights, in the last of which he'd stopped Leigh Allis, who went on to turn pro – agreed. 'Harry's right. There's no rush, is there? For all you know he could be like

Harold,' he said. Harold was also a veteran of more than fifty fights. 'You wouldn't want to get in the ring and box him in a real fight, would you?' asked Dave.

No chance, but I was still too new to boxing, which, with a lack of awareness of the calibre of many white-collar boxers, meant that I was not capable of making a properly informed judgement. Added to which, my fitness was good. I'd done a triathlon in September, entailing a 1000-metre sea swim in six-foot surf. I'd completed the daunting circuit in Perranporth, Cornwall, and felt great. I was sure I'd be OK. And then, one evening, I got smacked in the chest by young Danny Bharj.

Danny is a cocky lad, but, along with Jamie Cox, is the outstanding natural talent at Walcot. Who knows what he could achieve if he concentrated and took his boxing seriously? This is not to say that he does not box well. Rather, Danny has reached a level, in his mid-teens, with which he is comfortable, at which he can box well, with ease, but does not seem to want to push himself up another notch. He was a National Schools' finalist in 2002, and a Western Counties Schoolboys champion in 2003. He is devastatingly quick, a smooth, skilful boxer who has a lot more power than one would at first imagine. In Umar-speak, *he can bang as well as move.*

Sparring against him one Wednesday I felt the full force of one of his punches. He was toying with me for about two rounds as I landed the occasional jab or right on his head. Dave Holyday was telling him off, enumerating the points he was giving away. 'There's another!' he would shout, when one of my rare attacks produced a result. Danny decided he'd had enough of this and hit me with a combination so fast that I didn't even see it. I could barely breathe for the third and last round.

Harry Scott saw all this and shook his head. 'Don't take that fight,' he said. 'Don't do it.'

Dave Veysey grumbled his agreement. 'You're standing square on,' he said. 'Boxing's a sideways sport. You want to have a think about that fight.'

But the night after Simon Dowson-Collins' fight, I made my way back to Walcot. 'You still having that fight?' asked Harry. 'I think I am,' I said. He shook his head, and told me to see Dave Veysey about training. I spent the evening sparring with Dave and Amy. The chest held up as Dave took it easy and I became Amy's *de facto* punchbag. It was astonishing to see how much she had improved. Her technique was virtually flawless. All I could do was cover up and let her hit me. I hadn't the wherewithal to give her a better workout – to slip and move and throw the occasional gentle jabs and rights, as Dave did – but I think she enjoyed herself.

I kept coming back for more over the next few weeks. Some of the sessions were dreadful, others were good. I started to look forward to fighting The Judge. I boxed through a heavy cold, and was still up for it when Lacey rang me one day as I picked the children up from school.

'I've had to pull the show,' he said.

'What?'

'Yeah, not enough interest from the members of your profession. Bloody lawyers!'

'Bloody hell, Alan, I was all set!'

'I know, son, but there you go. I just can't take the risk.'

So that was it – 'A Legal Minefield' had bitten the dust. Lacey had struggled to find enough lawyers to do battle in the ring, and the idea of the event hadn't proved as much of a winner as he'd hoped. He would be putting together another dinner show in three weeks, on 10 December 2003, to take care of those law firms that had bought tickets, but this time its remit would be expanded to embrace the City and, indeed, Wall Street. Would Phil Maier be coming over to fight in this one? Did it fit in with his schedule? Could I still fight him?

A few days later Lacey dropped me a line. 'As far as I know, Phil is unable to make 10 December.'

It was December, the festive season, and the invitations were stacking up. I breathed a sigh of relief. I could go out and have a few drinks and not worry about jeopardising my fitness, let alone being on the receiving end of a welter of blows from a judge who hit like a truck.

PART THREE

PART THREE

13

ON THE CANVAS (2)

Beano had me in one corner and was landing punches at will. He was too big, too strong – and, at twenty-four, too young – and there was nothing I could do. It wasn't like being Amy's punchbag – every one of Beano's shots hurt. I don't know what I'd done to upset him, but he was showing me no mercy. Again and again the blows crushed me; lefts and rights, hooks and straight punches, and then he started using uppercuts, sweeping up my chest and pummelling my chin, which I found impossible to protect at the same time as my head and body. It was horrible, I started to feel sick and I wanted to get out of there, to be anywhere but in the ring at the back of the old warehouse used by Walcot, taking a pounding from a heavyweight at least two stone heavier than me and three or four inches taller, a man whose sometime job as a doorman meant that violence was, if not his trade, something with which he had more than a passing familiarity.

I'd started brightly, tearing into Beano as best I could, but within about thirty seconds he had manoeuvred me into my own corner, where I'd stayed, trapped, for the next excruciating minute and a half. The bell sounded and round one was over. In between rounds I desperately tried to catch my breath. It was Sunday 20 December and the festive season had taken its toll. What fitness I'd reacquired in training to fight Phil Maier had soon evaporated in the obligatory December nights out. It was agony, and I yearned for Harold or Dave or Harry or whoever was taking training – I felt so exhausted, I no longer knew – to say 'OK, that'll do you, Alex', and haul me out of the ring. But no one said a word, and the bell rang for round two.

After about fifteen seconds, Beano dropped me with a straight right to the chin. I sank to my knees and looked again at the frayed carpet that stood in for canvas at Walcot ABC. There was a hush in the gym as the young lads wondered if I was all right. It was the same hush that I'd felt at the Mermaid when I had watched Paul 'Mad Manx' Beckett floored by a man he should never have been fighting.

I didn't fall flat on the floor, as I did when Harold Scott dropped me, back in the beginning. I fell directly on to my knees, and at once went to stand up, pushing out my right leg and trying to plant its foot on the carpet. It was useless. As I shifted my weight on to my foot I knew that I would fall over if I made another move. So instead I shook my head. 'It's no good,' I said. 'That's it.' I let a few more seconds go by and got to my feet. My head was spinning, as if from too much cheap white wine. I climbed out through the ropes. En route I was met by a concerned and frowning Beano.

'Are you OK? Mate, seriously, are you all right?'

'Yeah, no worries,' I said, with a smile.

I didn't feel fine, I felt groggier than ever. Beano climbed out of the ring and I heard him talking to Harold Scott as I took my gloves off.

'The thing is,' said Harold, 'you didn't hit him that hard.'

I didn't hear Beano's reply, but I did think: Jesus, how hard is hard for you guys? Minutes later, time was called on sparring. We went outside for sprint training. Harold split us into two teams, and we did shuttle sprints along the side of the County Ground. My head cleared, and I drove home thinking that that was one hell of a workout, a decent counter to the booze that I'd poured down my neck in recent weeks. I was back two days later, just before Christmas, but my neck was giving me grief – it had been sore from the battering dished out by Beano – so I didn't spar, just worked on the bags. At the end of the session I gave Harry Scott a bottle of whisky, thanking him for his help in getting me in shape for the fight against Vince Dickson earlier in the year.

'Alex, you're a gentleman,' he said.

It was good of Harry to say so, but I couldn't agree with him. Things were slipping, yet again. I was drinking too much, and would spend the next few weeks feeling *slightly rough* on a near-constant basis. Worse, my neck pain became so bad that I couldn't stand up straight. The nerves were twisted, 'consistent with severe trauma', said the doctor. So I couldn't box, as the New Year rolled round, and if I couldn't box, I reasoned, I may as well drink. Who knows, maybe a massive session would somehow cure my neck, unravel all the bewildered nerves? I drank more and more, in the pub, at home, at dinner parties, all the time smoking, losing my sense of self, obliterating everything as I always have done. Then one night, as I left a friend's house, where I'd been for dinner, I tripped over a concrete block in the driveway. I was so drunk that I had not seen what to everyone else was obvious, and I was so drunk that I did not react by putting my hands out to break my fall. Instead, I landed full on my chin. Blood cascaded down my neck, ruining yet another shirt, as I stumbled down the hill, to the home that I had re-established with Karen. It was everywhere. I added another scar to the one acquired in the Oscar's fight, and also broke a tooth. The dentist took it out a couple of weeks later when I finally got round to going to see him.

'Those Walcot boxers, they can move.'

The twentysomething lad behind me was admiring the footwork of Danny Bharj in a fight hosted by Walcot ABC at the Crosslink Centre, in Stratton, Swindon, on 12 December 2003. On what was billed as 'A Night of Top Quality Boxing', Walcot's boxers were taking on fighters from a variety of other clubs in an amateur home show. Amy was due to fight at the end of the evening, as was Beano. I attended the event with a motley crew from my village, including Joe, the former prizefighter in his sixties, and Robin, one of the veterans from CHQ football club. Also with us was Beano's namesake, Mark Reynolds, a man who, if anyone did, deserved the Rotella tag of being *good with his hands*. A stocky man in his late-thirties, Mark lived in my village, looked like Popeye and was twice as strong. He had powerful, gnarled hands and was a master craftsman, able to create anything from wood and stone. There was little doubt that he had had a few scraps in his time, but he had long since grown out of them and, like everyone in the village save for Joe, couldn't understand why I was involved in boxing. Nevertheless, Mark enjoyed the show. We sat on a row of seats at the back of the Crosslink Centre, supping our pints of lager and, in my case, covertly smoking. The young Walcot boxers – from southpaw, twelve-year-old Luke Osman to young teenagers Michael Liston and Richard Spruce, to Jake Sheppard and one of my sparring partners, Jaggdave Singh – put on a display of class that saw the club win seven of its ten bouts. Ben Fitch, the other fighter I'd sparred with in the lead-up to my fight, was unlucky to lose to Bristol boxer Jake Whitehead, taking four punches in the second round that forced a standing count and eventually losing on points. The other two Walcot fighters to lose – Luke's older brother Josh and young Breon McPherson – were both unlucky, and the biased home crowd loved every minute of it, no more so than when Danny Bharj, using every ounce of his talent and switch-hitting prowess, appeared to have clattered Droitwich opponent Adam Mytton into retirement. Mytton quit, sure enough, at the end of the second, though it was a sprained ankle that did for him.

'Those Walcot boxers, I tell you, they can move!'

Again, the voice behind me could be heard above the din, as its owner demonstrated his knowledge of boxing and, moreover, Walcot's boxers.

'They're slick, man, I tell ya! That's the way that Harry teaches 'em. Class. A real solid club. You watch. I bet that girl'll be just as good.'

The girl in question was Amy Wharton, making her debut against Jackie Masters of Droitwich, in what would be the first all-female boxing match to be staged in Wiltshire. I was looking forward to this, and so were the rest of the crew. But we didn't get to see Amy. Instead a collective demon possessed us and we made our way back to the Cotswolds for last orders, where we drank in our local for another couple of hours.

Beano's opponent didn't turn up but Amy won her fight. By all accounts, she was awesome.

'Alex, you have to make a decision.'

The man saying this to me was a top executive at a prestigious multinational. I wanted to like him, and I think he may have wanted to like me, but in the end we didn't see eye to eye.

He was standing over my desk, in his uniform of cuff-linked black silk shirt, grey slacks and black shoes, a smart look curiously offset by his mane of shaggy black hair and habitual designer stubble. We were arguing over some untoward conduct, specifically the sending to a shareholder of a document which purported to contain my signature. I had neither sent it nor signed it, and nor had the man in the black shirt, but someone had, and I had a good idea who. To make matters worse, I was a company secretary of a subsidiary of the multinational, a role of theoretical if not arduous corporate responsibility, and it was as a blend of company secretary and lawyer that my signature had, not to put too fine a word on it, been forged.

The background to the incident arose from an increasingly acrimonious shareholder dispute. Eventually, one side sought to gain an advantage by drafting what appeared to be minutes of a directors' meeting, in which it was decreed that various things would happen, to the conceivable disadvantage of the other shareholder. My signature, as company secretary, was required on the minutes, but I was away from the office. In my absence it was appended by someone with a hitherto unheralded talent for counterfeiting. Whoever decided to sign the document in my name no doubt thought it was the right thing to do, for themselves and their side of the dispute.

Perhaps it was. But they did not stop to consider what I would have to say, just as the man who floored me and broke my jaw on an anonymous south London football pitch didn't think whether what he was doing was right or wrong. He simply acted, and, it seems to me, those in the corporate and legal worlds, where action is apparently intellectual rather than instinctual, are not always above such a charge. At the very least, the appearance of a signature that was not mine compromised my sense of personal integrity; it could even have led to legal problems. I did not want to cause trouble, but felt that I couldn't let this pass. I took my disquiet beyond the legal department to the senior executive, whose unkempt hair suggested affability but who was aloof and elusive to a fault. For good measure, I pointed out that the overall conduct – aggressive, sharp, Machiavellian – of the shareholder employing us was giving me sleepless nights, but talking to the silk-shirted exec was like shooting a ghost.

He fiddled with his cufflinks and pondered my woes, before announcing that a decision had to be made. It was: 'You have to decide what kind of lawyer you're going to be. Are you going to be the sort of lawyer who helps a company like ours?'

It wasn't a hard decision to make. I had clambered back on to the legal treadmill following my demise in the Cotswolds, first with a temporary job with Theodore Goddard before moving to the then lauded but now defunct, because ultimately insolvent, German multinational in the sports rights world. On paper, it was a good move. The company's head office was in Germany and its core business the licensing of 'must-have' sports TV rights. On the back of the dotcom boom it had diversified and set up subsidiaries to exploit other possible revenue streams in betting and third-generation mobile phone technology. The offer of a job came less than a year after I had been sacked and with a pay packet that meant I could turn round to my father and say: *Remember what you said about never earning any decent money again? Well, I now earn more than I ever did, in Cheltenham or anywhere else.*

But money, and, still less, The Law, does not necessarily make for happiness. Not for me, anyway. I was more miserable for the eighteen months that I worked for the corporate giant than I had ever been.

The company inhabited the top two floors of Centre Point Tower, a dinosaur of a building as high as anywhere else in central London. The views were wonderful and I could look down on law firms I had worked for or across to the Northern & Shell Tower on the Isle of Dogs and scan the horizon to the west safe in the knowledge that Cheltenham was invisible even with a telescope. There were many in the company who travelled the world, business or even first class, and tickets to sporting events were plentiful. I made it to New York and Los Angeles, and, less dramatically, Brussels, Gibraltar and Munich. We wore shirts and slacks, there wasn't a tie to be seen. It should all have been so glamorous, a heady combination of laid-back cool and cutting-edge legal work.

But the job was soul-destroying. Day after stultifying day would pass, as I and almost everyone else spun helplessly in a vast Teutonic machine, as useless as cigarettes on a seabed and yet still seeking our synergies and honing our mission statements. Everyone was accountable, no one could do anything without innumerable apparatchiks dispensing their approving nods or, more usually, commenting, analysing, interjecting, scuppering, thwarting and annulling because their role was to comment, analyse and interject and they were never happier than when they had done so with the result that something innocuous like *a good idea* or *a sensible solution* had been scuppered, thwarted and annulled.

A friend of mine, who works in business, has a saying. When he is on the brink of concluding a deal, he says: 'Let's get the deal-breakers in.' In come the phalanx of lawyers, with their indemnities, warranties and entire agreement clauses, their intellectual property carve-outs and property law caveats, their terms of art and artful drafting, deliberate ambiguity if such is required, never one page when sixty-seven will do, lest an event of *force majeure* occur, God forbid but even so, a lawyer could spend a lot of time and rack up a lot of bills working out whether the event in question – Act of God, flood, fire, riot, labour dispute – was really, when all was said and done and it never is, a *force majeure* event but let's not get carried away, the lawyers have an indispensable role to play, they have to tie up the deals struck by the likes of my friend so that *just in case* anything goes wrong – and we hope, most sincerely, that it won't – everyone knows who to sue, who to blame, who to accuse of negligence or some other heinous crime because unless we knew that, where would we be?

A few weeks after I was asked what kind of lawyer I wanted to be, I left the corporate giant. My departure was a 'mutual termination' of my contract. The multinational was as pleased to see me go as I was relieved to be gone. I knew that my days in The Law – at least, on a full-time, employed and conventional basis – were at an end. There are other people who have the wherewithal for the legal profession, for its normalcy and rigour, its politics and its compromises. Many are decent and upstanding and everything that lawyers should be; some are charlatans, still others have no ability and some are even as intelligent as they claim to be. But most, somehow, fit in. The man in the black shirt had found his niche; he fitted in and in doing so – in coping with the pressure of his role and – who knows? – his own compromises – had little time for what must have seemed the petty laments of someone who, if the truth be known, had failed to correct his tendency to hungover lateness and consequential inattention to detail. I was *slightly rough* far too much in my eighteen months in his company's legal department, unacceptably so. For all that I loathed the job – the commute alone, at three hours, was enough to dismay even the most committed of employees, and then once in the office the interminable politics were insufferable – it was my choice to take it, and it was my choice to leave if I didn't like it. Instead, I would leave work and go drinking, staying over in London rather than trying to get the eternally delayed or cancelled train to the Cotswolds. Because one drink is never enough when ten are available I would get drunk and stagger in the next day at a time that would, no doubt, have appeared to be whenever it suited me but was, in reality, the best that my reeling, booze-addled body could manage. The senior executive saw all this, and so, when my signature was forged, and when I objected to this, he heaved his own ephemeral sigh of relief. Here, as he put it, was the possibility of an 'agreed exit'. Hence, the decision that he asked me to make: not to agree, as a matter of principle, that I supported the forging of signatures (which he expressly condemned), but *whether or not I was the sort of lawyer to help a company like ours.*

In short, was I the sort of lawyer who would fit in? Who would help the executives do their jobs? Who would stop raging against the machine?

But at last, after years of trying to fit in, and after hauling myself *back in* when I'd got myself thrown out, I knew that I couldn't maintain the pretence any longer. I felt like a fraud. I knew the answer to the question, but I had no idea what I would do next. If I was still a lawyer, I was in exile. In exile from The Law.

14

A HEATED EXCHANGE

'Well, I'll be damned!'

Alan Lacey wasn't expecting to see me. I had driven over to Oxford to watch the Varsity boxing match in early March 2004. Before the fights, held in the Oxford Town Hall (and reputedly the scene of rioting by fans two years earlier), I went to the bar with Mark Reynolds, aka Popeye, to get a swift lager or two. Lacey was there, with a rather beautiful brunette whose company was sponsoring the seventy-ninth battle between Oxford and Cambridge.

'What are you doing here?' asked Lacey. 'Working? Or are you an ex-Oxford man?'

'Neither,' I replied. 'Just here to watch the fights.'

If Mark had rarely looked so much like Popeye, Lacey looked more than ever the quintessential boxing promoter. Perhaps it was the surroundings. Young men from Cambridge strutted in smart slacks and light turquoise blazers and there wasn't a mashed-up face in sight. The women ranged from pretty to gorgeous and there was barely anyone who hadn't made some effort to dress for the occasion. The prefight atmosphere, at the bar and in the hall, was good natured, even rather decorous. In all this, Lacey – with his slicked-back grey hair, goatee, long dark coat and East End patter – was from another world, one of quick deals and ready cash, oodles of charm and plenty of risk. He introduced me to Suki, the brunette accompanying him in her guise as sponsor, and a large, tough-looking character who was either deliberately a skinhead or bald.

'Alex is a white-collar boxer,' said Lacey.

Embarrassed, because by this juncture with my ongoing neck pain I had not been near a boxing gym for two months, and, when all was said and done, I had had just the one fight, I blushed slightly. Lacey asked me when I would be fighting again.

'Soon. I've just got to get this neck sorted.'

'You have. You can't be going near a boxing ring with a dodgy neck,' said Lacey. Then he perked up. Gesturing at his male acquaintance, he said: 'He's going to fight Danny Mardell for the British heavyweight title!'

Suki looked on and said nothing, as did Popeye. The large man grinned proudly and I said something pointless like 'is he?' to Lacey. I couldn't seem to find anything else to say. Lacey curtailed what might have been an awkward silence by telling me that an Oxford boxer on the show had made an appearance in a Real Fight Club event.

'Justin Bronder. Good fighter, super-fit. Have a look at him.'

We got our chance in the third fight of the night, when Bronder, boxing as a light-welterweight, took on Jarungwit Wonsaroj of Hughes Hall, Cambridge. How Bronder made the weight as a light-welter was baffling. He was packed with muscle and looked at least a super-middleweight, if not a light-heavy. Like James Glancy, the captain of Oxford's team, he was in the services. He had graduated from the US Air Force Academy and was a second lieutenant in the US Air Force; he was also a member of the 'Wings of Blue', the Air Force Academy's elite parachuting team. He was a student at Exeter College. The programme for the night cast an image of the man every bit as impressive as his physique: 'An avid fan of both physical and mental challenges, Justin has balanced his time in the physics laboratory with intense competition with the University cross-country club in addition to serving as the secretary of the Boxing Club. On the rare occasions when Justin is not working out or studying, he enjoys spending time with his girlfriend, travelling, and tall pints of Guinness with friends from around the University.'

He was up against a Cambridge boxer better known as 'Ming', who was in his third year of a Ph.D. in civil engineering. Ming was specialising in tunnelling technology and was born and brought up in Thailand. The programme said he had no boxing experience prior to 2001, but, watching him fight Bronder, he looked like he'd been learning Thai boxing from the cradle.

In what was by far the best fight of the show, Ming was superb. The programme described him as 'a fanatical trainer with the physique of Bruce Lee', and as he battered Bronder's heavily muscled body into submission it seemed that he might even have a little of the Kung Fu master's power, too. The previous two bouts had had their share of drama, with an illegal hook by Oxford's Fred Brown flooring Cambridge's Phil Gaughwin in the second fight and the gutsy novice Peter Ho being stopped by his Cambridge opponent in the second round of the first fight, but both had gone Cambridge's way. Bronder needed to get Oxford back on track but Ming put in a virtuoso performance. Two rows in front of us, Lacey was clearly enjoying it, hands and arms moving to throw punches in a way that he never let himself at Real Fight Club shows. The velocity of Ming's punches was borne out in sound as they connected with Bronder: fat, lumpen cracks echoed in the hall, to the delirious cheers of the Cambridge faction who were watching what would prove to be their third victory of the night. Soon, Bronder's nose was bleeding profusely, but in the third round he staged a remarkable recovery, tagging Ming with a jab or two and then clumping him with one decent left that was as hard as any shot he had taken. The third round might just have gone the Oxford man's way, but it was too late. Ming had taken him apart in the first two rounds, throughout which Bronder smiled often, as if to say *you're hurting me, and I admire how you're doing it. It gives me pleasure. So don't worry, carry on.* At the end of the fight, both boxers embraced with gusto and genuine respect for the battle they had just waged – for what it meant to them as individuals, and for what it meant to those of us at ringside and in the hall. But it was 3–0 to Cambridge, and, with six fights left, Oxford were going to have to turn it on if they were going to prevent a hat-trick of Varsity wins by Cambridge.

It was not to be. James Glancy, Oxford's captain, was next up, and won his fight despite a performance in which he seemed distracted, almost perplexed, as if wondering what he was doing there. 'I don't know what was up with me,' he told me later. 'I just couldn't get into it.' Glancy's victory was greeted with surprise even by the Oxford fans, who knew that in Cambridge's Michael Dunning their man had more than met his match (no wonder: Dunning boxed as a junior with Merseyside's Towerhill ABC, winning five of seven bouts, and his stepbrother, Gary Jones, turned professional after winning a bronze at the 1998 Commonwealth Games). Glancy showed immense heart to keep going against Dunning, but his victory had the whiff of the political rather than merit.

Still, Glancy won, but then the light-middleweight Cambridge captain, Jonathon Pope, restored Cambridge to a three-fight winning margin, beating Oxford's Oleg Papazov. (Pope's biographical details were intriguingly unserious, perhaps even ironic given his army cadetship: 'He has captained the Light Blue Under 21s at Twickenham and is a member of the Hawks Club committee – with whom he likes to maraud in fancy dress, throw shapes on the dance floor and round off by diving into the Cam for his mobile phone. He is looking forward to returning to 83kgs on his customary Guinness-and-chocolate diet. Popey is on an Army Cadetship with the Royal Engineers, but hopes to be in a boy band when he grows up. Allergic to dark blue, he holds a W4-L1 record.') Pope had little trouble winning his fight, which sealed victory for the Light Blues (though for Papazov there was honour in defeat: he became the first Russian to win an Oxford Blue). Though there was brief respite for Oxford, as Mark Hudson and Charles Ogilvie won the next two fights, David Amiekumo and James Boyle also lost, making it 6–3 to Cambridge overall.

Aside from Bronder v. Wonsaroj, and, at the end of the night, Amiekumo v. Oliver Bowles, the standard had not been hugely impressive. There were moments when neither

Popeye nor I could muster much enthusiasm but Lacey was animated throughout, showing people moves in the intermission, slipping and ducking, throwing combinations into the rarefied air at imaginary foes, just as he had done a year earlier in the less salubrious smoke of The Light Bar in Shoreditch. His acquaintances bore contrasting demeanours. Suki appeared entirely disinterested. The large tough-looking lad was enthused and talked to Lacey a lot. Perhaps he was doing what so many boxers do, when watching boxing: thinking to himself, *I can't wait to get back in the ring*.

Popeye asked me on the way home how the Varsity fighters compared to Walcot and The Real Fight Club.

'The Walcot lads are in a different league,' I said. 'And The Real Fight Club are about the same. Mind you, some of those fighters tonight were quality.'

Quality and a radical reappraisal of The Real Fight Club were, it turned out, awaiting me. But that night, as we drove home, the conversation turned, as it often did, to our sons and their futures.

'The atmosphere was electric,' said Mark. 'And all those people, the opportunities, just amazing. It would be fantastic if my boys could go to a place like that.'

I understood exactly what he meant, and that sense of wanting the best for one's offspring had been in my father, when he had stood in Honiton Magistrates' Court and pleaded for leniency, when he had found the money to send me to public school, when he had hoped that I would secure a place at Oxford University.

Before we left, James Glancy came up to us. He was looking a lot better than he had in the ring. Clean-cut, focused; fit and intelligent; of the right sort and immensely likeable: Glancy was a bright young thing with a future. He and Justin Bronder and almost everyone at Oxford's Town Hall that night were tomorrow's white-collar warriors, undergoing their elite training before they seized their rightful spoils. How many of them would go on to enjoy wealth and privilege of a kind utterly absent from Umar's life, from the lives of many boxers I had met? The overwhelming majority. And how many would keep fighting, wearing the T-shirts handed out by Alan Lacey for Real Fight Club shows, rocking up to York Hall in their thirties, as I had done and as I planned, yet again, to do?

I shook hands warmly with James Glancy. He was a decent man and deserved his likely future successes. He knew that I boxed and invited me to come training with OUABC. 'We only train a couple of times a week in the summer, but you should come. You're welcome anytime, just give me a call.'

Once I had dropped Mark home back in the Cotswolds, I sat in the car, in the darkness of an empty country lane, and I remembered watching my father delivering his plea in mitigation, hearing him say *He has a lot going for him, with the prospect of a place at Oxford*, and my father's lips were quivering as he said those words, his voice had lost its usual firmness and strength, there was a subtle, regretful sympathy in the courtroom as everyone present knew how hard it was for him to be there that day, and for a moment or two I indulged a fantasy of redemption that saw me doing an MA at Oxford, perhaps at Michael Beloff's Trinity College. I could even join the boxing club, lie about my age and get an Oxford Blue.

Like all fantasies, this was pointless. I went back home to find Karen and the boys asleep, and thought of all that I had lost and all that I had recovered, and said to myself that it was about time I stopped disinterring the demons and got on with the future.

The twenty-fifth anniversary Real Fight Club show started with a minute's silence. There was so much noise as the MC announced what was happening that I couldn't make out for whom the audience at York Hall was suddenly standing respectfully. Billed as 'A Heated Exchange', and held on 25 March 2004, the show attracted the now-familiar blend of East End fight fans and City types there to watch their colleagues become 'Heroes for Six Minutes', as the ITV documentary on white-collar boxing described them. All – fighters, medics, stewards, fans, photographers, bar staff – were still until the ringside bell rang to announce that our minute of reflection was over. I was ringside, alone, and had no idea who had died. I assumed it must have been a famous old-time boxer.

I had arrived early for the show and watched as York Hall turned from a sparsely populated, sad old hulk into a thrumming arena brimful of those on or curious about The Real Fight Club's bandwagon. A much tougher looking audience than had been at the Oxford event congregated at the bar and gradually took their seats. Nearby, ringside, the same doctor who had been at my fight sat reading a medical journal. Simon White was talking to Alan Lacey, who looked less harassed than usual. White would be refereeing. The Pink Pounder was at the back of the hall, evidently acting as a whip for the night. Adrian King, Lacey's executive producer at The Real Fight Club, wandered around glad-handing, and Spencer Fearon, whose comeback had been dramatic but had resulted in defeat, mooched at the ringside tables, awaiting his role for the evening as timekeeper. King saw me and we swapped updates. He told me he was going to set up a pole-dancing club. 'It's the new yoga,' he said. Two card girls meandered through the crowd, with buckets to collect money for The Daisy Fund, the same charity that Lacey had helped at his 'Girls On Top' show. One was brunette, the other blonde; both wore skirts that would have the crowd craning their necks whenever they climbed through the ropes. Behind me sat Ann 'Sweet P' Parisio, and a glance at the flyer for the fights showed that at least two old hands would be in the ring: Vince 'Dynamite' Dickson and Thomas 'The Marauder' Lloyd-Edwards.

They were all there. The Real Fight Club was ready to rock.

Two months into 2004, my neck finally settled down. It had been excruciating and I recall one night in January, when I was unable get comfortable let alone sleep for the pain of the trapped nerves, saying to myself: 'That's it. Boxing is stupid. It is absolutely, utterly and completely stupid. Nothing could be more stupid. I am never going near a boxing gym again.' My neck hadn't hurt when Beano had dropped me, but about two days later everything had gone haywire and the two events could not but be connected. But by early March, just before the Varsity contest in Oxford, the pain vanished. At last, I could run and lift weights. And I could get my act together, with the focus of another fight. So I stopped drinking and gave Umar a call. I didn't want to roll up at Walcot again after a lay-off – going straight back to the club's regime would kill me. And just as for the fight against Vince Dickson, I wanted the blend of Umar and Walcot as the basis of my training.

'Hey, haven't heard from this geezer for a while,' said

Umar, recognising my number on his phone. 'How's it going?'

I told Umar all was cool, and that I was planning to have another fight. 'Good enough,' he said. 'You been off the sauce?'

There was a strong feeling of *déjà vu* as I admitted that I hadn't, but that things were going to change.

'They'll have to if you're serious,' he said. 'But this time, you're going to take your time. Train hard and have a fight when I say you're ready. Don't rush it. Listen to what I have to say and above all *be good*.'

That sounded fine, and we arranged a training session at his Chiswick flat. *This is where it starts*, Umar had said, more than a year earlier, and now here we were again, Umar barking orders, me sweating buckets as I ran and did press-ups and sit-ups and star-jumps, all the rigmarole of boxing training, until it was time to slip on the same red sixteen-ounce gloves that Umar had bought for me in the run-up to the fight against Vince. Umar set the timer, and held the pads in front of his face.

'Come on, let's see what you've got,' he said, pushing his left arm slightly further forward, to signal that I should throw a jab. 'Again!' he shouted. 'Keep jabbing! Now the right! Left hook! Cover up, don't let me hit you! Jab again! Right! Left hook, right uppercut! Don't get caught! Come on, man, you're slow! Jab! Jab! Again! Uppercut combination! Come on! Faster! Jab!'

And so it continued, for five two-minute rounds, until Umar decreed that I'd done enough.

'Not bad,' he concluded. 'You're not as out of shape as I thought you'd be.'

For the next two months, I turned up at Umar's Chiswick

flat whenever I was on my way into London, and got back into the Walcot routine. I felt heavier, and slower, than a year ago, but stronger and more durable. My boxing technique was at once better, in the sense that I had a better idea of how to defend myself, but also worse, because I couldn't seem to land any decent heavy shots with my right. Where had it gone? Had the mess of nerves in my neck somehow corrupted it? 'You can still bang,' said Umar, 'you've got no worries on that score', but down at Walcot I couldn't seem to find that punch, even when the good fighters were taking it easy, letting me throw shots. I sparred with Jamie Cox and he let me hit him; I sparred with Marlon, a quick and rangy twenty-four-year-old who was returning to the club having virtually grown up there, and he let me hit him, too. But while their punches steamed, mine sagged. At least, though, Beano was taking it easy, and as for Harold, all he did was defend himself, afterwards often asking whether I thought QPR would edge it over Swindon for promotion to Division One. 'No worries,' I'd say, as convinced that Rangers would somehow ruin a superb season at the last as I was that what small ability I had shown for boxing had left me.

I learnt that The Real Fight Club had a show on 13 May, at York Hall, and dropped Lacey a line to say I was up for it. Umar was concerned that this time I wasn't in with someone like Vince Dickson. 'The Pink Pounder, he's your man,' said Umar. 'You should fight that geezer. Tell Lacey you want to fight the pinko.'

My face must have dropped. For although I had, at one stage, been lined up to fight Charles Jones, what Umar didn't realise was that this time there was an added incentive to have a serious and hard fight. I was sick of how I kept slipping into my old ways, and more than ever I wanted the challenge of knowing that I might get annihilated to force me to stay on the straight and narrow. Perhaps, too, I wanted to get a beating, for all my sins, for all that I kept binge-drinking, for all that I was not the son my father had wanted. In my mind's eye I envisaged fighting one of the bruisers I'd seen on the bill the night Simon Dowson-Collins fought. That would do the trick. Having seen Charles Jones fight that night, I wasn't convinced he was the motivation I needed. He was, technically, reasonable, but there was nothing to his punches and he looked more like a giraffe than a boxer.

'Hey!' said Umar. 'How'd you know he ain't gonna cane you? How'd do you know the so-called Pink Arse-Bandit ain't gonna starch you? And why's it got to be so difficult? Why not have a fight against someone easy? I'm not saying he is – I tell you, he's gonna want to beat you and he'll be up for it – but boxing's full of fighters who fought patsies at the beginning of their careers. Why's it any different for you? Why do you have to climb in with some hard case who's gonna spark you in the first round?'

I can't have looked too happy. The look Umar gave me was the same as I'd received when we sat talking on the sofa in Marc's Clapham flat, eighteen months earlier. After an intense stare, as I stood forlornly on the grass in his flat's communal gardens, Umar spoke again, this time more softly.

'Come on, man,' he said. 'You need to chill. Life's good, enjoy it. Enjoy your boxing. Take it easy, there's no rush. Forget 13 May, forget the lot of it. Have a fight when you know you're ready, have a fight in another year, or maybe don't ever have a fight again. But whatever you do, chill out.'

'Thank fuck they called time. I was fucked.'

So said fitness trainer Nicky 'The Waterloo Warrior'

Sandford as he climbed out of the ring, sweat glistening on his muscular body. His fight against Mark 'The Shark' Hudson had been stopped at the end of the second round. No wonder. The pace had been frenzied from the first seconds, with OUABC man Hudson (perhaps recruited by Lacey on his trip to Oxford) much more aggressive at the outset, only to find that Sandford rallied to pin him on the ropes in round two. Once he had his man where he wanted him, The Waterloo Warrior gave him a hammering. Hudson, sans nickname, had been one of the few Oxford boxers to win in the Varsity match, but in Bethnal Green he was finding out that roughhouse boxing is alive and well. Sandford whacked him with lefts and rights as Hudson vainly tried to protect himself on the ropes, covering his head and ducking, only to feel body shots on both sides of his stomach. He was saved by the bell, and the respite proved to be longer lasting than a mere minute. The fight was stopped before the blonde card girl could make it through the ropes.

By now, York Hall was packed for The Real Fight Club's night of heated exchanges. Next up were Vince Dickson and Jonathan 'No Fear' Reah, but theirs was a lacklustre fight, despite the fearsome appearance of Reah, a sizeable character with tattoos on both arms who, rather like Paul 'Mad Manx' Beckett, did not look desperately white-collar. He was, though, a different calibre of fighter from Beckett, handling Vince well albeit more by brawling and clinching than boxing. Rajiv was working Vince's corner, continually exhorting him to 'Jab! Double jab!', but to little effect. This was perhaps the poorest fight of the evening, to Vince's disgust. 'I don't know what was wrong with me,' he said later. 'I just couldn't get going. It wasn't a great fight, I know that.'

Better was to come from Thomas 'The Marauder' Lloyd-

Edwards, in the red corner, who faced blue's Roger 'The Superdodge' Cue. Lloyd-Edwards had, it transpired, been taken on by Lacey and by day could be found in The Real Fight Club's HQ, building up the brand. In the evenings he did more of the same. 'Some people just have boxing in them, they need the outlet it gives,' he told me, when I rang to speak to Lacey to find him answering the phone. Lloyd-Edwards couldn't wait to find his outlet, standing at the beginning of the fight like a sprinter about to launch himself off the blocks. Both he and his opponent looked extremely fit, as were almost all the fighters on the night (Vince Dickson must have been a stone lighter than he had been for our fight). But Superdodge Cue wasn't as fit as he looked, dropping his hands repeatedly and leaving opportunities that Lloyd-Edwards did not hesitate to exploit. Unsurprisingly The Marauder prevailed, even knocking the headgear from Superdodge in the third round with a left hook followed by a straight right.

Lloyd-Edwards reminded me of some of the Varsity boxers. He had a polished accent and an air of the army. He was not of the same lineage as a man I noticed stalking through the rows of fans. It was Danny Mardell, swinging his arms like an overgrown monkey. This was his jungle, but for all that he sported a casual manner there was nothing casual about Mardell. He wore a T-shirt and trousers, and spent a lot of time talking to Spencer Fearon, but I could never look at him without wondering whether behind the façade there lurked a ruthless man who had not amassed a small fortune – and was not set to continue to do so – without making a few enemies. If I was right, none of them was in evidence at York Hall for 'A Heated Exchange'. Mardell was in his element, enjoying the fights and swapping banter with the ringsiders.

My ruminations on Danny Mardell were interrupted by the start of the fourth fight, between film technician Tom 'Lightning' Lea and Daniel 'The Carrot Cruncher' Anstice, a civil engineer. Both were fighting at around twelve stone, but Lea, walking out to The Rolling Stones' 'Start Me Up', looked in need of more than a wake-up call. He had little answer to the superior power of Anstice in the first round, despite the continued encouragement of Rajiv 'Batta Bing' Bhattacharya, again working the red corner. Between the first and second rounds, the blonde card girl climbed through the ropes to predictable delirium, to wiggle her way around the ring, altogether a much more seductive way of moving than the clattering and jumping from toe to toe that preceded her arrival. Who knows, perhaps Lea was distracted by her, for at times in round two he adopted a strange, square-on posture, more akin to *shotokan* karate than boxing. Both fighters would have incurred the wrath of Umar, for both kept dropping their hands, but nevertheless theirs was an engaging, even contest, with plenty of movement and good punches thrown by both men. They finished round three to huge applause.

In the intermission, Vince Dickson joined me. Showered and changed, no one would have guessed he had only minutes earlier been tussling with Jonathan 'No Fear' Reah. It turned out that this was Dickson's sixth white-collar fight. He was proud of the weight he had lost through training with The Real Fight Club at the Lennox Lewis Centre and at Gymbox in Holborn. 'You should come along, anytime, gave me a call,' he said. I said I might well do that, and observed that the standard of the boxers seemed to have gone up a notch.

'Definitely,' said Vince. 'The club's been going a while now, so people are getting better anyway, but also there are a lot of ex-amateurs turning up now.'

Before us the next fight was underway. In the blue corner, Adam 'Lights Out' Lycett, an IT controller weighing in at nine stone eleven, was shading it against a headteacher from Wales, Andy 'Welsh Warrior' Morgan. Before they began, a hefty security guard sitting ringside said: 'Watch blue, he's gonna be good.' He wasn't wrong, but Morgan, in the red of Wales and making his white-collar debut, was performing admirably. The two men were light and fast, buzzing around the ring as if errant children from Morgan's school, just released from detention. They traded blows with relentless vigour to the accompaniment of comments from Spencer Fearon that would not be heard in any other amateur fight: 'Let's hear it for the blue!' said the professional boxer and sometime Real Fight Club timekeeper, before changing tack as swiftly as a switch-hitter: 'Let's hear it for the red!' he cried, and Morgan and Lycett went at each other with undiminished momentum to growing applause from the crowd. This was a good, entertaining fight, with little separating the two men, but, good though it was, it was not a patch on Sergio 'The Rock' Luciano v. Dion 'The Rage' Page, in which Alan Lacey and The Real Fight Club put down a marker that anyone present would have found impossible to ignore. This was a classic fight, as thrilling as any boxing match anywhere: perhaps, in its nine minutes, The Real Fight Club came of age.

The fight looked like the real thing from the off. The dark-haired Sergio Luciano waltzed through the ropes wrapped in a boxer's dressing gown and warmed up with quick and aggressive combinations, while in the blue corner Dion Page exchanged jokes with his cornermen and seemed not to have a care in the world. Page had a goatee and short hair, and amid the ribald cheers from the large camps of supporters brought along by both men, I was unable to determine what the MC said he did for a living but it sounded as if he was a *proofreader*. Could this be right? Page did not look like a man who corrected grammatical errors to earn a crust, or, at least, he did not meet the stereotypical image of such a man, as characterised, for example, in Saramago's *The History of the Siege of Lisbon*, in which Raimundo Silva changes the course of history with a single, deliberate stroke of his proofreader's pen, ensuring that while the facts say that the crusaders helped liberate Lisbon from the Saracens in the twelfth century the truth is that they did not, a change in history that catapults the ordinarily timid Silva into a redemptive love affair with his sultry superior, Maria Sara, who evidently shares his view that *only the proofreader has learnt that the task of amending is the only one that will never end in this world*. Elsewhere, Silva has it that *we proofreaders are voluptuaries*, but for all the smiles and prefight chitchat, this was not a description that seemed to apply to Dion Page, who looked mean and ferocious, so much so that despite Luciano's bulk – he was very stocky, and very muscular – one could not but fear for him against Page. And hearing the respective weights of the men – Page at twelve-six, Luciano at twelve-ten – it occurred to me that if I were going to fight again, one of them might be my opponent. I settled down to see how Luciano would survive, and to determine my chances against these two white-collar warriors.

The first round was stunning, with Page living up to his ring name, battering The Rock with punches of sickening power. He was a switch-hitter, too, and Luciano seemed visibly disorientated both by the force of the punches crowding his head and the angles from which they were being launched. Clubbing hooks swept from nowhere, with Luciano moving backwards but keeping his stance throughout, tucking up well and popping jabs back at Page. Still, how could he withstand punches of such might, to the temple and sides of his head, even with headgear? Page had left his pedantry at home and was there for a fight; what's more, he was as comfortable having a fight as he would be unsplitting an infinitive. He seemed consumed with controlled menace, with enough malice aforethought to land him in a lot of trouble if he took it outside the lawful confines of the squared circle.

But in the second round The Rock made his move. To rapturous approbation from his massed fans, the man who looked the part before the fight began showing that appearance, this time, equalled reality. A booming straight right smashed into Page's temple, rocking him backwards, and Luciano followed it up with a virtuoso left hook, demolishing in two punches all the swagger and panache that Page had brought into York Hall. Dion 'The Rage' Page could not have mustered the anger to swat a fly: Luciano's punch was a KO, and, unlike that which had finished off Paul 'Mad Manx' Beckett a year earlier at the Mermaid, this time I was no more than two metres away from the action.

Page fell to the canvas heavily, his robust body reduced to a tangle of flailing limbs, of redundant muscle and brawn. For a second, our eyes met, but Page did not see me. He could not see anything. As he collapsed, grazing the ropes as he went down, his eyes were rolling in their sockets, momentarily seeming to settle but, in their disaffection, understanding nothing. He tried to stand up, and couldn't, slumping back to the canvas, unconscious. I know that feeling. The crowd went wild. Behind me, someone said: 'That's the first fight that looked like a serious boxing fight.' Vince Dickson took a deep breath, before saying: 'Christ, I'm supposed to be fighting that Luciano next!'

The doctor was promptly in the ring, as were a host of the kind of people who climb into boxing rings after a KO. After a couple of minutes out cold, Page was on his feet. He was smiling, chatting away to anyone near him. He had recovered already. He left the ring, and Sergio 'The Rock' Luciano took centre stage to celebrate with a display of rapid-fire punches that had a disturbing hint of hubris. Sure, he'd won, and knocked his man out to boot, but did he have to preen quite so aggressively afterwards?

I suppose he did. He looked the part from the off, had proved to be the part, and was finishing off his role with appropriate commitment. I turned to Vince. 'You sure about fighting him?' I asked.

'No!' said Vince, but he added that Sergio had seen him fighting, and had requested a match. Vince grinned. Something told me that he was inwardly relishing the thought of an encounter with Sergio 'The Rock' Luciano.

'Cool,' said Umar, when I told him about the fight. 'But it bears out what I've been telling you. If you're going to have another fight, you've got to get serious. Whether you're fighting The Pink Pounder or this Sergio geezer or someone in between, you've got to train hard and listen to what your trainer – me – says. So what's the score? You fighting pinko or what? Come on, what's happening? Tell me.'

'Don't know,' I said. 'I haven't spoken to Lacey yet. But, come on, I'm training, I'm here, I'm at Walcot, I'm feeling fit again. Maybe we'll have that fight on 13 May, or maybe in

June – there's an event then at Earl's Court that Lacey is putting together.'

'June would be better,' said Umar. 'It'd give you more time. Especially what with you going away.'

The 'going away' was to Albania, in mid-April, and Umar was right – it and other work commitments were interrupting training. A fight on 13 May was asking a lot, not least after watching 'A Heated Exchange'. If that was the standard, I could get hurt all too easily.

We were in Umar's gardens again, having just done a few rounds on the pads. I was exhausted, having trained at Walcot the day before. And I was depressed. However hard I trained, would I ever be a match for the likes of Page and Luciano? And however much I got into boxing, wouldn't I always blow it all with a night out of endless beers and thirty cigarettes? Who was I kidding, taking up boxing in my mid-thirties? Now I had turned thirty-eight, and what I was hoping to achieve through pugilism was starting to take on the quality of a chimera in a Renaissance painting.

Would mine be the fate of Steve 'Smokin'' Ford, or Adrian 'The City Destroyer' Cuthill, the last boxers to climb into the ring at York Hall for a heated exchange? Easily in their fifties, the two men had promised little but put on a fine display, especially Cuthill, who was squat and fat, a *doppelgänger* for white-collar boxing's most famous celebrity boxer, Ricky Gervais. 'He's a pocket dynamo, you watch his hands,' said someone near me, as Cuthill dug deep and found boxing skills that had clearly been learnt many years ago, taking the fight to his much taller opponent, Steve Ford, who, unlike many of The Real Fight Club boxers, was a visible presence in the hall before his fight, idly standing in white trousers and black leather jacket with a rather distinguished air. The trouble was that for all that he could box, Cuthill was desperately unfit, and soon resorted to charging bull-like into Ford. The crowd booed him, and Rajiv, working his corner, turned to them, hunting down the culprits with a murderous glare. 'Cunts,' he said, turning back to the skirmish, a victor from which it was impossible to declare.

Would I be like Ford and Cuthill, staggering on into my fifties, boxing at Real Fight Club events?

Just before the end of 'A Heated Exchange', in between the second and third rounds of Cuthill v. Ford, I read the back of the flyer for the show. It had the usual blurb, as well as a picture of Piero Severini, the man who had assessed me just over a year earlier. Beside a smiling Severini, wearing a Real Fight Club T-shirt, looking as if he'd just finished boxing or working out, were the words: 'TRFC Trainer – Piero Severini – ITALIA – passed away peacefully at home 2004 R.I.P.'

So it was Severini, a young man barely in his thirties, if that, who had been mourned before the show began. I turned again to Vince.

'What happened? How did he die? He was so young!'

'I know,' said Vince, his subdued voice at odds with the adrenalin of the environment. 'He killed himself. No one knows why.'

As soon as the last fight was over, I headed for the exit. It had been a superb show, but I didn't want to get caught up in post-fight talk. Outside York Hall, I was met by Jules, at whose flat I was staying for the night. I'd kept him waiting, and Jules hadn't been minded to join the throng inside. In fact, he looked a little ill at ease.

'You all right, lad?' I enquired, as we walked away from the spiritual home of British boxing.

He was quiet, then said: 'You know, it's not a great place to hang around.'

I glanced over my shoulder, back to the steps of York Hall, crowded now with heavy-duty blokes, glitzy females and City boys in suits, and it struck me more clearly than ever that Harry Scott was right when he said, 'boxing's not for everyone'.

15

IN THE LAND OF EAGLES

Umar was excited. 'I'm looking forward to this, it'll be cool,' he said as he squeezed into the passenger seat of my car. His thighs were three times the size of mine and he was way too large to wear a seat belt. I wondered if The Law made exceptions for people of his bulk. 'My client is innocent of the technical and minor offence of failing to wear a seat belt, for reasons, your Honour, that are all too apparent if you would just look at him.' Was this a statement made in court, from time to time? I should have asked Umar, who has been in court enough times to know, but it was a sunny day and we were both in the kind of rare and spontaneous good mood that it is churlish to interrupt.

My own high spirits were down to a draining morning session at Walcot. It had ended up comprising mostly bag and sprint work but started with Harry Scott ticking off some of the young boys for teasing the gypsies who turned up at the club. 'I don't care who you are, or who you think you are,' said Harry, pacing up and down in between the rows of bags and attentive boxers, his deep West Indian accent rising to answer the expectant silence. 'You don't take the mick out of someone just because he's different. I won't have it. You can train somewhere else if that's what you want to do. Makes no odds to me. I don't care. I won't have anyone here misbehaving like that.' When we got down to business, the work was as tough as ever, but I'd coped, and afterwards felt the peculiar satisfaction that comes of hard graft in a boxing gym. I drove up the M4 to Chiswick, purged and a million miles from feeling *slightly rough*, to find Umar in similarly fine fettle. He was full of enthusiasm about our impending trip to the National Portrait Gallery, where, on a spring Sunday afternoon, we were going to attend a lecture on a rarely visited topic, 'Byron and Boxing'.

As we walked into the National Portrait Gallery, Umar and I were far from typical attendees at a talk given for The Byron Society by the rather fey but highly eloquent scholar Anthony Peattie. We were ten minutes late, and, as is the convention when people are late for lectures, most of the assembled intelligentsia looked around to see who was making such a *faux pas*. The sight of Umar's gargantuan figure, clad in denim jacket and jeans, and my own less than delicate features confronted them, to prompt more than a few double takes, the majority aimed at Umar, whose size and colour, not to mention bald head and diamond-encrusted gold teeth, were far from standard fare in the lecture room.

We joined a friend, Isobel, an elegant journalist-turned-PR who had alerted me to the talk, and listened to Peattie explain how Lord Byron had been drawn to boxing throughout his life, his words accompanied by slides of

Byron in what passed for the boxing regalia of his age, images of other prizefighters and the occasional harmless interjection. Not only had Byron been drawn to boxing, but apparently he had been good at it, too, boxing for Harrow and delighting in the release of the bellicose emotions that led the defiant, melancholy and sexually unconstrained author of *Don Juan* into a series of controversies throughout his life. We learnt that Byron had been born with a club foot, was short and stout, and had travelled not merely to Spain, Italy and Greece but also to Albania. It is not known whether he boxed in Albania, but he did meet Ali Pacha of Tepelene, emissary of the Ottoman Empire, whom he described in a letter to his mother as 'very kind ... with a fine face, light blue eyes, and a white beard', and yet 'a remorseless tyrant, guilty of the most horrible cruelties, very brave, and so good a general that they call him the Mahometan Buonoparte ...'. In the same letter Byron wrote of Ali Pacha summoning 'my Albanian soldier, who ... like all the Albanians, is brave, rigidly honest, and faithful', and yet, just as Ali Pacha was evidently a man of contradictions, to Byron the Albanians were also 'cruel, though not treacherous, and have several vices but no meannesses'. Of them, Byron wrote also: 'They are, perhaps, the most beautiful race, in point of countenance, in the world; their women are sometimes handsome also, but they are treated like slaves, *beaten*, and, in short, complete beasts of burden; they plough, dig, and sow. I found them carrying wood, and actually repairing the highways.'

Byron's endless and indiscriminate infidelities were a strange, unharmonious counterpoint to his apparent empathy with the plight of Albanian women. Perhaps this note of dissonance was first subtly sounded by his own profligate father, albeit that he died when Byron was just three, the same age as my elder boy when I left Karen to be with Suzi (what damage is done by the absence of the father, whether absent of his own volition, or dead, of natural causes, or by the hand of another, or even as a suicide?). Thereafter, the '6th Baron Byron of Rochdale' was raised in Scotland by his mother, to take his seat in the House of Lords in 1809, having inherited the family title and estates through the death of his great-uncle in 1798. He was twenty-one but Parliament did not suit him: by 1811, he had completed his odyssey through the Mediterranean, returning to England to write *Childe Harold's Pilgrimage*, a fictionalised account of his travels that was an overnight success. Still he boxed, some fifty years before the Marquess of Queensberry codified the sport, sparring with the well-known prizefighters of the day. In 1815, he left England, never to return, after his wife, Anne Isabella Milbanke, walked out on him, his promiscuous behaviour insufficiently countermanded by the birth of their daughter. Perhaps, as he lived successively in Switzerland, Italy and Greece, his boxing came to an end. Or were there like-minded pugilists on his travels? Did Shelley – with whom he lived for a while – indulge him with a show of fists on the shores of Lake Geneva, so that on those cold autumn nights the waters of the lake echoed to the sound of flesh hitting flesh, bare knuckles rapping soft cheeks, Romantic poets heroically bludgeoning each other until Shelley's wife, Mary, could stand it no more and had to run inside and hurriedly create *Frankenstein*, anything to get away from those two fools muddied and bloodied, after all, hadn't they got better things to do than stand out there in the cold and beat each other up?

Umar thoroughly enjoyed Peattie's tour of Byron and

boxing. We spoke briefly to him at the end, hovering like two tricky individuals to say our piece once everyone had gone. After congratulating him on an interesting talk, Umar turned to serious matters.

'Do you box?' he asked, leaning down to Peattie, who was about a foot shorter than him.

Peattie laughed, as if the thought could hardly be more absurd.

'No, no, no I don't,' he said, not quite sure what was coming. Was Umar about to lay into him for some dreadful misrepresentation of the noble art?

'You should,' said Umar. 'I'm a boxer.'

'You *do* surprise me,' said Peattie, laughing a little more easily but still on his guard.

'Here, take this,' said Umar, handing Peattie a flyer for 'PBT4U', and explaining what he did for a living. 'Look at the Hemingway quote. That's straight up.'

Peattie looked at it and mouthed the words: 'My writing means nothing to me. My boxing means everything to me.'

'The first lesson's for free,' said Umar. 'Call me.'

Later, we went for a coffee across the road in St Martin's Lane. Years ago I had wandered there with Karen, to visit the National Gallery and its little sister, the National Portrait Gallery, in the days when everything was possible, even fidelity. Isobel was not convinced that she would be taking up boxing, despite Umar's best efforts. 'I prefer gardening,' she said. 'Honestly, I don't think it's for me.'

'You should try it,' said Umar. 'I'd work with you in a way that no other trainer would, and you'd see that it's not at all what you think it is.'

I didn't think Isobel would be calling Umar and I wasn't sure that Peattie would, either. But I had to admire him. Only he could tout for business in a lecture room at the National Portrait Gallery. I was due to fly to Tirana in a week or so, in another quest to sell sports TV rights, and found myself wondering what it would be like to be there with Umar. Knowing him, he'd take his flyers with him, and by the end of the trip every Albanian we met would know precisely what Hemingway thought of writing and boxing.

Umar would have enjoyed Tirana. In between meetings with broadcasters I met, for the second time, Hamdi Uka. The man with the sideways nose remained the boss at the Palestra Dinamo, which still housed a collection of lean and hungry Albanian boxers, now training under the name 'Klajd Klub'. Uka supervised a sparring session between me and Artur Muhedini, a twenty-two-year-old welterweight and Balkans champion. This was not undertaken without nerves on my part, not least because of feeling predictably *slightly rough*, and advancing to the centre of the ring, to hear Uka's command ('Box!' he said, in English), it was impossible to determine what the inscrutable Muhedini would do. Would he take it easy? Or would he delight in teaching the man who was perhaps the first Englishman to box in Albania a painful lesson? I remembered Umar's endlessly recycled Frank Maloney line: *if you can't jab, you can't fight*. I stuck out a jab and hoped for the best.

I had no need to worry. Muhedini was a gentleman. The language barrier may have meant that we would not have been able to converse for longer than thirty seconds, but it took him less than that to work out that I was easily within his capabilities. Despatching me would hardly be a source of pride. I was soon sweating and huffing my way around the ring, absorbed in trying to avoid getting hurt and doing my best to land a punch or two on Muhedini, a young man who, like Shatrolli a year and a half before, was the antithesis of my *slightly rough* self. I caught him with one left hook that surprised me more than it did him, but he resisted any urge to avenge himself. Besides, as Uka said at the end, after three rounds that I found exhausting but which served as a mere warm-up for Muhedini: 'In Albania, we like to be nice to our guests.' Before I left, Uka told me that Muhedini should be having a pro fight in England within six months. I told him I'd be there if he did.

'*Pac fat*,' I said, as I left the Palestra Dinamo, and the recipients of these two words from my limited Albanian vocabulary smiled. This time, though, I could walk away and think that for all that I still hadn't sorted everything out, for all that there was probably a myriad of problems waiting to assail me and for all that I still didn't behave in exactly the way that I thought I should behave, I was a hell of a lot further down the road than the last time I'd said *pac fat*. And for that, as much as anything, I had boxing to thank.

Karen did not want to join me for another Walcot boxing event, this one entitled 'A Night At The Boxing' and taking place on 7 May 2004. Walcot shows were devoid of the hype attached to Real Fight Club bouts, their titles never embellished with the wit of Lacey's linguistic promiscuity, but, hyped or not, Karen was not interested. 'Go with your mates,' she said. 'Just sleep in the spare room if you get back drunk.'

The spare room. How many times had I been consigned there? When I was living in Wandsworth, picking up the debris of my life, I would arrive in Cheltenham at weekends to see the children, and take up residence in the spare room.

From that room, I had looked out of the window during one trip home to see my boys playing in the garden. Karen had been wined and dined by Don Addler for a couple of months by this stage. He even took her to New York. This I knew, and hated. I loathed the man coming to our house (I still called it our house) in Cheltenham and courting my wife while the children slept upstairs, while I drank like a degenerate in the worst pubs of south London that I could find. On weekends, I would try to forget all this, and remember that I was the one who had behaved deplorably, that I deserved everything I got, but that the children were sacrosanct and themselves deserved a decent dad.

Watching my boys from the spare room, I saw Karen running around with them, laughing, looking pretty and selfless. How much I had hurt her, and how much I had let everyone down. I made my way downstairs and we sat outside on the patio, the boys delighted that their father was home, jostling for attention as Karen and I tried to talk. About what? Everything and nothing, the quotidian reality of marriage, even when it has fallen apart, the bliss and difficulty of children, my feelings for Suzi, hers for Don. And we looked at each other and suddenly it dawned on both of us that everything else was a waste of time. The only thing was the family, and in it we were immersed and always would be.

Retrieving our relationship was predictably battle-scarred. Every time I get drunk, Karen fears the same loss of control that has led to infidelity and fights. And every time I get drunk, I fear the loss of everything. And yet I still drink – not as much, in fact less and less (and no more by way of curiosity than compulsion), but enough. And at Walcot on Friday 7 May, I drank as pointlessly as ever. Joe and Mark Reynolds and another friend called Simon and I watched the young Walcot boxers get the better of virtually every opponent, downing the red wine as we did so, as former world champion and sometime Real Fight Club referee Charlie Magri looked on from the top table and next to us cruiserweight Phil Day, just retired, contemplated the action with the equanimity that comes of having been there before and done it a hundred times. The Walcot boxers were superb, as they always are, but there was disappointment: Amy's fight was called off. Her adversary, Jane Masters of Droitwich ABC, had got injured just before the fight. Once again, we would not see Amy box, and once again, we headed back to our local in time to cram in some extra lagers. I slept in the spare room and threw up for the whole of the next day.

On Sunday, still feeling the effects of Friday night's binge, I made my way to Walcot to train. It was a typically cathartic experience, distinguished, though, by the presence of a film crew from Albania. They were there to interview young Jorgen Catej, whose family, like Agim's, were émigré Albanians from Kosovo. Jorgen had beaten Jake Childs of Enfield on points to become the Junior 'A' (class 1) schoolboy champion. Harry Scott was justly proud of Jorgen's achievement, which had crowned a good season for the club, with local recognition for its work coming with the award of the Phoenix Trophy from Lord Lansdowne, president of Youth Action Wiltshire.

Jorgen seemed to take everything in his stride. He is a boy of great potential, not merely as an athlete but as a man. Intelligent and strong, cheeky and quick, but also modest, he quietly answered the questions of the Albanian journalists. When the interview was over, Dave Veysey gestured to me. 'He's a journalist as well,' he said, to the Albanians. I wandered over and talked to them. They were astonished to find that I had visited Tirana and that I knew various broadcasters and journalists. We talked for a while and, as I left, I couldn't resist those two words of Albanian.

'*Pac fat*,' I said, and I drove home to my wife and sons.

16

AMY ROCKS

Amy was on the canvas within five seconds. 'She got hit by a left hook that came from way back when,' said Harry Scott, after the fight. He was right, and when she went down I couldn't believe it. Now, when I was finally watching her box, in the Female Senior ABA finals in Huddersfield Town Hall on 29 May 2004, it looked as if her fight would be over within another ten seconds. Her opponent, Heather Mackie of Hedfit ABC, was set to tear Amy apart.

Before Amy's fight I had sparred a couple of times with her. Angry at the hangover following the Walcot event earlier in the month, I was boxing a lot at the club, and turning in sessions with Umar in London, too. I felt fit and positive, convinced afresh that I could turn things around, that boxing was my salvation. I derived a perverse pleasure from being hit by Amy. I would cover up and move around the ring, taking as many shots as she could throw, occasionally sticking out a left jab. She hit me with all her might, and some of her shots hurt like hell.

She delivered one body shot to the waist that left me with a bruise the size of a tennis ball, and I gave myself rope burns on my lower back, crashing along the ropes as I tried to evade her.

I showed Amy the bruise before her fight in Huddersfield. 'Did I do that?' she exclaimed. 'Yes, you did,' I replied. 'Hit as hard as that in there and you'll be fine.'

Karen was unsure about the whole thing, and the boys were more intent on spending their pocket money than watching the boxing. But we were there, as a family, on an outing that owed more to those black and white photographs of her mother and father than I could ever hope to explain. Karen met Harry and Amy, as well as Ben Fitch who had made the trip to help out. She loved Harry. 'You said he was a man of few words,' she said, after I'd left her talking to Harry to wish Amy luck. 'He's a charmer!'

This was, it is true, a side of Harry that I had not seen. Stern and taciturn and a man to respect, yes, but a charmer? No, that did not compute. 'He's lovely!' said Karen. I introduced our sons and asked if it would be OK for my Harry, the elder one, to come down to the club. Harry Scott said that would be fine, and chatted to him. 'Come down when you're ready,' he said. 'It's a man's game.'

It may be a man's game, but Amy and five other women were boxing on the card at Huddersfield. The female ABA finals were a prelude to the boys' National Junior ABA finals, the event hosted by local club Rawthorpe ABC. Huddersfield Town Hall – an excellent venue with a balcony, rather like a neater, better preserved and smaller version of York Hall, complete with ground-floor windows like ships' portholes – was packed with friends, families and fight fans. Before the bouts began, Amy radiated health and appeared confident, sitting on a bench outside the hall with Harry and Ben.

Underneath the bench was her kitbag, red and with the words *Amy Rocks* in thick black ink at one end. I wondered whether Amy had written the words, or if it was one of the Walcot lads, as I watched her bouncing on her toes waiting for the bell to ring. *Amy Rocks*, I thought, as Amy got to her feet after that knockdown in the first few seconds. A lesser person would have crumbled but not Amy, who got to her feet quickly and clapped Mackie and her knockdown punch as she took a standing count of eight. For the rest of the round, though, she continued to look doomed. I had a dreadful, sickening feeling during the interval, as Harry Scott fanned her with a white towel, that she was going to get hammered in round two.

But she didn't get a hammering, and round two was even. Both the women were orthodox boxers, and both had technique every bit as good as many male boxers', myself most certainly included. In round three, Amy took the fight to Mackie, constantly hounding her around the ring to the cheers of her vociferous supporters. She let go with one six-punch combination towards the end, and I had a feeling that she might just have nicked the fight.

It wasn't to be. Mackie got the nod, though the officials apparently agreed that if there had been another round, Amy would have won. The result did not seem to worry her. She was happy to have fought in a national amateur final, and, who knows, there is always next year. Moreover, in boxing as she did, Amy had shown the kind of character that boxers describe as *heart*. If it was a man's game, she had shown enough heart to earn her stripes for life.

We left Huddersfield immediately after Amy's fight, taking the scenic route back to the Cotswolds over the moors where the Pennine Way begins. I had walked most of it over a two-week period two months before being sacked. My boss at the Cheltenham firm had seen signs of increasingly unstable behaviour as I sought to juggle my torment over having left my family, obsession with Suzi and the requirements of working as a solicitor, and had allowed me leave to go off and clear my head. That was the idea, anyway. Instead, though I completed most of the Pennine Way, I managed also to get hopelessly drunk at the Tan Hill Inn, the highest pub in England, as well as various other pubs en route, so much so that in Dufton, near the splendour of High Cup, two walkers I met put two and two together and said: 'Are you the bloke who's been walking twice as fast as everyone else and getting pissed every night?' The benevolence of Caroline, in letting me undertake the Pennine Way, failed to result in any tangible benefit save for a healthy tan (as if to obscure my inner disarray), and now, as Karen and I drove around the hills of Edale, I felt battered by the past, by memories of just how far over the edge I had been a few years earlier. Why had I behaved with such spectacular rage? Why was I a wrecking machine? Why, when I had met him, had Umar looked me in the eye and seen at once the kind of man I am?

I thought of Amy fighting, of Karen and how important it was to me that she had accompanied me to Huddersfield, I thought of my beautiful sons, with whom I collected granite rocks – or fossils, as they would have it – during a brief stop on the way home, I thought of my father and had the peculiar sense that both he and I had let each other down but that it was down to me to achieve the still point in my life and our relationship, and I thought of my fight against Vince Dickson, of the fights which were supposed to have happened against Charles 'The Pink Pounder' Jones and Phil 'The Judge' Maier, and again I thought of the past, of my infidelities, of Suzi and her family, of everyone I had ever betrayed, but most of all I thought of Karen and her mother and father, of a wedding morning conversation I had had with her father in which I had promised that I would look after his daughter, *whatever happened*, and I could not but feel sad and bewildered and yet glad that we were all back together, as a family, as we should have been all along, until my identity as a wrecking machine had moved from the occasional and the covert to the consistent and the public, and I felt angry, angry that I had not done better against Vince, angry that injuries or whatever else had meant that I had not had any more fights, angry at myself and my failings, angry at my inability to belong and I resolved that come what may I would have another fight and that it would be a fight from which I would emerge with dignity, pride and respect and that from then on that was how I would view myself and the world.

That was in late May 2004. I went down to Walcot regularly, trained with Umar and arranged with Alan Lacey that I would fight on the card for a 'West End v. East End' event on 23 September. By now, I no longer cared whether I would ever fight Alex Mehta; it did not even occur to me to suggest to Lacey that now was the time to match us. To this day, I have no idea how I would fare against Mehta, and realise that he was only there at the beginning, rather as there are challenging ridges on the outriders of the mountains around Mont Blanc. I did once train with Mehta, having interviewed him for *The Lawyer*; he was his usual loquacious and enthused self as we talked near his company's offices in the City, before heading across the river to London's very own, recently opened, Gleason's Gym, in Bermondsey. There Mehta was greeted with respect by the other boxers, though he lamented that work was preventing him training as much as he would have liked. I watched him shadow box and work the bags. It was clear that he had good technique and excellent balance, though it was impossible to tell if his punches had any power. I did a couple of rounds on the pads with a heavyweight pro by the name of Michael Steed, and asked Mehta if he would like to spar. He declined. He said he'd like to be 'properly back in the swing of things' before he did any sparring. 'Besides,' he added, 'I've got a feeling you'd kill me.'

I have no idea whether this is true, and know enough now to conclude that Mehta – a decent, if sometimes rather odd, man – was probably ameliorating my evident disappointment with a compliment.

I got into a decent rhythm of my own with the focus of the 'West End v. East End' show. I drank less and rarely smoked. We went to Spain for a week, and I kept up the regime, swimming at least two miles in the sea each morning and running in the evenings. I felt superbly fit, and was enjoying life. Work had blossomed so that I was writing regularly. I still did a few night lawyer shifts for *The Times* and *Independent* and some globe-trotting for Rob Pickles, trying to develop markets for sports rights sales in Central Asia, but writing had become my core activity. At last, after all these years, I was doing what I had always wanted to do, and I was happily with Karen. In August, we took another week's break in Cornwall, and, despite being tired from a day on the beach with the boys, I hauled myself out for a run on the cliffs near Pendeen in the late afternoon. Near me were the disused workings of Geevor tin mine, whose tunnels had stretched half a mile out beneath the Atlantic. I jogged down the cliff path, towards the sea, and just as it occurred to me that the surface was unusually uneven – doubtless, because of the area's mining heritage – my right ankle caught in a rut and turned over. I heard the crack of the ligaments snapping cleanly. Such hideous pain. An ambulance came and I was taken to Penzance Hospital. Discharged later in the evening, I was met by Karen and the boys, alerted to this latest self-inflicted disaster by the excellent people of Geevor. I spent the week on crutches and sent Alan Lacey the inevitable email telling him that there was no way I would be fighting on the West End v. East End show. 'Life is full of little disappointments,' he replied. 'Next show is 25 November.'

In our holiday cottage, once the children were finally asleep, Karen and I took stock of things. A family holiday was, if not ruined, seriously compromised by an injury that itself was caused because I was determined to have another fight. I had been too tired to train but had forced myself out running, on ground that was unsuitable. It was stupid and she had every right to be annoyed. 'What next?' said Karen. 'What if you recover, have a fight and really hurt yourself? Is that when you'll stop, when you'll finally be happy? If that happens, what about us? Look around, at me, the boys, your life. *You've done it.* You've made things right again. What more do you need to prove?'

I lay in bed, unable to sleep because of the pain. And yet, somehow, I needed one more fight. I knew that I would make the 25 November show, even if Alan Lacey had to winch me into the ring. *In the destructive element immerse, one more time, and then, maybe, you'll be at peace.* That's what I told myself. And yet, as the weeks went by, for the first time in a life in which I have broken many bones, acquired numerous scars and ruptured tendons and ligaments doing one thing or another, I could remember the pain of an injury, of tearing my ankle ligaments on the cliffs at Geevor tin mine. Still, now, I remember it, a sharp crack and then unquenchable pain, pain that made me scream and writhe on the grass like a slug splattered with salt until a walker came upon me with her astonished daughter. I didn't want that pain again, and though there was no question that I would fight in November, I was deeply worried that, on the night, the same kind of pain would return and that it would all go horribly, desperately wrong.

17

AFTER WORK FIGHT NITE

'When are you fighting?'

I told Sean Lynch, City trader, Real Fight Club trainer and man of considerable boxing pedigree, that I was due to fight on 25 November, in six weeks, on a York Hall show billed simply as 'After Work Fight Nite'. Lynch was not impressed.

'I'll be honest with you, mate, you're not ready. You need more time.'

'Not an option,' I replied. 'I'm determined to have this fight.'

Lynch looked almost aggrieved. Now thirty-five, he had boxed from the age of nine at reputable clubs such as Repton and West Ham, reaching four national ABA semi-finals in successive years by the time he was seventeen. He quit a year later and obtained his professional boxing training licence, becoming the youngest trainer ever across Europe. He trained professional boxers for another six years, during which time he also built a career as a trader on the Liffe exchange. More recently he had got involved with Alan Lacey and The Real Fight Club, in particular organising its popular Hedge Fund Fight Nights. A little overweight and with glasses, not to mention a penchant for fag breaks, Lynch did not look the part but I had seen him box at the 'Girls On Top' night, when he'd stepped in to cover for a boxer unable to make the show. He had been light years ahead of his opponent.

'Look, boxers are at various different levels,' he told me in an East End accent. 'There are the really good ones, then there's ones quite near them, then there's the ones in the middle, then ones who aren't much cop, and then the ones who are useless. I don't mean to diss you but you're average. Bang in the middle. You need more time. The standard of white-collar boxing has gone right up across the board. It ain't what it was when you fought Vince.'

I had a strong feeling that what Lynch was really saying was that I was nearer to the bottom of the pile than the top. But I refused to be deterred. 'Trust me,' I said. 'I'll be all right. You'll see a big improvement in the next few weeks.'

Earlier Sean, whose father, Brian Lynch, has trained world champions including Nigel Benn, Terry Marsh and Dennis Andries, had watched me sparring against Alex 'The Suffolk Punch' Goldsmith. It had been a tough session, no less raw for its glitzy surroundings: The Real Fight Club had, for the past few months, been running a boxing facility at the Top Notch Gym on Tudor Street, Blackfriars. Just up the road was Carter-Ruck, the libel firm with which I trained and qualified as a solicitor, and within five minutes was the Temple, home of many of the UK's leading barristers. In between Carter-Ruck and the Temple was the Royal Courts of Justice, to which I had been dispatched for hearings and trials in my early legal life, and on its eastern flank was Chancery Lane, where the Law Society elected its representatives and drafted its codes and regulations and sat in judgement of the errant, the negligent and the disreputable, all the solicitors who ended up not being PLU. It was legal land, my old stamping ground, an area whose copious wealth was evident in the first-class equipment and upmarket clientele of the Top Notch. I had started turning up at the Top Notch about seven weeks after tearing my ankle ligaments, having heard about it from Alan Lacey. Before a night lawyer shift, I would park the car at Shoe Lane, underneath the International Press Centre (which houses Carter-Ruck), and walk the five minutes down to Blackfriars. Discovering the Top Notch solved the problem of where to train when I was in London and, for all that I kept in touch with Umar and, indeed, missed him, it was more convenient than stopping in Chiswick. Initially Sean had me doing the usual exercises and a gentle spar against him (in which the gulf in our ability was so pronounced that he found time to nod and say hello to people arriving, while swapping jabs and keeping me at bay), and then the second time he had me trained by a Scottish ex-pro called Mikey Callum, who works with him at the Top Notch. Again, though physically it was hard, a boxer like Callum could beat me even if he had a tranquilliser dart in each arm. Sean had an idea of my technical skills, such as they were, but in putting me in against Alex Goldsmith for a serious spar on my third visit to the Top Notch would find out what other qualities I might have.

I had a feeling I'd seen Goldsmith before, and he proved to be the blond man who had hurt his shoulder when I sparred against Rajiv 'Batta Bing' Bhattacharya at the Lennox

Lewis Centre all those months ago. Since then, he had had three white-collar fights, but though of the same height had a smaller build than me. I thought I would be OK, but what I didn't know was that Goldsmith, a thirty-seven-year-old derivatives broker, was an ex-amateur who had returned to the sport. Hailing from Chatteris in the Fens, whose more famous boxing son is Dave 'Boy' Green, Goldsmith had sixteen amateur fights and became both a regional ABA champion and a Schoolboys champion in his teens. Quitting boxing was a regret: 'I should have kept on with it, but the family moved and for various reasons it wasn't possible,' he told me. 'That regret spurs me on now. I believe in pushing boundaries and parameters and I believe there's something to be gained by the discipline and commitment of boxing.' There were, indeed, some parallels between myself and Goldsmith, whose return to boxing, under the aegis of Alan Lacey and The Real Fight Club, had come as a consequence not merely of regret at abandoning a good amateur career but also on account of personal problems. Perhaps, as with me, boxing was a corrective to the sense of having got things badly wrong: Goldsmith's marriage had foundered, and though now he and his former partner were on amicable terms, the break-up had been painful. As he said: 'I met Alan Lacey when I was at my lowest ebb. Some people might say he's a lovable rogue but he inspired me. I'm not joking when I say that boxing saved my life.'

In our three rounds of sparring, however, any potential comity was not immediately apparent. The Suffolk Punch hit me so hard on the nose that, if it wasn't broken, it had definitely moved so that my retroussé snub was no more. He also dished out a body shot that left me doubled up and gasping for breath, and a sock in the jaw that hurt for days. I split his lip and landed a few shots but Goldsmith was the better man. He was charitable in his obvious superiority, telling Sean that I had done well given that I still wasn't able to run, because of the ankle, and had barely trained for three months. 'His fitness is the main problem, not his boxing,' said Goldsmith. 'He's got a decent dig on him.' As ever, the principal attribute I had shown, if it can be described as such, was my determination, but overall this spar had been a demoralising experience. As Sean said afterwards, *You're in the middle. Your fitness ain't there and you need more time.*

Alan Lacey broke into a familiar chuckle before telling me of my opponent's pedigree. 'He's taller than you, fitter than you, and he's going to hit you hard,' he said. 'But I'm assuming you're going to want to come out and try and kill him.'

'Is he my level, or what?' I asked.

'I'd say he's fitter than you but not as good. It'll be a good fight.'

I never got the name of my would-be adversary, whom Lacey had told me about some four weeks before the show on 25 November. As it turned out, he loomed large in my mind for only a week or so. At another Real Fight Club show three weeks before the 25th, he was knocked out. As with amateur boxing, this meant that he couldn't spar, let alone take another fight, for twenty-eight days. Yet again, it seemed, I had got to the brink of having a second fight, only for it to fade away at the last. But what relief. For a day or so, I didn't box, I didn't run, I ate takeaways and took it easy. But also, I didn't drink, and I didn't smoke. I didn't want to ruin the fitness and sense of well-being acquired through weeks of concerted training. And soon enough, Lacey was on the phone.

'I told you I'm a resourceful man. I've found you another opponent. You're still on for the 25th.'

'Who is he?'

'He's fifty-two and he's an accountant.'

I breathed a sigh of relief and said that that sounded pretty good.

'Don't be fooled, and don't take this fight lightly,' said Lacey. 'He's good and knows what he's doing.'

I asked if it was his first fight. Lacey said that it was and denied that he had ever done any amateur boxing. 'He's called 'The Amazing' Alan Fitzgerald,' he said. 'His wife came up with the name.'

Later that day I was training at the Top Notch. It was an evening session and Sean was taking five or six fit-looking and well-spoken thirtysomethings through their paces. I arrived too late for any sparring but found the exercise alone draining enough. Sean told me he'd find out about the 'The Amazing' Mr Fitzgerald in the next couple of days. I duly arrived a couple of days later to be told to climb through the ropes to spar with a boxer called John. He had black hair and a bit too much weight, and was building up to a Real Fight Club fight in early December. The going was about even, and Sean, who spent every session teaching me how to move more like a boxer, ducking and weaving ('cos that's your build, you're stocky and need to get inside'), seemed a little happier. 'You've come on a lot. You'll be all right on the 25th. Just practise moving your head, bob and weave all the time. Oh, and I've talked to Lacey. You ain't gonna be stitched up.'

I arrived at Walcot for a Friday evening session, with just under a week to go before my fight against Alan Fitzgerald. I was feeling fit but now, with the fight so close, did not want a hard spar for fear of sustaining an injury that would ruin the months of training. I saw Harry Scott and asked him if I could take it easy. 'Don't worry,' he replied. 'Glove up. You'll be all right.'

Jamie Cox was told to climb into the ring. He was training furiously these days, perhaps inspired by Amir Khan's silver medal at the Athens Olympics: Khan and Cox are in the welter to light-welter divisions, and Jamie, who in the summer had rued his form when he had sparred with me and suffered a cut lip, had got his act together with the aim, I am sure, of turning pro and making the big time. If Khan could do it, why couldn't he? Once, when running together, he told me he wasn't sure whether to join the army or turn pro, and admitted to the distractions of girls and booze. He had been only briefly distracted and now was boxing with ever more astonishing power and speed. First up against him was Jamie Husband, a twenty-year-old light-heavyweight, tall and rangy and always on his toes. Cox took him apart. One body shot was so hard that the onlookers winced, as Husband doubled up, as if about to retch. Punches of terrifying velocity continued to slam into Husband, himself a decent boxer but unable to come up with anything to answer Cox's onslaught. On the chair beside the ring, Harry Scott kept shouting: 'Not so heavy, Jamie! Not so heavy!' But Cox, who is unfailingly respectful of Harry, didn't seem to hear. A severely battered Jamie Husband left the ring after two rounds, to be replaced by Ben Fitch, who was back at the club after a lay-off. Fitch took a beating, too, despite Harry's increasingly heated demands that Jamie back off. Again a wicked body shot left Cox's opponent crumpled, though Ben did land one straight right that caused bleeding from Cox's nose. At the side of the ring, I stood gloved up and with my headguard on, dreading the possibility that I would have to spar against Jamie. In this form, he would kill me. The same fear was shared by other boxers watching, and gradually an uneasy silence settled in the febrile air as we watched Cox destroy Fitch, leaving him looking profoundly worried when he climbed out of the ring, an expression shared by the next boxer to take him on, young Jake Sheppard. A tall and wiry kickboxer in his late twenties called Dan, who had recently started coming to the club, caught my eye and we raised our eyebrows as if to say *This is serious, but I tell you what, if we spar each other, we'll take it easy*. No such luck for Sheppard, a talented and strong young boxer but not in Cox's class. Yet again Cox dished out an immense right-hand bodyshot, so that Sheppard, too, could do nothing other than double up with pain. Harry Scott had to scream 'break!' as Cox seemed about to annihilate Sheppard once and for all with a flurry of hard lefts and rights to the body. 'Jamie, you've got to calm down!' shouted Harry. 'You're the best in the club but these are the people you spar against. If you kill them they're not going to spar you, so then what are you going to do?' Faintly, Cox slackened his pace for what proved to be the last of his six rounds. Thank God, Harry called time on his sparring and ushered me through the ropes.

I had hoped my opponent would be Dan, with whom I had reached a tacit agreement to calm things down, but I was in against Jamie Husband, the first boxer to suffer at Cox's fired-up hands. Everything went well in the first round. Though I always find him difficult to box, because of his height and range, I managed to catch him with a couple of good rights, to Harry's surprise. 'Good, Alex, good! That's it! More of that!' And so, in the second, I went for more, steaming into Husband with a combination that ended with as hard a right as I could manage. I think it grazed the side of his head, but it was not, ultimately, the right move. Husband was riled. It is one thing to get a pounding by Jamie Cox, another to find oneself on the ropes against someone of my calibre. He decided that enough was enough and snapped out of the perilous position he could have been in by launching a left uppercut on to my nose. I saw it coming, up through my inadequate guard, but could do nothing to stop it. It wasn't a knockout punch but it was one hell of a blow. I could feel blood cascading everywhere within seconds. Harry stopped the sparring and looked at my nose. 'Box on,' he said, to my dismay. We did, for another twenty seconds or so, but by then there was so much blood that it was coming up into my mouth, my T-shirt was soaked with it and I couldn't concentrate. Harry stopped the session. Afterwards he held my nose, head tilted back, for an age, as the other boxers looked on. It took forever for the blood to stop. There was a pool of it on the floor, reminding me of the pool of blood left outside Oscar's when I was eighteen, which my father had photographed and which remained discernible even three days later, when once again we walked past the scene of the crime. Harry looked at the blood on the floor at Walcot. 'Bloody hell, Alex, it's like a slaughterhouse in here!' he said. And as I left for the evening, half an hour later, we talked again. 'I don't know what happened in there tonight,' he said, in a puzzled tone. 'I've never seen anything like it. Never in all my years here.'

Two days later I was back. My nose, already mildly rearranged by Alex Goldsmith, had moved sideways and had a new bump on its bridge. Karen took one look and said that it was broken. It felt broken, too, but if I went to hospital and they told me it was, I couldn't have the fight, now only four days away. And so, rather like a child who knows that he or she has to climb back on a bike after a fall, I forced myself back to Walcot that Sunday.

At the beginning of the session Harry had all the boxers stand still. 'You all know Alex,' he said, and young Jorgen Catej, standing next me, smiled, so too Amy and Beano standing in the ring. 'He's a writer, does this and that. He always helps us out and he always tries his best. He's got a fight this Thursday so I want you to wish him all the best.' They clapped, and, unlike the first time Harry gave this speech, I didn't feel embarrassed. A voice was murmuring in my head, saying *A lot has changed, you've come some way to earning your place here, stick with it and keep working hard*. Harold took training and, after sparring with the other senior boxers, told me to get into the ring. 'Can we take it easy?' I implored him, as once again I bent to slide through the ropes, noticing for the first time that Walcot's old, frayed, off-green carpet had been replaced by a rather more colourful, patterned affair. 'You'll be all right,' said Harold. I had no conviction that I would be and Harold then put me through nine minutes of continuous boxing. The bell came and went but there was no rest. 'Box! Come on, keep going!' said Harold. 'Keep your arms up! Jab!' The pressure was unending and, sure enough, blood flowed again from my nose, though not as freely as on Friday night. For the last minute Harold pushed and boxed and shouted at me to keep going, to box on, until finally it was over. 'If you can do that, you'll be all right for the fight,' he said afterwards. And for all the pain and exhaustion, still there even as I got changed and Jamie Cox had a word with me and told me to *come back a winner*, I knew he was right.

The look in 'The Amazing' Alan Fitzgerald's eyes was

constant throughout the fight, a look of unwavering, impenetrable blackness even as I hit him with the hardest rights I could find and never more so than in the third and final round, when for every ounce of strength that was ebbing out of my body he seemed to find another punch, another left jab and another straight right, despite my grabbing him and holding him, trying to push his solid frame down towards the canvas, because in doing so, as Umar had told me, *you wear the other geezer out*, but the truth was that I was shattered, in the final thirty to forty-five seconds of that third round I had nothing left, nothing but the ability to remain upright as Fitzgerald stalked me from one side of the ring to the other, clattering me with punches that somehow I knew would not knock me down, not that night and perhaps never, because before the fight began, when for a short time I was left alone for a minute in the dressing room, I took my wedding ring out of my jacket pocket where I'd left it for safekeeping hoping it would be OK and kissed it and said *This is for you, for you Karen and for you Harry and Elliot, my sons, I am not going to let you down*, and walking down the steps from the stage at the back of York Hall, preceded by Alex Goldsmith and Sean Lynch, brokers and boxers both, hearing the bass of Jean-Jacques Burnel setting up The Stranglers in 'Hanging Around' (chosen, having served me well once before, out of superstition), I felt more up for the fight than I had ever imagined possible, despite the knowledge that my nose was broken from Jamie Husband's uppercut and the certainty that it would bleed even if caressed by the gentlest of jabs, which Fitzgerald duly dispensed after about ten seconds and thereafter with increasing power, power that I had imagined he possessed when I had first set eyes on him, late that afternoon when I had wandered into a near-empty York Hall

310

with Mark Reynolds and Ian Smith to bump into an uncommonly relaxed Alan Lacey who introduced me to Fitzgerald with the words *Meet your opponent* and at once I sized up the man who had stepped in at short notice to fight me and observed his formidable bulk and slight height advantage and felt wholly disturbed until I heard him say *I'm feeling terrified, absolutely terrified* and then as I walked the streets of Bethnal Green to kill the hour or so before the fight I started to think that if this man was that nervous I had a chance, I could sock him with those rights and try and deserve my *nom de guerre* of The Slugger, I had trained hard I hadn't smoked I hadn't been drinking for months so I should get out there and enjoy it, a conceit that seemed absurd on so many occasions in the two years since I had started boxing, for this is the hardest game at any level and is not, surely, about fun, whatever Alan Lacey might say and yet as I climbed through the ropes and heard the shouts of encouragement from the crowd intermingled with the boos from Fitzgerald's contingent I lost consciousness of all fear and shuffled and shadow-boxed for just a few seconds and felt completely in control, an emotion that was not dented even by that look of chthonic blackness in The Amazing's eyes as we touched gloves and ignored all the words from the referee not because we were two streetfighters who had no intention of adhering to the Queensberry Rules but because we were both lost in the moment, unable to register the exhortations to have a fair fight and not dish out any low blows or whatever it was that was being said to us but despite the absorption in the impending confrontation I still found the possession to say *Good luck, mate* because I remembered how scared this man had been when first I had met him and knew exactly how he felt but when the bell went regretted being so soft, so gentlemanly, so white-collar, for instead of the customary touching of gloves in amateur boxing (a ritual often if not universally observed even after the bell has signalled the formal commencement of hostilities) The Amazing did not respond to my proffered left glove and I knew that I had a fight on my hands as we spent the rest of the round hitting hard and trying to figure each other out with no clear conclusion when the two minutes were up but, at that point, I had reason to be confident, not least because of a nice early combination ending with a short uppercut to the body but also because of some decent overhand rights and the feeling that tricky though he was and implacable though his eyes were if anything Fitzgerald's being radiated fear more than menace, a feeling bolstered when I sat down in my corner and felt Sean Lynch staunching the blood from my nose and listened to Alex 'The Suffolk Punch' Goldsmith telling me to keep bobbing and weaving and to *hit him with that right*, a right that had hurt Goldsmith himself a few days before the fight in my last spar, in the rather more luxuriously appointed ring of the Top Notch when Lynch had told me that I was going to do three rounds *as if it's Fight Night*, heedless of my laments about having done nine continuous minutes with Harold the day before because as he said *You need it and I want to see what you've got*, and so Goldsmith and I had boxed hard for three three-minute rounds in the course of which I connected with a straight right to the Chatteris man's sternum which was still giving him problems on the 25 November show (*You hurt me the other day, I'm having trouble breathing*, he said, as Sean wrapped and taped crepe bandage around my hands in the shabby dressing room backstage at York Hall, occasionally interrupted by one of the whips for the night, Igor Kennaway, pianist and conductor, tall and

well-spoken, veteran of two white-collar fights and able
unlike my friend Jonathan Phillips to transcend the barrier
between pugilism and art), a show billed by Lacey with both
uncharacteristic simplicity and a concession to the linguistic
flexibility of text-speak as 'After Work Fight Nite', and at
which Vince 'Dynamite' Dickson was appearing, indeed he
was sharing the same dressing room as me and had Lynch
and Goldsmith in his corner as well, we nodded and shook
hands and I recalled the hideous feeling of losing my legs and
dancing drunkenly after he had hit me fifteen months ago
but it felt good in some obliquely talismanic way to have the
same cornermen as Dickson, described by a friend who had
seen our fight as *lethal* and yet who couldn't seem to get going
in his, the first fight on the card, one which seemed to entail
more by way of pushing and holding than the crowd had paid
money to see which was far from the case in my fight with
Fitzgerald, a man whom I had reeling in the second round
from at least two heavy right hands, punches that if only they
had landed flush on his chin would have knocked him to the
canvas but which I saw landing on his cheekbones and the
side of his head, hard enough to dislodge his headguard on
two occasions, meaning that the referee had to stop the fight
to allow Fitzgerald's blue corner to fix it and allowing me to
suck in some much-needed oxygen and think to myself *I'm
in control, I'm completely relaxed up here, in front of all these
people, and I can knock him out*, which proved to be Alex
Goldsmith's thoughts in the interval between the second and
third rounds as again Sean Lynch stopped the flow of blood
from my nose and The Suffolk Punch said *You can knock this
fella out, get out there and do it*, advice which Umar had
dispensed when he had rung me before the fight (*Clean his
clock*, he said, *don't mess about and hit him with that right early*

doors), advice which I tried to put into effect the moment the bell for the third rang, moving purposefully towards The Amazing and in my desire to get out there forgetting to let Goldsmith put my gumshield back in, so that I had to return to my corner, to stand by the ropes in front of an array of friends including Louise who had helped get me to my feet at the *Independent* and Paul who had done so similarly and Simon who had put in a word and many others who had stuck by me even Nigel from the Carter-Ruck days was there and now I was standing in front of them and had to wait to feel the blood-spattered piece of rubber lodged around my upper teeth before I could turn around and march towards Fitzgerald and let go of some more looping rights but again, somehow, they refused to follow the trajectory I had set for them, for Fitzgerald was a skilful boxer, evasive and able to parry, a man who felt he had edged it in sparring against the master of white-collar boxing himself, Alan Lacey, whom he described as *a clever boxer, but one I could handle*, a view that I was able tentatively to endorse having once trained with Alan at the Paragon Gym in Hoxton, it was a humid summer's day not long after my fight with Vince Dickson and lunch was arranged with Alan, but the traffic was hell so I rang him to say I'd be late and he said he was having a lousy day too so why not relieve the stress with some boxing so half an hour later there we were working with Stuart Lawson, British full-contact kickboxing champion, with endless pad and bag work and shadow-boxing and my glances at Lacey told me that he knew what he was doing, he had a very slick, flash style and knew all the moves and, who knows, *coulda been a contender* if he had started when he was young but now was the same age as The Amazing, fifty-two, the man who suddenly turned his fight around in the third round was fifty-two, built like a rock and tearing into me inexorably, fifty-two, an accountant, in amazing shape for a man not merely of his age but any age and able to find reserves that afterwards he told me he didn't know he had and come back into a fight that I had been winning, smashing punch after punch at me as I tired and could barely throw out even a lukewarm jab until in a neutral corner he struck me flush with a right beneath my right eye and I felt my head snap back but like all his other punches I knew, *I knew* none would knock me down because at that juncture, on that night, boxing defined me and I was not going to let anything get in the way of giving the best performance of which I was capable so that Karen and my sons would never, ever be able to say that I was the kind of man to quit and I knew that I was fighting for the three of them, for us as a family, to annul once and for all that part of me that had so nearly destroyed everything and I felt strong and confident and aware that I would not go down even as The Amazing came at me, not tonight, and I hoped that I would not go down again, in another fight, at another time, for other reasons, and so despite the lassitude beginning to ooze into every limb I found the strength for another couple of jabs, I knew that even as I took some more punches I would keep going, until the end, because as turn-of-the-century heavyweight champion 'Gentleman' Jim Corbett says you *fight one more round, when your arms are so tired that you can hardly lift your hands to come on guard, fight one more round, when your nose is bleeding and your eyes are black and you are so tired that you wish your opponent would crack you one on the jaw and put you to sleep, fight one more round – remembering that the man who always fights one more round is never whipped*, and I know exactly what those words mean, in boxing and beyond, *you fight one more round*, when you have lost your job and dignity, when your marriage is in shreds and your former lover wishes you were dead, when your friends of old can barely look you in the eye, when you have behaved with intemperance and enormity and brought everything upon yourself and even if you know the potential is still there inside you, probably always will be, simmering away, *the possibility exists of being a wrecking machine*, but not if I can help it, and so you keep going, *in the destructive element immerse*, you take the shots and get up for more, you never give up and not least when children oh my beautiful sons are concerned, you turn round and refuse to be the father whose children cannot look up to him because there is nothing to look up to and still less do you suffer your own traumas on your sons, you try instead to behave with commitment, with control, with confidence, qualities that I had in abundance in the first two rounds and yet which were sorely tested in the third only for the last seconds to approach as again The Amazing hit me and again I looked into those unforgiving, relentless black eyes and knew that the end was near, the bell must be due and yet I had nothing left and wondered if I could take much more and then it was over, it was done, save for the congratulations and the instant sense of camaraderie with Alan Fitzgerald, fifty-two, the man I had just had the fight of my life with and who later agreed that calling it a draw was a decision that had both honour and objective fairness, though immediately my corner thought I had shaded it, with Fitzgerald's men over in the blue corner holding the converse view, thoughts that were destined to remain imponderables in the no-decision world of white-collar boxing and which meant little to Alan Lacey who climbed through the ropes and almost swaggered to Sean Lynch and said *Am I a fuckin' good matchmaker or what?* and handed me my trophy and wished me well, later to say that *it was a cracker of a fight that had an elemental honesty to it that's missing from real life*, and I was all set to leave the ring when Sean and Alex told me the doctor wanted to examine me and so he took me to the corner and peered at my nose and said *You've broken your nose* and I heard Alex saying that he and Sean knew it was broken in the third and I said *I didn't tell you but I broke it at Walcot a week ago* but it didn't matter, Doctor Rashid straightened it backstage in the dressing room and for a minute or two I was again left alone and I caught sight of myself in the mirror with a bloodied face and black eye and realised that I had never felt happier and rang Karen and told her: 'I've done it.'

18

OUTSIDE

For many years, I have had a dream in which I see my father approaching a bench, in a park in Exeter, near the prison. He is wearing a grey suit and looks sad. He walks up to the bench and sits down. He is alone, and stares into space, at the green trees and grass, at one or two young mothers pushing prams. There is a plastic bag fluttering in the gentle breeze, and it is summer. My father's hair is as white as it has been for a long time now, and as he sits down on the bench, he clasps his hands together. He sits down because he is tired. He has finally, at last, grown tired of life and the battles that have come his way. Sitting on this bench feels like the first time he has ever sat down for the past forty years of toil and worry, forty years in which he has kept the practising certificate issued by the Law Society and run his own, successful law firm. He sits and stares and doesn't move, and just at the point when someone friendly – an unexpected arrival, coming from the direction of the prison – is about to lay a hand on his shoulder, he looks round. For many years that would be the end of the dream, but a few days after the fight I dreamt it again. This time, my father turned to look at me. He had a smile on his face and reached out his hand to mine. I shook it with more affection than these words can convey.

'I shouldn't keep on with the boxing,' said my father, a few days after my fight with Alan Fitzgerald. 'It's a young man's sport.'

My father is right. But unlike others I have met in the world of boxing, I have no illusions. I am, at best, an average boxer. I am clumsy, inelegant, overly aggressive, and what to some is a right-hand punch of pedigree is, to others, nothing. I am too old. To a good boxer, my skills – if that is what they can be called – are mediocre at best. To the likes of Jamie Cox, who I watched from ringside in the 116th senior ABA finals at the Excel Centre in London's Docklands on 18 March 2005, I am far from problematic, still less a threat. Cox's massive left hand once broke Kevin Fertnig's nose so badly in two places that when Fertnig went to casualty, the nurse and doctor couldn't believe that a punch had done the damage ('They told me, "No one can punch that hard,"' said Kevin). In the ABA light-welterweight final, against the slick and more experienced London boxer Michael Grant, Cox impressed the crowd and assembled boxing writers with his strength, fitness and power, and, if Grant marginally deserved his 16–14 win, Cox did more than enough to merit a special award bestowed upon him at the end of the show as 'Prospect of the Night'. That night, at ringside sat the illustrious Amir Khan, who himself would surely have been in the final had he not controversially withdrawn from the 2005 championships over the ABA's allocation of tickets for the quarter-finals in Gorleston, Norfolk. I observed Khan, the British boxing prodigy, as the evening wore on, and doubted that he regretted not appearing in the final against Grant or Cox. On the brink of turning pro, Khan looked composed and yet seemed to have his mind on other things, no doubt the imminence of his professional career. He handled both the media and autograph-seeking fans with the maturity of a seasoned champion. This, of course, is what he aims to be: 'When I'm 25,' he has said, 'I want to be retired, a world champion and a legend.' Speaking later to reporters, Khan said he had no doubt that he would have beaten Cox or Grant, had he fought either of them, and yet, certainly so far as Jamie Cox goes, I am not so sure. For unlike me, and unlike the pugilists drawn to The Real Fight Club and white-collar boxing, Cox is unquestionably the real thing. Less than forty hours after his narrow defeat to Grant – whom he nearly knocked out of ring in the third round – Cox was training again at Walcot ABC, as ever watched over by Harry Scott. As he always does, he was working twice as hard as every other boxer, and just as predictably, he was polite and modest. Time will tell how Cox fares, as it will Grant and Khan. But one thing is certain: Jamie Cox is a contender.

And yet for all that it is too late for me ever to be in the same bracket, for all that my boxing will never equal that of countless pugilists in amateur gyms up and down the country, and for all that I will never be a contender, I have become, as the cuts man and writer F. X. Toole has it, *a member of the fancy*. And because I have become a member of the fancy, I experienced the greatest high of my life after I fought Alan Fitzgerald. Nothing can ever compare to the adrenalin running riot in my body and soul when the contest was over, a sentiment endorsed, when I spoke to him a couple of weeks later, by Fitzgerald. We both had a sense of unprecedented exhilaration, swiftly followed by the comedown. 'What next?' we thought. And yet, speaking for myself, I know that I will keep going down to Walcot, as I did the Sunday after the 2005 ABA finals; I know that I will give Umar a call from time to time, that I will slot in the odd session at the Top Notch with Alex and Sean. For despite my initial doubts, through The Real Fight Club and boxing I have experienced camaraderie, I have seen showmanship, and better yet I can see the prospect of sustained control and from it the confidence not to binge, the commitment not to destroy everything all over again. I might one day have another fight through The Real Fight Club, or I might not. I might 'get starched by some heavy geezer', as Umar puts it, or I might put in a great performance thanks to him, thanks to Alex and Sean, thanks to Harry Scott and everyone at Walcot. Who knows? What I do know is that having tried so hard to fit in all my life, there is a place for the likes of me.

That place is on the outside. It is a place similar to that which boxing occupies in society. That I inhabit a psychological space akin to boxing owes much to issues from my childhood that may never be resolved. Likewise, to the fact that I spent so many years *inside*, trying to belong, fettered to a construct of self that was predicated on fulfilling my father's image of me, or, at least, what I imagined was my father's image of me. And all that time that I'd been on the inside, I kept going *outside*, to the danger zones, looking for trouble, courting disaster, until finally the annihilation I had craved came to me. The tension existed because I was neither *outside* nor *inside*, but shuttling catastrophically between. Now, I box. I no longer feel defined by being a lawyer. There are echoes of my past identity, occasions when

I might use my legal skills for money, but they are determined by choice, not fear. And when I write about The Law and its guardians, its practitioners and developments, when I'm interviewing someone from The Law, I wonder whether he or she also wants to wreck everything, to dismantle the carefully ordered legalese of their lives, that which annulled my sense of self to the point when it felt like I had nothing *of me* left to wreck.

I do not know whether I have the commitment to stay here, on the outside, free of guilt, but I have sworn that for as long as I can I will keep boxing, and that I will try to be a decent father and a better son, try to be a husband who when faced with the choice of whether to be a wrecking machine again says No, those days are over, I am at ease with everything, No, I now understand my father, my upbringing, my mistakes, the hurt I have caused, I see from my own experience of fatherhood what my father wanted for me, what he dreamt of, what he tried to do as my father, so No, if I am not of the right sort and not from the right place, if I am on the outside, it does not matter, the only thing to do is to keep going, to keep fighting, for as we know *the man who does will never be whipped*, and Yes, I regret so much and remember it all, the women I have let down, the absences from my home, the outbreaks of violence, the enmity to The Law, the meaningless drinking sessions and the impossibility of everything, the rage, the endless unspeakable rage, but now it is time to forget and perhaps even forgive so No, No and again No, please, I am no longer a wrecking machine.

ACKNOWLEDGEMENTS

I owe a tremendous debt to many people but, in a book such as this, it is appropriate to start with those connected to boxing. I thank Walcot ABC for getting me in shape and teaching me the camaraderie of boxing. Everyone at the club deserves praise but none more so than the boss, Harry Scott himself. Dave Veysey and Harold Scott also put time into my efforts and to all there – Dave Holyday, Bobby Gwynne, Jamie Cox, Beano, Ben Fitch, Jake Sheppard, Jaggdave, George Cook, and the town girl herself, Amy Wharton (to name but a few) – I will always be grateful. It is obvious, too, from the preceding pages that Umar Taitt is another man whom I cannot thank enough. He is an inspiration as much through his strength of character as his patient ability to teach the noble art. But without Alan Lacey and The Real Fight Club this book would not have come into being. I thank Alan for his drive, determination, flamboyance and endless imagination, and I thank Sean Lynch and Alex Goldsmith for moulding an out-of-shape boxer into something half decent when it mattered. To

Mike Higgins – thanks for 'The Slugger', and thanks too to all those who turned up to watch me at York Hall.

Outside boxing, certain people helped me when things were at their worst. Thanks to: Rich, Darren, Jules, Al, Barney, Marc and Elliot.

I am grateful to Michael Beloff QC, President of Trinity College, Oxford, for giving me a copy of his First Annual Espeland Lecture, 'Advocacy – A Craft Under Threat?', delivered on 28 November 2002 at Universitetets Aula, Oslo, Norway. I am indebted, too, to Merlin Holland's *Irish Peacock and Scarlet Marquess: The Real Trial of Oscar Wilde* and to John B. Cunningham's *Oscar Wilde's Enniskillen*.

My emergence from a self-created gutter would never have happened if The Law had not thrown up the best of its progeny at crucial times. Louise, Paul, Simon and Tom played roles that they perhaps did not realise were so vital; so too did all those at *The Times*' legal department, Jan at the *Independent* and Frances, Clare and Alan at *The Times*. To all, once again, my sincere gratitude.

There are other people who were instrumental in my life moving on – my agent, David Milner; my editor, Andrew Gordon; Rob Pickles, who gave me a shot; Ronnie Anderson, for being himself and Julia Silk, who was the first person to believe that I might one day publish a book. To my mother and father – without whom, nothing – my love and thanks, and to all my family, not least my indomitable grandmother, thank you. Truly, though, there are so many people that I cannot hope to thank them all here.

What I must do, however, is say that without Karen, Harry and Elliot my life would have been nothing. To the three of you, who are everything: my love and thanks.